The Medals Year Book
1999 Edition

The Medals Year Book
1999 Edition

LEO COOPER
LONDON

First published in Great Britain in 1998
by
LEO COOPER
an imprint of
Pen & Sword Books Ltd,
47 Church Street,
Barnsley, South Yorkshire S70 2AS

© Pen & Sword Books Ltd 1998

A CIP record for this book is available from the British Library

ISBN 0 85052 573 X

All rights reserved. No part of this publication may be reproduced, in any form or by any means, without permission from the publishers.

Printed in Great Britain by Redwood Books, Trowbridge, Wiltshire

Contents

An Auction Review vi
Orders of Knighthood 1
Decorations 12
Campaign Medals 31
Long Service and Good Conduct Medals 102
Coronation and Jubilee Medals 146
Life Saving Medals 162
Index 172

Auction Review

by Gavel

The process of reviewing British auction sales of orders, decorations and medals only serves to underline the impressive range and quality of awards sold through the sale rooms every year. During the period under review from the beginning of 1996 to the end of summer 1997 (press date of this Yearbook), over eleven thousand lots came under the hammer at the four main British sale rooms - Dix, Noonan, Webb; Glendining's; Sotheby's; Spink - with many more appearing at smaller houses - such as Bonhams; Bosleys; Wallis & Wallis.

Even a brief survey of the many medals and other awards on offer and their associations conjure up famous moments of history such as the classic actions of the Napoleonic campaigns, the Charge of the Light Brigade, Rorke's Drift, the Somme, the Battle of Jutland, the Battle of Britain, D-Day and so on. Although many items relate to military engagements, there was much else besides; for example, medallic awards for Polar explorations, for Royal events, particularly Coronation and Jubilee celebrations, for Police service, for civilian bravery and for achievement in civilian life and more.

Inexperienced collectors may consider the idea of bidding at auction to be a daunting prospect, particularly at high profile auction houses with international reputations. The reality is somewhat different. Bids can be executed in a number of ways - by bidding in person, by placing a postal bid, by a telephone bid, or by appointing an agent (a service provided by several medal dealers). The pre-sale viewing also provides an opportunity to gain experience by examining medals that are of interest.

The medal specialists within the auction house are most approachable and willing to give advice to both potential vendors and purchasers. Key names are Nimrod Dix and Pierce Noonan at Dix, Noonan Webb; Andrew Litherland and John Millensted at Glendining's; Edward Playfair at Sotheby's; David Erskine-Hill, Brian Simpkin and Nicholas Watts at Spink, in addition their consultant John Hayward, is available within the Department from Monday to Thursday each week; Daniel Fearon at Bonham's; and Roy Butler at Wallis & Wallis.

Prices over the period 1996-97 were generally firm and better for good quality items, rarities, pieces with interesting historical backgrounds and/or interesting recipients. Although the market is not especially large when compared to many other areas of collecting that are more financially accessible to a wider public, the interest from medal collectors, dealers, military museums, and collectors with other focuses but occasionally attracted by medals that fall within their collecting themes, has been and is on a scale to

An Auction Review

keep the hobby buoyant. Inevitably most sales have their disappointments, although the reasons for these are always diverse and debatable - but key factors can be over optimistic estimates and reserves, items which though good fail to find a special niche in any collection, a market over abundant in a particular type of item, something about a medal or group that 'is not quite right' etc.

The British premier award for gallantry, the Victoria Cross, has performed particularly strongly over the period under review. A forceful factor here has been the increasing interest over recent years from a private collector who is known to bid on most VCs. But lately, with growing interest in Great War period issues from other parties, not to mention obviously Lottery-backed museums and local councils, his strike-rate has not always been successful. Indeed increasing publicity and Lottery funds will make his task all that much harder.

Inevitably any review of this nature can only focus on a very small percentage of items that came under the hammer and for those that are included there are inevitably many more that are worthy of inclusion. The fact that some auction houses have been given more extensive attention than others is not necessarily intended to suggest that they are more commendable, just the fact that they have in the eyes of the reviewer seemed to have had a good number of especially interesting items and important collections during the period under consideration. It is hoped that the details given for the items mentioned will give a clear indication of why they were 'special' and will present a clear picture of the range of factors and themes that make the collecting of orders, medals and decorations such an interesting hobby.

DIX NOONAN WEBB

1996

Dix & Webb (to become Dix, Noonan, Webb in 1997) opened their 1996 season with a 5th March sale which offered a good selection of single campaign medals spanning both nineteenth and twentieth centuries, a collection of medals to the Essex Regiment, and gallantry groups representing all three armed services. There was a strong emphasis on First World War medals and groups, a period which attracts a strong body of collectors; these lots included many items awarded to those who were war casualties, and for whom there is generally more research material available.

An early item brought a disappointment: this was the Naval General Service Medal 1793-1840 (NGS) with the emotive Trafalgar clasp to Commander Hugh Entwisle RN for services aboard HMS Bellerophon, sold with a portrait miniature, which found no buyer willing to offer close to the rather progressive estimate of £4,000-5,000. In contrast another NGS with a Trafalgar/Egypt clasp combination to a Royal Marine Private attracted more interest and made £2,700 (estimate £1,500-2,000). He had served aboard HMS Victory at Trafalgar - one of only 21 Royal Marine recipients of this clasp for service on Nelson's flagship and his medal was one of only nine Royal Marine medals with this particular clasp combination. Another lot to a Marine recipient was the Nile campaign Distinguished Conduct Medal group of four to Colour Sergeant John Drew, Royal Marine Light Infantry and Guards Camel Regiment , on which the bidding soared to £3,600

An Auction Review

(estimate £2000-2,500). His recommendation noted his coolness and considerable exertion in bringing the sick convoy to safety when in came under attack in 1885.

Similarly a Jutland CB (Companion of the Order of the Bath) group of eight representing very varied service to Lieutenant C.E. Collard, the Senior Royal Marine Officer afloat during the battle more than topped its estimate at £3,000 (estimate £1,400-1,800). His East and Central Africa Medal 1897-99 clasp Uganda was probably unique to the Royal Marines; whilst the Rhodesia clasp to his Queen's South Africa Medal 1899-1902 was one of only two to a Marine officer serving with the Army; additionally his was one of only 12 King's South Africa Medals 1901-02 to the Marines. Collard had materially assisted in controlling the gunfire of HMS Benbow at Jutland in 1916.

What appeared on the surface to be an interesting group, not least to a Canadian audience, was a Great War Military Cross group of three to Prince Antoine of Orleans and Braganza, Captain, Royal Canadian Dragoons. It spanned service in Natal 1906 and also included a French Legion d'Honneur (5th class) to a recipient who had been Intelligence Officer to the Canadian Cavalry Brigade and ADC to its Major-General during the First War. Somewhat marred by a brooch fitting, it remained unsold at £1,100 (estimate £1,500-2,000).

The 11th June sale at Dix & Webb grabbed the newspaper headlines with the auctioneer's assessment that the Victoria Cross and South Africa Medal 1877-79 pair to Private Robert Jones, 24th Foot, earned at the famed defence of Rorke's Drift 1879, was the last remaining VC for this historic incident not accounted for in a museum or other institution and hence the only one still available for public sale. Eleven Crosses were awarded for this most famous action, seven to the South Wales Borderers. It was thought that the final price might even exceed the buoyant estimate. However with just one interested buyer at this level, the group sold at the lower estimate of £80,000 (estimate £80,000-120,000). Private Robert Jones had acted gallantly in saving the lives of six hospital patients at the defence of the remote mission station. It is worth mentioning that virtually as the sale was taking place, the news broke of another such Victoria Cross. Held by Spink on behalf of a client, it had long been considered a cast copy, but the outcome of scientific tests at the Royal Armouries resulted in a statement that there was no reason to consider it other than a genuine Rorke's Drift VC, given that the analysis had shown it to be comparable to other Crosses of the period.. In addition the fact that there was still another VC for this action which could come on to the market, further excitement was generated by the news that this was the Cross awarded to the legendary Lieutenant Chard., Royal Engineers.

The sale extended its South African theme with a single South Africa Medal 1877-79 clasp 1877-8-9 to Sergeant Robert Maxfield, 24th Foot who was killed in the hospital at Rorke's Drift by an assegai. He was the Regiment's most senior ranking casualty. Although the medal had the disadvantage for some collectors of having a slight official correction to the naming, it quickly sold well within the estimate at £7,200 (estimate 6,000-8,000). On offer also was the Companion of the Order of the Bath (CB) group of four to Assistant Commissary Colonel W.A. Dunne, in charge of the stores at Rorke's Drift, who had been recommended for the Victoria Cross. Presumably collectors considered the estimate to be too progressive, as this good group failed to sell when bidding ceased at £15,500 (estimate £20,000-25,000).

An Auction Review

Rarity is not just a facet of highly priced items, rarities also occur within middle and lower price brackets, and on this occasion a Royal Marine Meritorious Service Medal with date '1848' below the bust, of which only 40 were issued to the Marines, sold for £1,250 (estimate £800-1,000).

Medals can sell for a host of different reasons, and here a single unnamed specimen Polar Medal 1904 with four clasps for Scott's last expedition, Mawson's Australian expedition, and Shackleton's Trans-Antarctic expedition made a hammer price well over estimate at £720 (estimate £400-500), because, it was rumoured, there were specialist collectors who required the clasps. During the period under review several sale rooms offered items to interest the small but enthusiastic Polar collecting fraternity. Here Dix & Webb sold what was probably a unique combination of awards to Petty Officer Alfred R. Pearce, RN whose Arctic Medal 1876 came together with an Abyssinia Medal 1867 and a South Africa Medal 1877-79. Having survived the severe conditions in the Arctic, including those on the 'Furthest North' Sledging party 1876, he was to die of dysentry in 1879 during the Zulu Wars. Bidding on his group soared to £4,000 (estimate £2,000-3,000).

Most sales have their disappointments and here it fell to a section of fairly basic First World War trios on the one hand and on the other to a group of five awards to Alice, the Honourable Mrs George Keppel, mistress of King Edward VII. Interest in the latter item petered out at £1,450 (estimate £2,000-3,000), the extensive catalogue details of her rarified social and intriguing personal life having failed to attract interest at the required level.

Although Museums do not always have the funds to buy everything they would like, on this occasion the National Army Museum, a regular bidder at auction, was able to secure a rare Egyptian Army group of five to Bash Shawish (equivalent of Sergeant) Fudulula Ali, 9th Sudanese Regiment which covered service in Egypt and the Sudan in the last two decades of the nineteenth century. The Khedive's Sudan Medal 1896-1908 came with 10 clasps - the maximum number known to have been awarded. The Museum had to part with £1,800 hammer price (estimate £700-900) from their budget (plus of course the buyer's premium).

THE DOUGLAS-MORRIS
COLLECTION OF NAVAL MEDALS
PART 1

All eyes were on Dix & Webb (soon to become Dix, Noonan, Webb in 1997 with the arrival of a new partner) as news broke that they had been chosen to dispose of the post-1840 pieces from the magnificent naval collection of the late Captain Douglas-Morris RN, some of which was familiar from having been on loan to the Portsmouth Royal Navy Museum and from being recorded in the Captain's two published volumes on naval medals. The extensive material was sold in two separate sales, the first in October 1996, the second in February 1997. Until the publication of the catalogue of the first part of the sale there was much speculation as to how the collection would

An Auction Review

be split for auction. Part one contained over 700 lots spanning campaign, long-service and gallantry from the beginning of the nineteenth century right through to Korea.

The disposal of this first part witnessed a full saleroom with many more postal bidders. The auction of an important collection always creates a special frisson among the collecting fraternity with interest focused on the whole sale as opposed to just the most exciting items as is usually the case with a more general sale.. Estimates were considered to be strong, posing the inevitable question of how easy it would be to move such a volume of material at these price forecast levels, especially when it is acknowledged that pure naval collectors are spread quite thinly when compared to collectors of Army material. It was to the collection's benefit that Captain Douglas-Morris had not focused solely on rare and expensive items, but had aimed for completeness, and that in his aim of achieving a comprehensive collection, he had acquired runs of relatively ordinary medals - these were given an added gloss by having been part of his collection but their inclusion nonetheless ensured that there were items to attract all levels of collectors. Further there were items whose appeal extended beyond the naval collecting community.

The Captain himself undertook endless research on his medals and presumably the cataloguers had an enormous job in producing succinct historic accounts of the medals and recipients. However, for potential bidders the catalogue was very informative without being over long and bogged down with inessential detail of interest only to the successful purchaser. Those prepared to persevere and work systematically through the catalogue would have been able to pick out information which added considerable interest to what might on the surface have appeared to be fairly ordinary medals. An example of this was the single India General Service Medal 1854-95 clasp Persia to Lieutenant M.A. Sweeny, Surveying Brig Euphrates. His conduct in the Mutiny met with the approval of Queen Victoria and during the Persian War he was commended by his Flag Officer. Accompanied by much more service detail, the medal proved attractive, selling at £520 (estimate £250-300). A similar medal to Mr G. Beyts, Master of the Hired Troop Steamer Scindian, was on line to attract interest as he was probably the only person from that ship to qualify for the medal which brought £260 (estimate £200-250). A trio of Naval General Service Medal 1915-62 clasp Yangtse 1949, Korea and United Nations Korea Medals 1950-53 to a Stoker Mechanic Bannister RN was accompanied by details of personal courage exhibited during the evacuation of Rose Island and his time as a hostage of the Communist Chinese prior to the escape of HMS Amethyst down the Yangtse River. This elevated the trio to something even more fascinating than it appeared at first glance and it sold at £1,800 (estimate £500-700).

The sale contained something for collectors at all levels, and it is worth stressing again that scarcity and interest was not only manifest in the more highly priced items but also in some of the more modestly estimated pieces as well. Most naval engagements were represented and in some cases there was either a medal or a group to a recipient from a majority of ships (sometimes all) involved in each action - from the classic actions of the Napoleonic Wars, through the Crimea, Indian Mutiny, the three China Wars, to the wider world panorama of the two major conflicts of the twentieth century. Recipients varied from historic naval figures to unknown, yet nonetheless intriguing, individuals such as the African Seaman Tom Dollar, born in the Gambia, who served in the Navy for 20 years before earning a Conspicuous Gallantry Medal for his gallant service in the Ashantee War 1873-74 as an irregular Army Scout under the then Lieutenant Lord Gifford VC, who recommended Dollar for the award. This realised £2,200 (estimate £1,800-2,000).

Private John Bunton, whose Crimea group of four included a Naval Long Service & Good Conduct medal for gallantry, was one of only seven Royal Marine NCOs and privates to receive the medal with gratuity for gallantry as a result of his actions at Inkerman clearing some caves occupied by enemy sharpshooters when he was severely wounded in the forearm. His Crimea Medal 1854-56 was presented to him by Queen Victoria in 1855 at Horse Guards Parade. The group sold for £1,550 (estimate £1,200-1,500). A contemporaneous group of nine to a higher profile figure was that to Admiral HSH Prince Victor Hohenloe-Langenburg GCB, RN, nephew of Queen Victoria and Governor and Constable of Windsor Castle decorated for gallantry in the Crimea. He had landed with the Naval Brigade in the Baltic 1854, was slightly wounded when in charge of the field guns at the capture of Bomarsund, was present at the capture of Kertch and Anapa, at the battle of Tchernya and was distinguished for his bravery during the taking of the batteries at Sebastopol. For later services in China he was mentioned in despatches and recommended for the Victoria Cross. The group sold at the low estimate of £8,000.

The range of naval forces often comes as a surprise to those not familiar with the naval services. A quick survey of the two Douglas-Morris auction catalogues is enlightening with examples of awards to the Royal Marine Forces Volunteer Reserve, the Royal Naval Auxiliary Service, Board of Trade Rocket Apparatus Medals, and all manner of Volunteer Force Medals, and even to those serving with Anglo-Russian Armoured cars. Sections that appear to contain less glamorous items, such as medals for meritorious service, and for long service and good conduct, can often be more interesting than at first sight. Some of these pieces are scarce and are therefore especially attractive to the medal collecting fraternity, for example a rare Meritorious Service Medal for Russia to a Royal Naval Air Service recipient - only 27 MSMs to the RNAS - who additionally served with 20 Squadron Armoured Cars went to £850 (estimate £200-250), similarly Naval Long Service and Good Conduct Medals with the scarce 'anchor' reverse 1830-47 attracted sustained bidding (estimates in the region of £250-400).

Collectors looking for the unusual were rewarded by the inclusion of medals named to unusual rates and ranks such as the Canada General Service Medal 1866-70 clasp Fenian Raid 1866 to Able Seaman and Trained Man which sold at £150 (estimate estimate £140-160).

The excitement generated by medals relating to famous naval actions particularly if the groups included gallantry awards was inevitably strong - the Distinguished Service Order and Bar group of seven to the Commander of the Q-ship Cullist soared over estimate making £3,900 (estimate £2,000-3,000). Both DSOs were awarded for the hazardous Q-ship activity of acting as decoys to draw out enemy submarines to positions which made them easier targets for destruction.

Medals sold together with archival material or associated commemorative items usually find favour as with the Distinguished Service Medal group to Acting Chief Petty Officer W. Waterhouse, who took part in the Tanganyka naval expedition in 1916 to oust the German Navy from the lake which first had to cover the 3,000 arduous miles fully

An Auction Review

equipped from Cape Town to their objective by land, water and railway; his medals were accompanied by his handwritten diary which together were bought for £3,300 (estimate £1,500-2,000).

There are specialist collectors of life-saving medals, and inevitably a sale of items which focuses on the sea services included lifesaving awards. An example was a New Zealand Medal 1854-66 reverse dated 1860-61, a scarce item to those on HM Colonial Steamer Victoria, but here also enhanced by the company of two Royal Humane Society Medals in bronze, large and small varieties, which brought £3,800 (estimate £1,200-1,500).

For the purist fascinated by rare and interesting combinations of awards and numismatic rarities the sale was a feast. One such example was the triple gallantry group of Distinguished Service Cross, Distinguished Flying Cross, and Air Force Cross to Group Captain Edward Burling, Royal Naval Air Service and Royal Air Force, who was one of only three officers to win this particular gallantry combination and was 'the first pilot to be launched by catapult from a ship under way' in 1925. It was secured by a bid of £9,200 (£6,000-8.000).

Inevitably a sale of this stature included a Victoria Cross, this to Seaman Joseph Trewavas for bravery in the Sea of Azoff 1855, during the Crimea campaign. His VC was in the first list of winners of what was then the new premier award for gallantry and he was present at the first Hyde Park investiture; he was also awarded the Conspicuous Gallantry Medal. A Cornishman from Mousehole, Trewavas was honoured by his locality when the Penwith District Council and Penzance Town Council successfully purchased the group for £29,000 (estimate £24,000-28,000) to go on display in the local Penlee Art Gallery and Museum, Penzance.

Between selling the two parts of the Douglas-Morris collection, Dix, Noonan, Webb managed to squeeze in a late November auction of about 500 lots. The opening single campaign medals included the unique Naval Small Gold Medal to Vice Admiral Sir William Parker RN for the action against the French Fleet in the Channel three days prior to the Glorious First of June 1794, an integral part of Earl Howe's famous victory, which realised £10,000 (estimate £10,000-12,000). Parker was later the recipient of a Naval Large Gold Medal for the battle of Cape St Vincent, not being offered on this occasion. In general the 140 or so campaign lots which carried estimates ranging from £30-12,000 did well securing prices at about the estimated levels, except for a small run of Waterloo Medals 1815 which were probably too expensive (estimates £800-1,000).

A rather handsome silver medallion known as the MacGrgegor Medal, awarded to Captain G.E. Leachman for exploration work in North East Arabia 1910, later murdered in a rebellion in Iraq, which probably had good amount of research potential, was subject to very competitive bidding and brought £1,500 (estimate £250-350). Another purchaser was presumably enticed by the catalogue description that a combination of Air Efficiency Award, Cadet Forces Medal (both EIIR) and Rhodesia Medal 1980 was probably unique and hence paid £650 (estimate £500-600).

This was just one of the auction houses who during the years 1996-97 offered small runs of engraved silver regimental medals; on this occasion there were just three items accompanied by the usual caveat that they were being sold as seen and not subject to return due to the difficulty of establishing authenticity. These items can be very attractive, but experience and the occasional good hunch play a large part in acquiring 'correct' pieces.

Among the campaign groups and pairs were a couple of items that carried what is often viewed from hindsight as the romance of the Napoleonic era. First was the wonderful Naval group of CB, KH (Knight of the Royal Hanoverian Guelphic Order) with both Naval and Military General Service Medals 1793-1840 and 1793-1814 and a Sultan's Gold Medal for Egypt 1801 (third class) to Colonel Sir John Morillyon Wilson, 1st Foot who was wounded 13 times during service in the Peninsula and North America; it brought a hammer price of £11,200 (estimate £6,000-8,000). The second was a KCH (Knight Commander of the Royal Guelphic Order) with Field Officer's Small Gold Medal for Salamanca to Lieutenant General Sir Henry John Cumming, 11 Light Dragoons which realised £4,800 (estimate £3,500-4,500).

The gallantry section contained some notable pieces: a rare Artillery Dongola campaign 1896 Distinguished Conduct Medal group of seven to a Royal Marine Captain, whose part in the action was well documented, and whose DCM was presented by Queen Victoria at Windsor, which brought a healthy £4,500 (estimate £3,000-3,500), also another DCM group this time to an Omdurman 1898 charger, a Lance Corporal with 21 Lancers, sold very reasonably for £3,100 (estimate £3,000-4,000) given that details were available of his gallant act in helping to bring a wounded man out of action. The Royal Air Force also figured in this section, particularly noteworthy was an outstanding First World War Distinguished Service Cross and Bar with Air Force Cross group of six to Group Captain Vivian Gaskell-Blackburn RAF and RNAS who saw service with a wide variety of units and took part in the world's first Carrier Air Strike in 1914, flew in operations against the Kπnigsberg in East Africa, and was decorated for Kut-el-Amara and operations at Ctesiphon 1915-16, which produced a top bid of £6,200 (estimate £3,000-4,000). For naval enthusiasts there was also one of only two Distinguished Service Orders awarded to the Royal Indian Marine for the Boxer rebellion, China 1900-1902 (only 25 such awards for the whole campaign) - this rare Edward VII DSO was bestowed upon Commander Alexander Rowand RN, late RIM and sold at £3,700 (estimate £3,000-3,500).

One of the famed 'six before breakfast' VCs in a group of nine to Lieutenant Colonel Richard Willis, Lancashire Fusiliers, won during the Gallipoli landings April 1915, a famed episode in the Regiment's history, attracted much interest, being secured by a possibly unexpected bid of £54,000 (estimate £30,000-35,000).

The second part of Captain Douglas Morris' naval sale held in February 1997 was eagerly awaited by collectors anxious to purchase their first or further items, by dealers buying on commission or hoping to spot a real bargain, and by many interested onlookers interested to simply watch the disposal of such an important collection rather than engage in the bidding. There was further speculation as to whether the market for naval items was reaching saturation point. Some 650 items were described in the second catalogue the emphasis of which was very much on later nineteenth century campaigns, runs of Meritorious and Long Service Medals, together with gallantry items especially from the two World conflicts of the twentieth century. As with the first part of the sale, the material offered was most varied, ranging from simple campaign medals to illustrious combinations of gallantry awards.

An Auction Review

Earlier conflicts were represented, by such as a First China War 1842 group - gold CB, China Medal 1842 and Baltic Medal 1854-55 - to Captain Harry Eyres, HMS Modeste, the most actively employed RN ship in the China conflict, which took part in 12 of the 13 actions that conferred eligibility for the campaign medal and whose Captain was nine times mentioned in despatches. Despite this, it failed to live up to expectations and brought £1,800 (estimate £2,000-3000).

Significant naval names also figured in the sale - an outstanding group of 10 items to Admiral of the Fleet Sir Charles Hotham GCB, GCVO covering campaigns in New Zealand 1845-66 (where uniquely he was theoretically eligible for New Zealand Medals for two differently dated actions, actually resulting in the additional details being engraved on the edge of the medal), and in Egypt and the Sudan 1882-89 also failed to meet the expected figure and sold at £4,500 (estimate £5,000-6,000); the awards to Admiral of the Fleet Lord John Hay GCB, Commander-in-Chief in the Mediterranean during operations in the Sudan 1884-85 brought a top bid of £5,200 (estimate £5,000-7,000); while the group to Admiral Sir Michael Hodges KCB, CMG, MVO, who commanded one of the Powerful's 4.7 inch naval guns at the Defence of Ladysmith found a buyer at £3,000 (estimate £3,000-4,000). A Defence of Legations group to a member of the 78 strong Royal Marine Legation Guard which defended the British Legation at the Siege of Peking 1900 was the subject of sustained bidding, which rose to £4,100 before a sale was made (£2,000-2,500).

Overall single campaign medals presented a more buoyant picture in contrast to some of the more substantial groups that sometimes struggled or brought little more than their lower estimates. Indeed some rarer single items also proved very attractive as with the North West Canada Medal 1885 clasp Saskatchewan, one of 34 to the Steamer Northcote which made a hammer price of £920 (estimate £600-800); so too an East and West Africa Medal 1887-1899 with unique clasp combination - Benin River 1894 , Brass River 1895 and Benin 1897 - which brought £800 (estimate £300-400)

There were no shortages of numismatic rarities, including the China Medal 1900 with no clasp to Commander E.R. Connor, Second in Command, New South Wales Naval Contingent, who left behind private diaries, which was fancied up to £2,500 (estimate £2,000-2,500), or of unique combinations such as that to the Royal Naval Division of Great War Military Cross, Distinguished Conduct Medal and Military Medal group of seven to Sub-Lieutenant C.B. Wheeler, Royal Naval Volunteer Reserve, who served with the Anson and Nelson Battalions, Royal Naval Division during the Great War but who went on to meet his death in action during the Second World War during the defence of Singapore 1942, which brought £5,200 (estimate £3,000-4,000).

A recipient, five times decorated for gallantry whilst serving in Q-ships, which engaged in most hazardous activities by acting as decoys for enemy submarines, was Petty Officer Ernest Pitcher, whose gallantry awards were headed by a Victoria Cross in combination with Distinguished Service Medal, a Mention-in-Despatches, and French M≥daille Militaire and Croix de Guerre in a group of nine might have brought more than the £28,000 for which they sold (estimate £30,000-35,000).

The wealth of historical research extended to all levels of items, even the more modest. A

An Auction Review

1914-15 Star trio with Long Service & Good Conduct Medal to K99 P.D. Ellender SPO, RN, which came with a manuscript certificate of service bearing he annotation that the recipient 'Participated in the Ballot for award of the Victoria Cross granted for operations against Zeebrugge and Ostende' in April 1918, realised £330 (estimate £100-150).

Particularly noteworthy, from a small section of trial and proof pieces, was the RN Long Service and Good Conduct Medal, Edward VIII, silver proof without suspension, obverse bust by Paget as for coinage patterns. The estimate was undoubtedly low, but the strength of bidding was nonetheless unexpected as it soared to £2,600 (estimate £200-250).

Inevitably the release of this amount of naval material on the market did lead to some ups and downs. Nonetheless overall it sold well, with pieces accessible for all ranks of collectors. Very little in the medal world remains secret for long, and given that all the major auction rooms were given the opportunity to 'tender' for the auction of the collection, it was widely rumoured that the vendors and their advisors had hopes that the whole collection would bring as much as £1 million. Some thought that this was probably always over optimistic and the end result was that just over £600,000 was realised.

1997

Dix, Noonan Webb had a special two catalogue sale on 25 March, the first was devoted to the Dr A.W. Stott collection to 20th Foot, Lancashire Fusiliers and the Royal Regiment of Fusiliers, also Second War medals to all services which totalled 300 lots.

The second catalogue included more general lots, also medals from the estate of a deceased collector, and an important collection of very varied and exciting awards to the SAS and Special Forces, formed in the 1960s during the collectors own service with these units. The cataloguing of these latter items included some most awesome tales of daring.

Both parts of the sale brought some strong prices. From the Stott collection a First War Distinguished Conduct Medal, Military Medal and Bar group of six to Corporal F. Palmer, 2/5th Battalion, Lancashire Fusiliers realised £1,400 (estimate £900-1,200); whilst in the afternoon the rare campaign medal pair of two General Service Medals 1918 62 and 1962 to Trooper F.M. Hamer, Parachute Regiment and 22 SAS Regiment, who was severely wounded in the assault on Green Mountain, Oman 1959, doubled its pre-sale estimate with a successful bid of £1,500 (estimate £600-800). There were other exceptional Special Service awards, for example, again from more recent history, the WWII Distinguished Conduct Medal group of six (one of only ten DCMs to the SAS Regiment, including L Detachment during the Second War) to an original 'L' Detachment member for 1944 service in France behind enemy lines, and who served with Major Roy Farran in Italy. The group, which was secured for £3,200 (estimate £4,000-5,000), was accompanied by items of memorabilia and documents, including the recipient's handwritten account of his wartime service. Another WWII DCM in a group of 15 including Belgian awards to a member of the Belgian SAS Detachment who won the American Bronze Star at the Battle of Imjin River and received his DCM from Montgomery, which sold for £3,000 (estimate £3,000-3,500).

An Auction Review

Dix Noonan Webb produced another varied sale of campaign medals and gallantry awards across all three services for their auction in June. Prominent among groups to the Navy was that to Able Seaman W.C. Williams which included the first ever posthumous Naval Victoria Cross, one of six to members of the crew of the SS River Clyde for gallantry on V Beach during the Gallipoli landings on April 25, 1915. The successful bid was a hefty £46,000 (estimate £25,000-30,000). He was also the first rating with the Royal Navy to be awarded the VC since 1864. Another substantial amount was paid for a group to another member of the sea services, this was to Captain T.J. Badlan, 40 Commando, Royal Marines who was awarded a Distinguished Service Medal for his participation in the Dieppe Raid 1942 (the only DSM for the Raid). The bid price of £5,000 more than exceeded expectations (estimate £1,400-1,800).

An unusual item to the Army was the Black Watch 'Wauchope' silver Medal for Gallantry - privately produced after the battle of Mushaidie, March 1917 by Colonel Wauchope, Commander of the 2nd Battalion in the Battle - which brought £950 (estimate £300-350). Apparently about 60 were issued to men recommended for gallantry at this battle and at Loos, also ten others to those involved in scouting activities in no-mans-land. The only Distinguished Service Order for one of those obscure 'small' wars was the Edward VII example in a group of six to Brigadier General C.E. Palmer CB, CMG, DSO, Royal Artillery, commanding the Kissi Field Force in Liberia 1905 during a three month long expedition against local chiefs who had been raiding territory to capture slaves. The group realised £4,800 (estimate £3,000-4,000).

The sale included some high quality Air Force groups, but the demand for these overall was less intense than for gallantry to the other services. An excellent Commander, Order of the British Empire (CBE), Distinguished Flying Cross, Air Force Cross group of ten to Air Commodore S.L. 'Poppy' Pope, RAF test pilot and First War Ace with 60 Squadron, Royal Flying Corps, which included a Distinguished Flying Cross for Iraq 1926 sold at a respectable, but not over zestful, £2,400 (estimate £2,500-3,000).

Some of the classic early nineteenth century campaign medals sold strongly - good examples are normally well sought after. For example an Army of India Medal 1799-1826 to an Indian native recipient with scarce clasp Corygaum sold for £1,450 (estimate £900-1,200); a Naval General Service Medal 1793-1840 with rare clasp 29 Aug Boat Service 1800, one of only about 25 such clasps issued, made £1,550 (estimate £1,200-1,400); and an excessively rare Military General Service Medal 1793-1814 with 14 clasp and Waterloo Medal 1815 pair - only 12 recipients received 14 clasps and only one other received them in combination with a Waterloo Medal - to an Assistant Commissary, Field Train Department of the Ordnance, sold at £7,500 (estimate £6,000-8,000).

GLENDINING'S

1996

Glendining's continued in line with its well established reputation for providing a good cross section of medallic awards. The first sale of 1996 on 21 March included some interesting foreign awards, also the CB and Small Army Gold Medal to Lieutenant Colonel Archibald Campbell, 46 Regiment, for the battle of Nive where he commanded the 16th

An Auction Review

Portuguese Regiment. These awards came from a section of awards named to Campbell and sold for £3,700 (estimate £4,000-5,000). Indian campaigns supplied a significant auction theme and among some choice pieces was an India Mutiny Medal 1857-59 to the son of Charles Dickens, a Lieutenant with 42 Highlanders, which had a progressive estimate and disappointingly failed to sell (estimate £1,500-1,800).

Gallantry threw up some notable medals such as the George Cross and Distinguished Flying Cross group to Squadron Leader Lieutenant Edward D. Parker. The former award - an Empire Gallantry Medal exchange - ensued from his bravery in saving the life of a member of his crew after their aircraft crash landed on take off. He carried his injured colleague away from the bombs which were then close to exploding. The group proved less popular than had been hoped and realised £4,000 (estimate £5,500-6,500). Also on offer was a Great War Military Medal to a woman with the British Red Cross, who saw service in France and Italy and who was commended for her gallantry and devotion during a 1918 air raid. This proved to be more in demand and sold at a £1,850 (estimate £900-1,100).

The following sale on 4th July was again wide ranging but with some emphasis on Long Service and Efficiency medals. It also contained another small Army Gold Medal for the Pyrenees with clasp Nivelle to Major William Campbell, 36 Foot, which was bought for £3,100 (estimate £3,000-3,500). This was part of a second offering of awards named to Campbell which again proved attractive and went for generally good prices. For example, a Military General Service Medal 1793-1814 with 12 clasps, which apparently should have been part of a pair with a Waterloo Medal 1815, to Henry Campbell, 52 Foot, was still greatly desired and sold at £2,200 (estimate £1,200-1,400).

Miniature medals, although unofficial items, continue to attract a loyal body of collectors who even comprise a special interest branch of the British Orders & Medals Research Society. This interest, together with that from a small group who collect awards to women and/or the medical services, meant that a miniature group to Dame Sidney Browne CBE, RRC, Queen Alexandra's Imperial Military Nursing Service spanning a period beginning with the Egyptian campaign 1882-89 and moving into the twentieth century, sold together with a gold brooch apparently given by Queen Alexandra, found favour and realised twice estimate at £800 (estimate £400-500). She had an interesting and varied public life which was recognised by a variety of honours, such as academic recognition.

It is worth commenting that amongst the foreign awards, several good quality Imperial Russian pieces brought excellent prices; this was in contrast to some USSR awards, several of which failed to find buyers. The market in these items has been somewhat volatile which makes it difficult to set accurate estimates and reserves.

The last eighteen months have seen tranches of engraved silver regimental medals on the market (a small number sold at Dix, Noonan, Webb has already been mentioned). Both in this sale and that earlier in the year, such regimental pieces from the collection of Captain E. Gale Hawkes, were preceded by caveats to the effect that, as it is difficult to distinguish genuine items from those executed at later dates to deceive, the items were sold as seen and not subject to return - prices swung somewhat in the £80-130 range as bidders decided whether or not to back their hunches.

One section of the sale comprised a collection of long service awards, the property of the late Mr J. Hobbs. On the face it, this was perhaps not a theme resounding with excitement, but nonetheless it was one which proved fruitful for the more knowledgeable or for those who had just done their homework, as the relative rarity of some items appeared not to have always been appreciated in the catalogue. For example Efficiency Medals with rare suspensions such as for Nigeria, Rhodesia, and Rhodesia and Nyasaland had been estimated at the level of more common varieties. The Rhodesia and Rhodesia & Nyasaland pair sold for £640 (estimate £100-130).

Occasionally sales include collections not of medals, but of related items of military interest, and on this occasion Glendining's offered part of the late Stanley Kretschmer archive of military photographs, postcards and prints which encompassed most British Regiments as well as many from the Indian Army. Included were photographs showed soldiers wearing their awards. This fascinating material came in quite large lots, which successful bidders must have found most exciting to sort through.

Glendining's continued to provide good hunting with their last sale of 1996 on 14th November; this included more items from the named collections already mentioned - those of Stanley Kretchmer and Captain E. Gale Hawkes. Generally interest held up, although caution resulted in some restrained bidding.

Again a small Army Gold Medal for Java was offered, this time to Lieutenant Colonel William Campbell, 1st Battalion 78th Foot, who had his thighs shattered in action by grapeshot and died of wounds. It proved attractive and went for £5,300 (£3,000-3,500). A Crimea Medal 1854-56 to a recipient who rode and was killed in the Charge of the Light Brigade, an item to attract strong attention when officially impressed, on this occasion still sold well at £1,900 (estimate £1,000-1,4000) although unofficially engraved. A Queen's South Africa Medal 1899-1902 with raised dates on the reverse is recognised as a numismatic rarity, and this sale offered such a piece unique to the Army Service Corps, which was part of a larger group, including medals for Great War service. Competition on his item was brisk and more than kept up with the estimate to capture a final bid of £5,100 (estimate £4,000-5,000). Another example, on offer as a single medal to a Private in a colonial unit, Strathcona's Horse, brought £1,600 (estimate £1,800-2,200).

In view of the prices secured at other auction rooms, particularly with Irish items at Spink, during the period under review, the £480 (estimate £400-500) paid for a 1867 Fenian Raid Irish Constabulary Badge of Merit was most reasonable and might even be regarded as a bargain.

From the section of foreign awards a collection of Russian jettons - normally elaborately decorated badges commemorating military and other achievements - was expected to be an attraction and indeed brought good prices overall. More remarkable from among the foreign orders were two separate lots of what the catalogue described as German Silver Crosses of later manufacture. However telephone bidders apparently recognised something of more interest as the two items sold for £1,950 and £1,000 respectively (estimate £100-120 on both items).

Collectors are always looking for medals with interesting stories and for interesting historical episodes, this sale provided several including a family group of a South Africa Medal 1877-79 to a Civil Practitioner Zeederburg who carried out a post-mortem on Cecil Rhodes, together with the Boer War medals to his son. However they failed to attract a buyer with a top bid of £620 (estimate £700-900). Among the gallantry section, a British Empire Medal to a prisoner of war in Korea, who was at the Imjin River action with the Gloucestershire Regiment, was disappointing in that it failed to sell, passing at £1,600 (estimate £2,000-3,000). Conversely, a Great War Ypres Military Cross including Italian Al Valore Militare, a medal which seems to be fancied, to a Captain with the Royal Scots, wounded at Ypres 1917, extracted a top bid of £1,350 (estimate £400-500).

1997

Glendining's opened 1997 with a 20th March sale which included a good run of about 100 bread and butter campaign medals. The gallantry included the highlight of the sale - the Victoria Cross, sold as a single item, to Captain George Forrest, Bengal Victorian Establishment, won in action at the Delhi magazine 1857, which was gallantly defended when attacked by mutineers. It made a hammer price of £27,000 (estimate £25,000-30,000) in line with the expectations. Also in this section was a group of nine representative of Canadian Service - the Distinguished Service Order, Officer, Order of the British Empire, Distinguished Service Cross and two Bars to Group Captain B.D. Hobbs RNAS, RAF, CAF, RCAF whose DSO was awarded for the destruction of the German Zeppelin L.43 and the DSC for the probable sinking of a submarine, and the Bar for another confirmed sinking. The group proved attractive and made £5,300 (estimate £5,000-7,000).

A rare group of miniatures sold with a considerable amount of documentation and memorabilia, including epaulettes, buttons, a Boatswain's whistle and two telescopes, was well contested by those interested in these unofficial awards. The group was attributed to Captain E.H. Bayly RN, Commander of HMS Aurora and first in command of the defences of Tientsin 1900. The successful bid was £1,050 (estimate £500-700).

Glendining's 17th July sale opened with the disappointing news that the Crimea Light Brigade group to Lord Lucan, Commander of the Cavalry Division, was withdrawn from sale due to family difficulties but it was hoped that they would be sold later in the year. The rest of this varied sale brought mixed results. Some of the more modestly estimated items were especially well contested. For example, a St John Ambulance Brigade group of four which included the Life Saving Medal of the Order, more than doubled expectations by selling at £470. A Great War trio and Memorial Plaque with four Second War Stars to a Captain in the Rifle Brigade realised £430 (estimate £100-150). A Baronet's Badge for Nova Scotia would doubtless have attracted attention from the strong band of Canadian collectors among others and a sale was made at £4,100 (estimate £2,500-3,500). This time Russian jettons were not as successful and several in this sale failed to find buyers.

An Auction Review

SOTHEBY'S

1996

Sotheby's 11th April sale, though relatively small in terms of the number of items sold, was big in terms of military figures. One of the most important Second World War groups to have appeared for sale, namely the treble Distinguished Service Order group to the legendary leader of the Chindits in Burma, Major-General Orde Wingate was the star item. It was Wavell's opinion that Wingate possessed 'a high degree of military genius' and this view can be supported in part by the range of circumstances in which he exhibited bravery and leadership and for which he was awarded three Distinguished Service Orders. The first was won in pre-War Palestine, where he was engaged in Special Night Squad (SNS) operations, the second for achievements in Ethiopia, including the relief of Addis Ababa, and the third for his first Chindit operation behind Japanese lines in Burma. On the day, an anonymous British bidder was prepared to greatly exceed the estimate to secure its purchase. The price of £50,000 was the highest ever at sale for a group of gallantry medals not including the Victoria Cross. The fact that the lot included a number of items associated with Wingate's career such as his service revolver and Wolseley helmet, the latter recovered from the aircraft in which he was killed in 1944, together with photographs and documentation, would have assisted the price.

Other important items in the sale were a Knight Grand Commander, Order of the Indian Empire (GCIE) group to a late nineteenth century administrator in India, Sir Owen Burne. As a subaltern he was recommended for a Victoria Cross for Lucknow; later, as a Private Secretary, he witnessed the assassination of the Viceroy of India, the Earl Mayo in 1872. His orders and campaign medals were accompanied by a presentation silver cup and an inscribed copy of Queen Victoria's volume Our Life in the Highlands and realised £10,000 (estimate £7,000-9,000).

Bravery in a wide variety of circumstances seemed to be a dominant theme of this sale as exampled by a Croix de Guerre group of three with mention in despatches to a Lance Corporal, Essex Regiment Commando who was taken prisoner of war in the St Nazaire operation. Though apparently estimated realistically at £500-800, together with associated militaria and documentation, it brought sustained interest and finally sold at £2,400. A group, including foreign orders and decorations, to Lieutenant-General 'Mike' Michaelis, twice wounded, who dropped on D-Day with the now legendary 101st Airborne at Arnhem, afterwards assuming command of part of the unit, then winning further recognition in Holland and at the Battle of the Bulge, and later awarded a Distinguished Service Order for Korea, disappointingly failed to find a buyer (estimate £4,800-5,200).

Unexpected was the £4,600 (estimate £1,000) paid by a private Irish buyer for the unofficially engraved Crimea Medal 1854-56 to Private Patrick Doolan who rode in the Charge of the Light Brigade at the Battle of Balaclava 1854. This group had sold unexceptionally at auction on previous occasions, however this time Sotheby's were adroit in attracting the eyes of the press who were keen to stress the Irish connection - Doolan was born in Tipperary - which undoubtedly enhanced the competition and spread interest so that on the day five telephone bidders came into head-on competition.

Among the section of foreign awards was an excessively rare Mannerheim Cross and Bar

An Auction Review

to General Aaro Pajari, Finnish Army, one of only four men, to have won this VC equivalent on two occasions. His long and distinguished career spanned three wars including the repulse of the Soviet Armies in Winter War 1939 and the War of Continuation 1941-45. Pajari was twice wounded and decorated many times; his extensive group of awards was accompanied by a substantial and important archive. Disappointingly, the group was withdrawn due to a dispute over ownership - a problem all auction houses have to face from time to time.

Among the more spectacular orders was a diamond set badge of the Order of the Golden Eagle of Wurttenburg which soon became obsolete when it was merged with another order to become the Order of the Crown of Wurttemburg. This example sold at £14,000 (estimate £15,000-20,000).

A collection of campaign awards formed during the 1950s and 1960s attracted a good deal of interest at Sotheby's 26th July auction. Among the lots was a unique nineteenth century nursing group to Joan Gray, the 14th woman to receive a Royal Red Cross (RRC). As a result of her nursing service, she was also the recipient of a South Africa Medal 1877-79, an Egypt Medal 1882 clasp Nile 1884-85, the Khedive's Star 1882, the Ashanti Star 1896, and Queen's and King's South Africa Medals 1899-1902. This unique group attracted collectors of medical, nursing, and/or women's items. An unidentified purchaser paid £9,000 (estimate £4,000-5,000) to acquire this wonderful group.

Several interesting Polar awards came up during the period under review, one of the best was an outstanding Knight Commander, Order of the British Empire (KBE), Companion, Order of St Michael and St George (CMG) group to Admiral Vice Sir Charles Royds, a prominent member of Scott's first expedition 1902-04, who led the Great Ice Barrier team in one of the greatest Antarctic journeys on foot, and latterly became Commissioner of the Metropolitan Police. His medals came with a variety of associated items including a presentation gold hunter pocket watch, a set of RMS Discovery buttons, a gold Metropolitan Police pass, and his collection of photographic slides from Antarctica. The final result significantly exceeded expectations with a price of £11,500 (estimate £6,000-8,000). A less substantial but nevertheless interesting Polar group was the Arctic Discoveries group 1875-76 including World War One medals to a Royal Marine Sergeant, later Captain, which attracted bidders to the level of £1,950 (estimate £800-1,000).

Understandably gallantry always attracts interest especially if for incidents that have a strong public appeal by being the subjects of well known films or books, on this basis one might have expected the Distinguished Service Cross to Warrant Engineer W.H. Locke RN, HMS Campbeltown, who participated in the renowned Second World War raid on St Nazaire, was taken prisoner-of-war and went on to serve in the Korea War to have sold for rather more up to estimate than the £2,500 it produced (estimate £3,000-3,500), but possibly the fact that another more significant St Nazaire gallantry award had produced an excellent result at auction some years previously may have led to rather robust expectations. Locke was one of only two officers to survive the incident when the Campbeltown rammed part of St Nazaire dock, the only suitable dry dock on the Atlantic coast from which the Battleship Tirpitz could operate. More modestly estimated, but still full of interest was the Distinguished Service Cross to a Fleet Air Arm pilot who torpedoed a major Italian ship and had to ditch his Albacore as a result of ack-ack damage £1,300 (estimate £700-900).

An Auction Review

Army gallantry was well represented and included a rare Royal Tank Regiment Military Medal for Tobruk with pre-war India General Service Medal 1936-39, whose recipient subsequently became a prisoner-of-war and filed war crime allegations against a German Captain. The lot made £620 (estimate £400-500)

Those interested in civil bravery were treated to the disposal of one of the finest collections of Edward Medals - awards from Edward VII to King George VI, for Mines and Industry, in silver and bronze, for incidents not just in the UK, but also elsewhere such as Africa and India. Scarce varieties in particular performed strongly against estimates, for example an Edward VII issue for Mines in silver (77 issued only 29 during this sovereign's reign) awarded for bravery in Fife produced a top bid of £1,550 (estimate £800-1,200).

Another famous historic event was represented by a South Africa Medal 1877-79 to a Private with the 1/24th Foot, killed at Isandhlwana 1879 which attracted a successful bid of £1,800 (£800-1,000), somewhat above the sort of prices such medals were generally making.

Medals to those who charged at Balaclava in 1854 and at Omdurman in 1898 are emotive items and several instances have already attracted comment in this review. On this occasion an Omdurman Distinguished Conduct Medal group to a Sergeant, 21st Lancers was not expensive at £5,200 (estimate £3,000-4,000) given that he was a proven charger, as opposed to one who might have charged, and in that his gallantry award was for bravery during this historic action and came with documentary evidence of his deed.

Elizabeth II gallantry awards are well sought after, hence the £950 (estimate £500-700) for a Military Medal pair to a Gurkha was a reasonable price and the Queen's Gallantry Medal for Northern Ireland to the Royal Artillery could well have brought more than £1,200 (estimate £900-1,100) had it been to a unit that collectors consider to have more charisma.

Numismatic rarities usually attract attention from serious collectors and here a Royal Marine Meritorious Service Medal with '1848' dated obverse, together with snuffbox, sword and photograph were snapped up against strong opposition, for £1,750 (estimate 1,200-1,500).

There are often lots on offer at sales of orders, decorations and medals the interest in which spreads far wider than the world of medal collecting. The buoyant price of £1,450 (estimate £600-800) for an unofficial SS Titanic and RMS Carpathia medal would indicate such an interest. - this award was given by Titanic survivors to the crew of the Carpathia who came to their assistance in 1912. A McDonald Moscow Restaurant Medal - given to staff members at the opening - was purchased for £110 (estimate £30-50); it would be interesting to know what sort of collector would be drawn to this item.

In November David Erskine Hill moved to Spink and his place was taken by Edward Playfair. The emphasis of his first sale on the 27th of the month was heavily on the air services with the awards to Sir Geoffrey de Havilland, the renowned designer of the Tiger Moth, Mosquito, Comet and others, which included his Order of Merit, CBE (Commander, Order of the British Empire) and other aeronautical awards, together with a quantity of archive material (estimate £8,000-12,000). The medals of his son Geoffrey Raoul de Havilland, a test pilot, were also for sale (estimate £500-800). Not surprisingly the Royal Air Force Museum was the successful bidder on both groups which brought £14,000 and £2,200 respectively.

Perhaps the outstanding lot of air gallantry was the Companion, Order of St Michael and St George (CMG) and Distinguished Service Order group with extensive archive to Air Commodore E.L. Gerrard, one of the four founding fathers of the Naval Air Service in 1911. Included was a typed memoir containing anecdotes, largely concerned with pre-1914 flying and other memorabilia. Another National Institution - the British Museum - acquired this group with extensive documentation for £8,500 (estimate £3,000-5,000). Other RAF gallantry which attracted sustained attention included Distinguished Flying Medal groups with several to Bomber Command crew, particularly Pathfinders, one to an extremely successful Typhoon pilot and two Distinguished Flying Cross and Bar groups to night-fighter aces.

The rest of the sale included a Queen's Sudan Medal 1896-98, one of 17 awarded to the Royal Navy, the East and West Africa Medal 1887-1900 with clasps Liwondi 1893 and Lake Nyassa 1893, one of only two such medals for those gun boat expeditions, both in a group to Rear Admiral C.H. Robertson CMG, MVO, who also served with the gunboats of the Nile Flotilla during the reconquest of the Sudan. A private collector was successful with this latter item but the final bid was high against estimate at £8,500 (estimate £5,000-7,000).

Although not associated with memorable moments of history, there were rare Efficiency Medals with Mauritius and Southern Rhodesia suspensions which realised £520 (estimate 180-220) and £220 (estimate £120-150) respectively.

Several of the lots already mentioned came with interesting archival material, so too did a CB, Distinguished Service Order group to Brigadier General H.D. Grier RA who was wounded at the defence of Kut-el-Amara in 1916. This included correspondence from his time in a Turkish prisoner of war camp. The medals and archive brought £1,300 (estimate £800-1,200).

1997

Sotheby's was the last of the four major sale rooms to hold its March 1997 auction on the 26th, though a small sale it included some fine pieces and groups. Foremost was the Indian Mutiny Victoria Cross group to Lieutenant Colonel T.B. Hackett, Royal Welch Fusiliers for bravery at the Secundra Bagh during the Relief of Lucknow 1857, which sold at double the estimate for £52,000 (estimate £18,000-22,000).

Items with overseas associations attracted interest such as the rare Soochow Creek Valour Medal, for that battle near Shanghai 1937 in a trio to Private A.G. Weller, Loyal North Lancs Regiment which realised £820 (estimate £500-700); and a group of medals to Captain M.A.R. Trotobas, Manchester and Middlesex Regiments, a Second War Resistance leader which brought £8,200 (estimate £2,000-3,000). Trotobas, alias Capitaine Michel was leader of Farmer Circuit, SOE, who was eventually betrayed by a colleague under torture, and was shot whilst attempting to avoid capture.

In the foreign orders was a rare Hawaiian Order of Kamehamehah I by Kretly of Paris

An Auction Review

1865-85 enticing to the strong band of bidders on foreign orders; it made £1,900 (estimate £1,200-1,500).

Also on offer were a fine selection of medals to Royal Marines, encompassing both campaign and gallantry items, the latter, for example, being represented by an Conspicuous Gallantry Medal for Egypt (only nine to the Marines) when at the battle of Tamaai 1884 the recipient , although surrounded by the enemy, carried to safety a Doctor who was speared in the chest. His award was presented by Queen Victoria at Osborne House. There was also an excessively rare Great War Military Cross and two Bars, Unique to the Royal Marines, named to the Major T. Buckley. His catalogue of gallantry included blowing up ammunitions dumps, fearlessly leading his company forward , and leading an advance bombing party, all while under heavy enemy fire. The former was secured by a final bid of £1,900 (estimate £1,500-2,000), whilst the latter realised £1,600 (estimate £1,800-2,200).

A group to an interesting recipient with very varied service was of CB, CMG, DSO and campaign medals to Brigadier General H.H. Austin, the author of a number of biographical work charting his career, who was awarded the DSO for his part in quelling the Sudanese mutiny at Fort Lubwa's, Uganda and the CMG for his achievement in leading a surveying expedition to Lake Rudolph when out of 62 men only 17 survived. His Naval General Service Medal 1915-62 with clasp Persian Gulf 1909-1914 for his work as a Naval Intelligence Officer was one of only 14 awarded to Army recipients. The group made £5,200 (estimate £5,500-7,500).

Sotheby's medal sale room is a good spot to visit especially during the summer months, due to its situation at Summers Place, Billingshurst, West Sussex. Among the 400 or so lots sold on 26th June was a superb Sash Badge of the Most Ancient and Most Noble Order of the Thistle (KT) - the chalcedony cameo badge set in a gold mount with green enamelling and gold lettering. The badge was that bestowed on the Third Earl of Warwick, Henry Richard Greville, in 1827. It was not surprising that it realised £13,000 (estimate £8,000-12,000). The section of foreign orders was less of a success, although a German 3rd Reich SS Long Service Award for 12 years brought £1,150 (estimate £200-300).

Although items associated with the historic Defence of Rorke's Drift usually find buyers unless estimated and reserved too ambitiously, which was presumably so in this case when a South Africa Medal 1877-79 with clasp 1877-8-9 to a Sergeant with the famous 1/24th Foot failed to sell (estimate £6,000-8,000), as did a piece of Rorke's Drift memorabilia - a silver propelling pencil in the shape of a Zulu assegai- presented to the legendary Lieutenant J.R.M. Chard VC, Royal Engineers by his fellow officers (estimate £9,000-12,000).

A item combining two themes was that to a City of London Policeman. His Olympic Gold Medal for participation with the winning Tug of War team in the Antwerp games of 1920 sold at £2,600 (estimate £2,000-2,500). It was purchased by the London Police Museum to add to its strong medal collection.

In a section of Royal Flying Corps and Royal Air Force awards was a CMG, DSO group to a Great War balloonist , the Officer Commanding 1 Balloon Wing RAF in support of the Canadian Corps during 1918 was fancied at £1,600 (estimate 1,200-1,500); it came

An Auction Review

with a variety of documents and artifacts., including a gold tipped swagger sick and original mention-in-despatches certificates. A British Empire Medal to a woman, Sergeant Hilary Terry, for her outstanding devotion to duty when her telephone room was bombed during a raid on RAF Warmwell brought £750 (estimate £500-700); while a Battle of Britain New Zealand Memorial Cross to a Sergeant with 264 Squadron RNZAF realised £450 (estimate £200-300).

Sometimes interesting items appear in the overseas sale rooms of major houses. Worth a particular note is the Carpathia Medal in Gold which was sold at Sotheby's New York - it was one of only 14 struck in gold and is believed to be the only example to come up at auction. This medal (issued in gold, silver and bronze) was presented by survivors of the Titanic to the officers and crew of the Carpathia who went to their rescue in 1912. It sold for US$50,000.

SPINK
1996

Spink's 12th March 1996 auction contained a range of general properties, including several small collections focusing on the Royal Irish Constabulary, Imperial Russian Orders, the Crimea War, and life-saving awards manly in gold; however a significant part of the sale concentrated on the disposal of the extensive collection of Gordon Lowther with just over 400 lots which included two Victoria Cross groups.

The sale room was packed as the bidding opened on the Lowther medals. In common with most collections, there were ups and downs but, generally speaking, interest and resultant prices were strong. The first Victoria Cross group to be offered also contained a Distinguished Conduct Medal to Lance Sergeant, later Lieutenant, E.B. Smith, Lancashire Fusiliers, while the second, to the same regiment, was awarded to Regimental Sergeant Major J. Clarke. Lieutenant (then Corporal) Smith's acts of gallantry took place in the same month during the Somme battles and the advance in Picardy; having won his DCM for conspicuous gallantry and devotion to duty during the Battle of Amiens on 10th August 1918, he went on to perform several gallant deeds in attack and counter-attack during the Battle of Bapaume on 20th and 21st August, which led to the award of the VC. Regimental Sergeant Major Clarke upheld regimental tradition a little over two months later when during the final advance in Picardy, he won his VC for several instances of conspicuous bravery in an attack during the Battle of the Sambre. These two groups crowned by the UK's premier award for gallantry sold to the same telephone bidder for £19,000 (estimate £18,000-20,000) and £22,000 (estimate £16,000-18,000).

Civilian gallantry in wartime conditions was represented by a Second World War 'Plymouth Blitz' George Medal group of six to Company Officer Cornelius Legg, London Fire Force, National Fire Service which realised £1,150 (estimate £750-800).

Sale catalogues include endless pieces of fascinating information and it would have been easy to pass by the entry for Private Thomas Byrne, VC, 21st Lancers in the knowledge that it was his duplicate Victoria Cross on offer, with the rest of the medals described as a display group. However, reading on, there came the most interesting information that after Byrne's original awards were stolen, the issue of a duplicate Cross was approved,

An Auction Review

apparently the only occasion when permission was granted for the official replacement of the Victoria Cross after the recipient's death. His Victoria Cross was awarded for gallantry in rendering assistance to a wounded officer during the famous charge at Omdurman during the Battle of Khartoum 1898. The successful bidder was prepared to pay £6,500 for this unique item (estimate £6,000-8000).

There were many good items later in the sale from the section of general properties. Good quality foreign orders attract a worldwide specialist audience, and in this instance an item that seems to have been significantly under-estimated was the Supreme Order of the Chrysanthemum Sash Badge which appeared to bring a sensational price of £3,400 when viewed against the estimate (£400-500).

All eyes were on the unique quadruple World War Two and Korea Distinguished Order group to Major General Sir D.A. Kendrew, Royal Leicestershire Regiment, Brigade Commander, and Governor of Western Australia. His Second War DSOs were won in North Africa and Italy. Only 17 officers have been awarded the decoration with three bars, of whom only eight were in the Army; Kendrew's three awards for the Second World War and one for a lesser conflict stand alone. The group sold respectably at £10,500 (estimate £8,000-12,000), but it would not have been surprising had there been sufficient competition to push the price higher.

Both the Crimea and life saving collections, the latter that of Captain Jack Boddington, proved attractive to bidders, but it was the items from a small Royal Irish Constabulary collection that locked two bidders head to head producing prices at twice estimate and more. For example, a scarce Fenian Rising Irish Constabulary Medal brought £2,400 (estimate £1,400-1,600); an Irish Constabulary Badge of Merit made £2,300 (estimate £1,200-2,400); and a King's Police Medal (GVR) cost its purchaser £950 (estimate £200-£300).

Spink continued the VC theme in their 16th July sale, although there was plenty for all ranks of collectors not just a minority with deep pockets. The India Mutiny Victoria Cross group of six to General Sir C.J.S. Gough, late Bengal Cavalry, Corps of Guides and Hodson's Horse was the peer of the groups on offer - his VC was awarded to recognise four separate acts of gallantry between 1857 and 1858. The Gough family were the recipients of two other Crosses, another for the Mutiny and the third for Somaliland 1903. This historic item easily found a buyer and sold at £36,000 (estimate £34,000-38,000). The three family Crosses provide one of four instances of two brothers winning the VC, and one of three instances of the award being given to both father and son.

A group which received good local newspaper coverage had both a sporting and an Indian interest, this was the Olympic team Gold Winners Medal with commemorative medals to Major L.C.R. Emmett MBE, Indian Army Medical Corps who was a member of the winning hockey team from India at the Berlin Olympics 1936. It had a special immediacy as 1996 was also an Olympic year. The group sold well, making £2,800 (estimate £1,400-1,600), although sadly the recipient, who was then over 80 and in ill health, died only a few days after the sale.

Gallantry was the byword for many of the most notable groups in this sale, which included some rare and interesting gallantry awards from a specialist collection of Distinguished

An Auction Review

Conduct Medals to the Royal Artillery encompassing decorations for the the South Africa campaigns 1877-79, the First Boer War, Maiwand, the Sudan, the Boer War, the North West Frontier 1897 and 1908, Nigeria 1900 and Dunkirk. They were well contested and the rarity of an award for Ulundi 1879 was underlined by a successful bid price of £7,500 (estimate £2,600-2,800). It is worth noting that whilst 23 Victoria Crosses were awarded for the Zulu War 1879, only 15 DCMs were granted.

It is invariably the case that good examples of the classic medals covering the whole Napoleonic period and the first decades of the nineteenth century can always find buyers if not unreasonably estimated. In this sale a small run of Naval General Service Medals 1793-1840 affirmed this statement. Attractive was a NGS to an officer who had served at Trafalgar and, as a First Lieutenant, had accompanied Napoleon to St Helena, where the two are reported to have played chess together on several occasions. Together with a portrait miniature, the medal sold within estimate at £2,400 (estimate £2,000-3,000)

At this sale a fresh example of a NGS to a recipient who served aboard Nelson's flagship HMS Victory surfaced for the first time, having come direct from the family. Awarded to Able Seaman James Hartnell, it sold for a healthy £4,400 (estimate £3,500-4,000). The number of known extant NGS medals with Trafalgar clasps to officers and men who served on the Victory is just under 40.

Collectors of miniatures again made their presence felt when a miniature Military General Service Medal 1793-1814 with engraved clasps, together with associated items including original documentation, attracted competition to a level of £800 (estimate £400-500).

Obviously items that only occasionally come on the market need to be snapped up, and here among the foreign awards was a cased military set of insignia of the Russian Order of the White Eagle. Only infrequently does a set with swords come on the market; and the selling price of £10,500 (estimate £8,000-10,000) was evidence of this.

Although good and interesting, some groups fail to sell simply because no-one has a niche for them or those that do find the price beyond their means. This may have been true of a rare life saving group of five medals to Commander T. Leigh, HM Coastguard comprising Matthew Boulton's Medal for the Battle of Trafalgar in pewter, Royal National Lifeboat (RNLI) Second Award Gold Boat, RNLI Silver Medal, two large Royal Humane Society Medals in silver, together with six boxed silver teaspoons engraved with elements from Nelson's crest. Bidding came to a standstill at £2,200 (estimate £3,800-4,200).

A historic group that came under the spotlight was that containing a Polar Medal with clasps for Scott's first and second Antarctic expeditions, together with First World War Medals and two related Royal Geographical Society Medals to Chief Petty Officer T.S.

An Auction Review

Williamson RN, one of the search party who discovered the final resting place of Captain Scott and his companions and who had also been on Scott's first and second expeditions (one of only seven men to receive the two clasps). It produced a most buoyant price, selling for £10,500 (estimate £6,000-7,000).

One of the finest and most comprehensive regimental collections to be disposed of for many years was that to the Connaught Rangers (88th and 94th Regiments) formed by Peter Power-Hynes. Composed of more than 250 items it covered the period from the Napoleonic Wars to the First World War. Overall the medals kept well up with estimates but with a notable number climbing even higher. The factors that combined to make this happen were sometimes easily discernible, for example a Waterloo Medal 1815 to Arthur Stewart MD, 71st Regiment, the Inspector-General of Hospitals 1785-1854 and the only officer also entitled to the Military General Service Medal 1793-1814 (MGS) with the 88th Foot, interested both regimental collectors and those that collected to a medical theme as well as apparently the owner of his separated MGS. Consequently the purchaser had to part with £1,900 hammer price (£750-800). Three groups of campaign medals were sold together in the same lot, all named to the Babbington family, this pitted a family member against a dealer buying for a client. The result was that the successful bid was an astonishing £3,600 (estimate £600-700).

A scarce Field Officer's Gold Medal for Cuidad Rodrigo with Sultan's Gold Medal for Egypt 1801 (36mm with original hook and chain) together with a forwarding letter from Frederick, Duke of York also produced considerable competition and realised £6,500 (estimate £3,800-4,200) The recipient had risen from the ranks finally to meet his death as a Major at Badajos.

The catalogue description of a unique Regimental Bravery Medal for Talavera with seven clasp Military General Service Medal 1793-1814 and Regimental Order of Merit First Class called into question some aspects of the latter medal. This did not deter potential purchasers who placed bids up to £5,500 (estimate £3,000-3,500).

Items from classic named collections are coveted and several items from the Power-Hynes collection had also previously graced that of the regimental historian Colonel H.F.N. Jourdain. For example a Crimea Distinguished Conduct Medal group of three to Private Michael Burke, 88th Foot sold at £950 (estimate £550-650).

Autumn at Spink brought a significantly more compact sale on 6th November of about 250 lots, although the diminution in the amount of material as compared to the earlier sales of 1996 did not lead to a diminution in quality.

Again Victoria Crosses headed the field. The first was an outstanding item to Canada's most decorated soldier of the First World War, Captain J. MacGregor, 2nd Canadian Mounted Infantry, consisting of a Hindenburg Line VC, a Military Cross and Bar, and a Distinguished Conduct Medal for Vimy Ridge (estimate £40,000-45,000). Doubtless this would have attracted a good deal of interest, but the medals had to be withdrawn before the sale because the Canadian vendor had not acquired the required export papers. Subsequently the group was purchased as a result of fundraising in Canada and is now on display at the Canadian War Museum in Ottawa. A Victoria Cross for the Battle of Loos posthumously awarded to one of the youngest ever VC winners, 18 year old Private G.

An Auction Review

Peachment, King's Royal Rifle Corps, exceeded the estimate, selling at a hammer price of £27,000 (estimate £18,000-22,000). The same purchaser bought the third Victoria Cross, awarded for gallantry in 1917 at Pickern Ridge, Ypres to Private G. McIntosh, Gordon Highlanders who went on to serve as a Flight Sergeant in the Second World War, but again he had to buy at a price well over estimate, £32,000 (£18,000-22,000).

Attractive was a group of family medals to four separate recipients of the Bishop family, ranging from a Military General Service Medal 1793-1840 to World War II medals, also included was a Meritorious Service Medal group to a Yeoman Warder of the Tower of London, late Colour Sergeant, 37th Regiment who served in the Indian Mutiny. The Bishop medals were secured with a bid of £1,700 (estimate)

Other rare items were a Military Medal to Tank Commander Senior Sergeant T.M. Sheshlo, Red Army, one of only four such Second War awards to Russian personnel. Although entitled to Russian awards they were not sold with this medal. Disappointingly it did not meet the urgent requirement of any collector and remained unsold at £1,200 (estimate £1,900-2,200). Another superb group, again with a Soviet interest, was that of 12 medals to Soviet Fighter Ace Major N.F. Denchik who had 13 victories to his credit. His group included a Medal of the Hero of the Soviet Union (gold star), Order of Lenin, and three Orders of the Red Banner. This group sold just below estimate at £2,400 (£2,500-3,000).

Also rare was a Constabulary Medal (Ireland) to Temporary Cadet George C. Gash, Auxiliary Division RIC (1921), although part of a broken group the scarce naming to a 'TC' ensured its success at £1,700 (estimate £800-900); it was sold with photographs of the recipient. A rarity among the foreign orders was the Imperial Austrian special Jubilee award of the Military Merit Cross set with cut diamonds and Burmese rubies which brought £7,800 (estimate £4,000-5,000).

1997

Spink's first sale of 1997 took place on 18th March - the first under David Erskine-Hill. Undoubtedly the most historically important item of the auction was the group of awards to Air Chief Marshal Baron Dowding GCB, GCVO, CMG, generally acknowledged as the architect of the crucial Battle of Britain. His leadership during the Summer of 1940 is generally recognised as being one of steadfastness in the face of a most difficult task and in face of the interminable opposition and squabbles that he had to encounter. His insight into the total strategy required to defeat the Germans came from his vast experience dating from his time as a frontline pilot in the First War through his interwar involvement in building up the RAF into a highly effective fighting force. However a private sale was concluded prior to auction, with the RAF Museum, Hendon apparently purchasing the awards for the higher estimate of £60,000 (plus buyer's premium) (estimate £40,000-60,000). The group, sold by Lady Dowding, widow of Dowding's son, were expected to go on immediate display next to Goering's wartime awards.

Another heavyweight item was the Bhootan campaign 1865 Victoria Cross group to Captain James Dundas, Royal Engineers, later killed in active service by a mine explosion in Afghanistan 1879, which made £38,000 (estimate £25,000-28,000). This was one of

An Auction Review

only two VCs for the Bhootan campaign in the mountainous territory on the Tibet border, where Dundas personally accounted for five or six Bhootanese with his revolver during a desperate hand-to-hand struggle inside an enemy stronghold.

Other items representative of the British period in India were the Indian Order of Merit, Military Division Reward of Valour 1st Class, one of only 42 awarded between 1837 and 1912, which realised £1,850 (estimate £1,500-2,000) and a well researched Army of India Medal 1799-1826 with rare clasp Kirkee and Poona awarded to the Honourable Mountstuart Elphinstone, Resident at Poona and later Governor of Bombay, which brought £6,500 (estimate £2,500-3,000).

The Napoleonic campaigns were represented by a trio of outstanding lots: firstly two Army Gold Crosses, one with five bars to Lieutenant Colonel Henry Hardinge, one of just 18 such awards, the other to Lieutenant General Sir Joseph Carncross with two bars, which brought successful bids of £18,500 (estimate £18,000-22,000) and £11,500 (estimate £10,000-12,000) respectively, also the awards to Lieutenant-General Sir Robert Garrett, Colonel of the 43rd Regiment, who was wounded three times in the Peninsula War and became Commanding Officer of the 4th Division in the Crimea some 40 years later. Accompanied by a fine set of miniatures, the group sold at £7,000 (estimate £6,500-7,500).

Moving on a century there was a small specialist section of campaign awards to the Special Air Service (SAS), including a General Service Medal pair 1918-62 and 62 pair with clasp combinations Malaya/Arabian Peninsula and Borneo/Radfan respectively to Corporal 'Mau Mau' Williams. The pair was much sought after and sold at £1,250 (estimate £600-800).

Naval service was represented by a Knight Grand Cross, Order of the Bath (GCB), Knight Commander, Order of St Michael and St George (KCMG) group of fourteen with First World War medals and some foreign awards to Admiral of the Fleet Sir Frederick 'Tam' Field who was wounded in the Boxer Rebellion, commanded the King George V at the battle of Jutland 1916 and served as First Sea Lord and Chief of Naval Staff 1930-33 during which term of office he had to deal with the famous Invergordon Mutiny. Despite the recipient's interesting service history, the group did not quite live up to expectations with a top bid of £4,500 (estimate £5,000-6,000).

Also on offer were Royal Household Service Medals, including a group of 12 to Frederick Finch, Manservant to Edward, Prince of Wales (later King Edward VIII) which realised £3,000 (estimate £2,500-3,000) and a group of seven to Lawrence Wrighton, Valet to King Edward VII from 1901-10 which sold at £1,500 (estimate £800-1,200). Royal household groups can be found at auction from time to time and usually attract sustained interest.

The Spink auction of orders, decorations, campaign medals and militaria on 17th July 1997 contained an impressive wealth and breadth of material. Inevitably this induced wide interest from a broad cross-section of collectors and others, resulting in strong telephone and book bids, together with a backed auction room and overspill outside.

The Van Trappen collection of commemorative medals, plaques and other memorabilia, mainly but not exclusively from the Great War, opened the sale. The Belgian Van Trappen family had acquired many of the pieces during the 1920s and indeed had known many of the designers and sculptors personally.

Much of the material was of a patriotic nature, mainly from France, Belgium and the Central Powers, and the collection was unique both in its extent and in its comprehensiveness. The items were unusual, particularly in this volume, for a sale room and it must have been very difficult, despite the quality of the pieces, to predict the outcome at auction. In many cases it was possible to lot up the collection according to some of the themes depicted, such as royalty, military and political leaders, even battle scenes. Many of the 250 or so lots contained quite a number of medals and/or plaques, sometimes over one hundred pieces. Collectors able to view the sale in advance had the greatest potential to do well and find both the unusual and what really interested them, in contrast to those who could only rely on the catalogue in which the majority of lots inevitably remained unillustrated.

On the day, a section of satirical, propaganda and political medals from the Central Powers by Karl Goetz brought variable results, with some subjects more popular than others. Two of the famous original commemorative medals for the sinking of the SS Lusitania (copies were also produced for British propaganda purposes) appeared in separate lots, one with the so-called error date (5 Mai 1915) made £380 (estimate £200-300) and the other with corrected date (7 Mai 1915) realised £200 (estimate £200-300). A lot containing a rare piece in commemoration of the execution of Sir Roger Casement seemed to find favour and sold at a hammer price of £480 (estimate £300-500). A small run of examples from World War Two also sold for solid prices.

More propaganda pieces by other medallists also attracted an enthusiastic audience, for example the eighteen medals relating to the German Air Force and Balloon Detachments, with depictions of a number of German fighter aces, the bombing of London by Zeppelins and the sinking of the Ark Royal; after sustained bidding these sold for £1,100 (estimate £400-500). Additionally 22 other propaganda pieces relating to naval events of the Great War brought £1,000 (estimate £600-800).

The final lots from this collection consisted of patriotic medallets, unit badges, stick bins and lapel ephemera of the Allies and Central Powers, mainly from the First War. Again these presented a challenge to the auctioneers who must have been pleased to find in some areas there was a strong demand. For example over one hundred Red Cross and related Badges sold at £600 (estimate 180-220), whilst what was said to be a most comprehensive run of 235 enamelled badges, mostly from identifiable army units, brought a top bid of £1,800 (estimate £800-1,000).

The auction recommenced after a break starting with single campaign medals, which sold well, like the campaign groups and pairs later in the sale. Collectors and museums with an interest in the early nineteenth century continue strong, and this generally guarantees a reliable demand for good quality, realistically estimated pieces. In this sale a Naval General Service Medal 1793-1840 clasps St Vincent, Trafalgar and Guadaloupe, fine and rare in original card box of issue, brought a hammer price of £2,100 (estimate £1,600-1,800), and an Army of India Medal 1799-1826 with clasps Argaum and Assye to Lieutenant C. Cobbe, 19 Light Dragoons, extremely fine and very rare, was subject to competitive

An Auction Review

bidding from, among others, a Regimental representative, and sold at £4,000 (estimate £2,000-2,500). A Kelat-I-Ghilzie Medal 1842 (unnamed as issued) more than doubled its estimate as potential buyers battled to secure such a scarce item - the successful purchaser paid £1,250 (estimate £400-500).

Medals for historic actions always have the potential to bring good prices, for example awards for the Crimea War 1854-56 to participants with the Light and Heavy Brigades. In this sale single campaign medals, one to a Heavy Brigade man in the 2nd Dragoons (officially impressed) sold at £650 (estimate £300-400), the second to a Heavy Brigade charger with 5th Light Dragoons (contemporarily engraved) made £340 (estimate £200-250). The Indian Mutiny Medal 1857-59 clasps Lucknow and Defence of Lucknow to a Private with the 84th Regiment - the latter clasp is rare to the Regiment - was considered by many to be a reasonable purchase as only 50 men participated in the Defence of Lucknow. It produced a successful bid of £520 (estimate £500-700).

As has already been commented on in Spink's own publication (Spink Medal Circular, October 1997) some years ago, British South Africa Company Medals 1890-97 were subject to a spate of 'naming up' which reduced their attraction to buyers. However in this sale a named two-clasp example sold for £780, more or less double top estimate (estimate £300-400) perhaps suggesting that a cautious confidence is being injected into the market for these medals. The Cape Copper Company Medal for the Defence of Ookiep 1902 turns up rarely these days, nonetheless the single example on offer was bought at a reasonable cost of £620 (estimate £350-450).

One of the most interesting facets of medal collecting is the fascinating facts that can be uncovered in connection with the circumstances surrounding the award of a medal. This was illustrated in this auction when medals with good stories were seen generally to be in demand. For instance a Queen's South Africa Medal 1899-1902 to Trooper C. Godden, South Africa Light Horse, which came with much information concerning the recipient's gallant service, made a hammer price of £700 (estimate £300-400). Trooper Godden was in small attacking party which made a courageous crossing of the Tugela River under enemy fire, an incident later described by Winston Churchill, then a Lieutenant with the Regiment, and for which Godden was mentioned in despatches. Soon afterwards he was seriously wounded in action which led to his death.

The awards for gallant and distinguished service included some outstanding items, a number illustrated in the catalogue by marvellous historic photographs of the recipients Òin actionÓ. Three superb Victoria Cross groups were all acquired by the same purchaser. The outstanding VC and Military Cross group of five to Captain J.A. 'Oozy' Liddell, Royal Flying Corps and Argyll and Sutherland Highlanders was one of the earliest such awards of this premier decoration for gallantry to a pilot. Liddell, though severely wounded, his right thigh shattered and with a lapse into unconsciousness, safely landed his badly damaged aircraft, which had dropped out of control for some 3000 feet, behind British lines thus saving the life of his observer. Liddell died later the same month. The group went for £85,000 (estimate £80,000-100,000). The same bidder had to part with another £70,000 to secure the unique Second War Victoria Cross group with escaper's Distinguished Conduct Medal in a group of six to Lieutenant A.G. Horwood, Queen's Royal (West Surrey) Regiment, attached Northamptonshire Regiment (estimate £70,000-

80,000). The VC was awarded for sustained gallantry over a three day period at Kyauchaw, Burma in January 1944, when he a established a forward position to locate the enemy who maintained intense sniper, machine gun and mortar fire on the forward troops both when stationary and as they advanced, Horwood led the final brave attack on the Japanese and in so doing was mortally wounded at point blank range. His DCM was for his conduct at the evacuation of Dunkirk.

Probably the last Arnhem related Victoria Cross likely to come up for sale was in combination with a Chindit associated Distinguished Flying Cross and campaign medals in a group of nine to Flight Lieutenant D.S.A. Lord - the only World War Two VC to Transport Command. Here strong bidding took the item over estimate; the successful bidder acquired his third VC of this sale but had to pay £110,000 (estimate £80,000-100,000) due to strong competition from the Royal Air Force Museum, Hendon as the underbidder. Whilst piloting a Dakota aircraft detailed to drop supplies on Arnhem, Flight Lieutenant Lord's aircraft was hit by anti-aircraft fire which resulted in his starboard engine bursting into flame; despite this, he made two runs to ensure that the last of the supplies were dropped (an eight minute procedure). Only one member was able to abandon the aircraft, Lord and the remainder losing their lives as the aircraft fell in flames. By remaining at the controls to enable his crew and passengers to abandon, Lord had ensured the sacrifice of his own life.

A good deal of pre-sale press publicity had been given to the gallantry group to Brigadier J.M. Calvert, Chindit Leader and Commander of the S.A.S. Brigade. It was, perhaps, predictable that the sale of this Second World War Distinguished Service Order and Bar group of 14 to such a colourful personality should have attracted attention, particularly with the almost concurrent of a book said to give a more balanced account of his life. Despite the more controversial nature of his later life, his military stature and exploits are well established and widely acknowledged thus it was no surprise that these awards to such a renowned military figure, who is associated with historic actions and units with superb credentials, should bring a price well over estimate - the group sold for £18,000 (estimate £12,000-15,000).

World-wide interest is usually assured for any auction containing foreign orders, decorations and medals, provided they are good pieces. As is usual for Spink, this sale was no exception and the foreign section brought essentially good prices with just one or two unsolds. Fine quality pieces of a good age produced a winning combination as far as the realisation of strong prices was concerned.

Rarely seen Manchukuo Orders such as the First Class sash Badge of the Order of the Auspicious Clouds and the Order of the Illustrious Dragon Grand Cordon Star sold solidly at £1,600 and £3,200 respectively (estimates £1,400-1,500 and 2,500-3,000). Unsold in this section were the rare Bulgarian Lesser Collar Chain of the Order of St Alexander (estimate £4,000-5,000) and a French Order of the Iron Crown, Chamberlain's key (estimate £1,500-1,800); as can sometimes happen, although of undoubted quality and interest, these pieces were more difficult to place.

Among the British orders and single decorations a CBE pair offered with a selection of memorabilia and documentation was that to a Political Correspondent, Parliamentary

An Auction Review

Lobby Journalist and Member of the Parliamentary Press Gallery, Guy Eden - this attracted sustained attention and sold at £920 (estimate £600-800). The pair seemed to offer great potential for research as the catalogue contained no real personal information on the recipient.

There were some astonishing prices in the sale of a collection of miniature Victoria Cross groups. Despite the fact that miniature medals are not official awards, coupled with the difficulties of producing watertight provenances, the strong body of miniature collectors ensured very strong competition, even where the provenance was particularly slight. The Crimea VC group of four attributed to Rear Admiral C.D. Lucas RN brought £2,400 (estimate £800-1000); the Crimea VC group of five to Captain A. Moynihan, 90 Regiment sold for £1,700 (estimate £600-700); and another group with apparently tenuous connections to Rorke's Drift VC, Colonel J.R.M. Chard, South Wales Borders, brought an astonishing £2,900 (estimates £400-500). For those not engaged in miniature medal collecting, the rationale behind such prices is difficult to understand.

A section of Meritorious and Long Service awards included a Coronation Medal 1953 which rarely turn up for the Mount Everest Expedition; this example, named to a Leading Sherpa, nonetheless sold within estimate at £720 (estimate £600-800).

The morning session of the auction had opened with the usual section of militaria which is now a feature of Spink and other medal auctions. A wide variety of items was on offer, some perhaps were of more interest to collectors of orders, decorations and medals than were others. The two final items of militaria were particularly fascinating because of their association with especially colourful military figures and both brought good prices. Field Marshal Montgomery's beret, together with a signed letter bestowing provenance on the item, was much in demand and sold at £12,000 (estimate £5,000-7,000), one lady bidder who went to 10,000 was bitterly disappointed not to be successful as her father had a connection with Montgomery. A pair of English riding boots belonging to General George Patton, who favoured boots of English manufacture, sold at £1,600 (estimate £1,000-2,000).

BONHAMS

1996

Although relatively new to medals, Bonhams, in addition to providing regular small runs of standard items for the average collector, were able to produce several interesting and desirable pieces and an outstanding collection in 1997. For example, their September sale included a short run of 32 medals, the most significant group being that of a Great War Distinguished Service Order and Bar in a group of 12 to Major General H.W. Higginson CB, Royal Dublin Fusiliers in Command of the 2nd Battalion 1915-16, who had seen varied service in Africa prior to the First War. The medals sold for £2,400 (estimate £2,000-2,500). A more modest but still interesting pair was the Crimea Medal 1854-56 together with a Scottish Naval and Military Academic prize medal for military history, together they realised £180 (estimate £80-120).

Their end of the 1996 year sale was held at the beginning of December, but this contained just a small section of medals, the most notable of which was a Great War Distinguished Service Order group of nine to Colonel C.F.H. Greenwood CB, Queen's Royal Regiment and 1/22 London Regiment who saw active service in the Boer War 1899-1902 and the First World War, it sold with the hammer at £1,100 (estimate £700-900).

1997

Bonhams pulled off a major coup in 1997 when they announced that in June they would be selling the impressive James R. Barracks collection which comprised every Japanese Order in all classes. This highly important collection of Japanese orders, medals and insignia formed 50 years ago was the most complete ever to appear on the market in the West and included examples of very rare pieces. Also offered in the same sale was the William Long collection of awards to Irish Regiments. Including a larger than usual section of general properties, in all the sale comprised over 300 lots. This was Bonham's greatest success story to date and more than lived up to expectations.

The highlight of the sale was the last lot, part of the Japanese collection, which was the rare collar and pendant badge of the Japanese Supreme Order of the Chrysanthemum: this sold on estimate at £55,000 (estimate £40,000-60,000). A Grand Cordon of the Order of the Golden Kite (First Class) soared to reach a successful bid of £12,500 (estimate £2,800-3,200), similarly successful was the Cultural Decoration Neck Badge which realised £11,000 (estimate £800 1,200).

The Barracks collection provided wonderful material for reproduction in colour in the catalogue, which is now a useful reference in itself. For example the colour plate of the star and badges of the Order of the Sacred Crown established in 1888 and awarded only to ladies provided an spectacular illustration - the star and higher class badges are all set with seed pearls. Other plates cover the Order of the Golden Kite, the Order of the Sacred Treasure, and the Order of the Rising Sun.

From the Long collection a rare First World War Military Cross and two Bar group of four, unique to the Regiment, named to Lieutenant M.F. O'Donnell, Royal Dublin Fusiliers made £3,200 (estimate £1,800-2,200). Most other lots were well contested.

BOSLEYS
1997

Bosleys, a newcomer on the medal scene, offered representative runs of material for the general collector In their June 1996 sale of military antiques, which included a First World War 1914 Star trio to a Private, Australian Volunteer Hospital together with his St John's Ambulance Brigade 1911 Coronation Medal, a Service Medal of the Order of St John, and a Serbo-Turkish War Medal 1912. The AVH was the only Australian unit to qualify for the 1914 Star and the group realised £900. Sales continued throughout the year, in August the highlight being a First World War gallantry combination of Distinguished Conduct Medal and Military Medal to a non-commissioned officer in the Tank Corps, which sold for £3,300.

In April 1997 Bosley's had more medals to offer, including a small collection of bread and butter pieces connected with Hampshire, which sold for prices between £20-160. RAF groups included a Battle of France 1940 Distinguished Flying Cross awarded to a pilot

An Auction Review

who, though wounded, managed to return to his airfield with valuable information about troop movements, this realised £900. A Member, Order of the British Empire (MBE) group with a quantity of photographs taken in Iran 1923-32 was that to Wing Commander Frederick Wall, which produced a top bid of £700.

In June, the sale included a variety of items including a St John Ambulance Brigade Medal for South Africa in bronze, one of 68 issued for home service, which brought £310 (estimate £100-125); an Ashantee Star 1896 to a Private in the West Yorks Regiment, one of about 420 (2000 or so issued in total) which were named by the Colonel of the 2nd Battalion, West Yorkshire Regiment at his own expense, induced a top bid of £300 (estimate £175-250); and a Royal Household group of seven to Queen Alexandra's wine butler realised £380.

WALLIS & WALLIS
1996

Wallis & Wallis hold very regular sales of militaria and medals at their Sussex room in Lewes. These include a general range of medallic items, with a number of items to attract more than average interest. In 1996 their sales contained a South Africa Medal 1877-79 to an Isandhlwana casualty, a Private R. Morse, 1/24th Foot which sold for £1,350; a much more recent award was the Gulf Medal 1990-91 clasp 16 Jan-28 Feb 1991 with the Saudi Arabian Liberation of Kuwait Medal and a Kuwait Medal 1991 to a Gunner, Royal Artillery was bought for £125. Their special Connoisseur sale in May included some fine British orders, most notably the eighteenth century gold and enamel Great George Collar Badge of the Most Noble Order of the Garter (from the collection of the Duke of Cambridge, son of George III) which brought £12,000; Breast Stars of the Orders of the Garter (1825), of the Thistle in metal, and of St Patrick (1855) with diamonds which made £3,200, £3,200, and £3,000 respectively. A Knight Commander's insignia of the Order of the Star of India Neck Badge and Breast Star with diamonds in original Garrard case sold at £5,100; and a Royal Order of Victoria and Albert 3rd class with pearls and diamonds for £7,000. Enticing too was a Royal Jersey Militia gold regimental medal in very fine condition to Private John Journeaux, 3rd East Regiment which may well have attracted strong interest from Jersey itself; the successful bid price was £1,750.

Their more general sale in June included an award that was apparently associated with a fascinating tale. This was an Imperial Russian Order of St Stanilas neck badge in gold and enamel attributed to Albert Bierstadt which was said to have its origins in the Wild West.. As a friend or good acquaintance of General W.T. Sherman, Bierstadt was asked by the General to include some North American Indians on a buffalo shooting party to be laid on for the Russian Grand Duke Alexis in 1871. Both Colonel Cody and General Custer assisted with other arrangements for this Russian visit to North America. The Order was apparently awarded for Bierstadt's services at this time and sold for £230.

1997

A variety of interesting items appeared in the March 1997 auction including a Borough of

Hartlepool Special Constable's silver medal with the reverse inscription 'Borough of Hartlepool. Special Constable. Bombardment 1914. Air Raids 1915-18. Zeppelin destroyed 1916', thought to be one of about 116 issued. In December 1914 Hartlepool, Scarborough and Whitby were bombarded by the German battle cruiser squadron with Hartlepool the worst hit. The item sold at £450. Among the more than 100 lots of medals was also a Naval General Service Medal 1793-1840 with rare clasp Cornet Aug. 1808 which realised £1,400.

In their first Connoisseur sale of 1997 in April, Wallis & Wallis offered the unique Military Cross group of four to Second Lieutenant H.A. Somerville, Royal Sussex Regiment, together with photographs and accounts both of his career and that of Max Ritter von Muller, the German First War top scoring fighter ace (37 kills) that he successfully shot down. Somerville earned his MC 'for most conspicuous gallantry' at Ypres, after which he took up an instructional course with the Royal Flying Corps. It was on his first flight on a photographic mission that he was attacked by seven enemy aircraft, to which he responded with 50 rounds setting aflame Muller's plane. The group brought a hammer price of £4750.

Orders of Knighthood

There are two opposing views on the collecting of orders of chivalry: dug-in medal collectors often tend to sneer at these pieces as mere 'jewellery' having no connection with real people, but simply a perk of the aristocratic or the rich and powerful. Those who collect them, however, will be happy to talk of beauty, craftsmanship and the freedom of not having to concern oneself with whole groups or the 'man behind the medal'. Whichever view is taken, it cannot be denied that the collecting of orders for their own sake, rather than as part of a person's group, is not as widespread in the United Kingdom as the collecting of decorations and medals.

Overseas, however, particularly in the United States, where there is not the same tradition of named medals, this area of collecting is a good deal more popular and some mouth-watering displays can usually be seen at the Annual Convention of the Orders and Medals Society of America.

British orders are presented to the recipient by the Monarch, hence the prices given below are for official issues manufactured by those under contract to the Central Chancery of Orders of Knighthood. It must be remembered, however, that many overseas countries have not and do not operate the same system, often simply presenting the recipient with a diploma and allowing him to purchase his own insignia wherever and to whatever quality he wishes. Orders of this type, therefore, can be manufactured by a variety of jewellers, both at home and abroad. Some small countries often had their insignia manufactured abroad and, for instance, it is quite usual to find Serbian pieces made in Vienna and Paris.

1. THE MOST NOBLE ORDER OF THE GARTER

The premier Order of Britain and one of the oldest in Europe, the usually accepted date for the foundation of the Order of the Garter is 1348. It consists of the Sovereign, the Prince of Wales and 25 Knights only (KG), but there is also provision for the admission of other sons of the Sovereign and a number of extra Knights who are mostly foreign reigning monarchs. During this century, reigning Queens have been admitted as Ladies of the Order.

The insignia of the Order comprises a mantle, hood, surcoat and hat together with the garter itself, worn on the left leg by Knights and on the left arm by Ladies. The Collar, only worn on special occasions, consists of alternate roses encircled by a garter and lovers knots. From this hangs the George, an enamelled figure of St. George and the Dragon. The Lesser George is similar in appearance but is encircled by an oval garter and worn suspended from the sash on the right hip. Finally, the eight pointed breast Star bears a central red cross of St George surrounded by the garter.

All items are returnable on the death of the holder which means that pieces are very scarce on the market. However, before the present century, many of those honoured with the Garter had parts of the insignia privately made, sometimes to a higher standard or set with precious jewels. It is these items which are sometimes offered for sale.

Collar Chain	Rare
Collar Badge (George)	£22,000
Star (metal)	£3,000
Star (embroidered)	£850
Sash Badge (Lesser George)	£6,000
Garter (embroidered)	£500
Garter (gold)	£2,500

2. THE MOST ANCIENT AND MOST NOBLE ORDER OF THE THISTLE

Established by James II in 1687 to consist of the Sovereign and 12 Knights (KT), the Order fell into disuse upon his dethronement in the following year. It was revived by Queen Anne in 1703 and extended to 16 Knights in 1827. Like the Garter, the Thistle was an aristocratic Order, but mostly reserved for the Scottish nobility. There has only ever been one Lady of the Order, Queen Elizabeth the Queen Mother.

The Insignia worn on special occasions consists of a mantle and the enamelled Collar of alternate thistles and sprigs of rue, from which hangs the Badge depicting St. Andrew holding a saltire Cross before him. The gold Jewel, which is similar in design, is worn suspended from the sash on the right hip and the Star bearing the cross of St. Andrew is worn on the breast. All parts of the insignia are returnable at death so, as with the Garter, any pieces offered for sale will be privately made.

Collar Chain	Rare
Collar Badge	£30,000
Star (metal)	£2,500
Star (embroidered)	£800
Sash Badge (gold)	£5,000

3. THE MOST ILLUSTRIOUS ORDER OF ST. PATRICK

The third of the 'Great' Orders, St. Patrick was instituted by King George III in 1783 as a method of rewarding his Irish peers. Originally to consist of the Sovereign and 15 Knights (KP), it was extended to 22 Knights in 1833. For obvious reasons, appointments to the Order ceased with partition in 1922 and the Order became obsolete in 1974 upon the death of the last holder. In addition to the Mantle, the insignia consisted of a Collar of alternate roses and harps linked together with gold knotted cord from which hung the Badge, a gold circle containing the red enamelled saltire Cross of St. Patrick on a white background with a green shamrock superimposed. The Sash Badge, worn on the left hip, is similar to the Collar Badge, but is oval in shape with outer blue enamelling. The Star is a circular version of the Sash Badge.

All items of insignia were returnable at death and privately made specimens appear very rarely on the market.

Further information may be found in the book, *The Order of St. Patrick*, by Peter Galloway, published Phillimore in 1983.

Collar Chain	£40,000
Collar Badge	£15,000
Sash Badge	£6,500
Star (silver and gold)	£2,500
Star (embroidered)	£650

4. THE MOST HONOURABLE ORDER OF THE BATH

Established by George I in 1725 as a single class Order consisting of the Sovereign, a Prince of the Blood Royal, a Great Master and 35 Knights or Companions (KB). In order to provide the means of rewarding the military at the conclusion of the Napoleonic Wars, the Order was reorganised in 1815 into two divisions, civil and military, with the military having three grades: Knight Grand Cross (GCB), Knight Commander (KCB) and Companion (CB). The civil division remained in the single class of Knight Grand Cross. A further re-organisation took place in 1847 when the civil division was extended to match the military. Throughout its history, the majority of appointments to the top classes of the Bath have been in the military division. Women have been admitted since 1971.

Knights Grand Cross wear the enamelled Collar and Badge only on special occasions; normally they wear the Badge on the left hip suspended from the sash and the Breast Star of the Order. Knights Commander wear the Badge from a neck ribbon and the Star and Companions wear the neck badge only. Prior to 1917, the Companion's Badge was worn on the breast like a decoration. The military version of the Order is an eight pointed white enamelled star with a centre consisting of a green wreath around a sceptre from which issues a rose, thistle and shamrock between three crowns. The civil version consists of the central design executed entirely in gold. Until 1887, all badges were of gold: since then they have been silver-gilt.

After 1857, members of the Order were permitted to retain their insignia, but the collar is still returnable upon death and other insignia upon promotion in the Order.

Further information may be found in *The History of the Order of the Bath and its Insignia* by J.C. Risk, published by Spink in 1982.

KNIGHT OF THE BATH	
Collar Chain	Rare
Collar Badge	£6,000
Star (metal)	£3,500
Star (embroidered)	£500
Oval Unenamelled Sash Badge	£5,000

Military Division		Civil Division	
Knight Grand Cross		*Knight Grand Cross*	
Collar Chain	£8,000	Collar	£6,000
Collar Badge	£4,000	Star (metal)	£500
Star (metal)	£750	Sash Collar Badge (gold)	£1,250
Star (embroidered)	£600	Sash Collar Badge (gilt)	£600
Sash Badge (gold)	£3,500		
Sash Badge (gilt)	£1,100	*Knight Commander*	
		Star	£225
Knight Commander		Neck Badge (gold)	£600
Star (metal)	£450	Neck Badge (gilt)	£185
Star (embroidered)	£200		
Neck Badge (gold)	£1,100	*Companion*	
Neck Badge (gilt)	£385	Breast badge (gold)	£450
		Breast Badge (gilt)	£250
Companion		Neck Badge (gilt)	£150
Breast badge (gold)	£850		
Breast Badge (gilt)	£500		
Neck Badge	£300		

5. THE ROYAL GUELPHIC ORDER

Instituted by the Prince Regent in 1815 as an Hanoverian Order for award to both Hanoverians and British in military and civil divisions. As the salic law of succession prevailed in Hanover, the Order reverted to that country upon the death of William IV in 1837 and was no longer available for award in Britain. During the 22 years of its existence, however, it was awarded quite extensively to British subjects in both divisions.

It was established in three classes: Knights Grand Cross (GCH) who normally wore the badge from the sash, but had a Collar for special occasions; Knights Commander (KCH) who wore a neck Badge and Star; and Knights (KH) who wore the Badge on the left breast.

The insignia comprises a gold cross very similar in design to that of the Order of the Bath, with the white horse of Hanover in the centre. Awards in the military division bear crossed swords between the cross and the crown suspender. The short life of this Order as a British award leads obviously to its scarcity.

Knight Grand Cross

	Collar (gold)	£12,000		
	Collar (gilt)	£5,000		
Collar Badge	Mil.	£5,000	Civil	£4,000
Star	Mil.	£1,500	Civil	£900
Sash Badge	Mil.	£4,750	Civil	£3,850

Knight Commander

Star	Mil.	£1,250	Civil	£850
Neck badge	Mil.	£2,250	Civil	£1,250

Knight

Breast Badge (gold)	Mil.	£1,500	Civil	£950
Breast Badge	Mil.	£750	Civil	£450

6. THE MOST DISTINGUISHED ORDER OF ST. MICHAEL AND ST. GEORGE

Established by George III in 1818, originally to reward services in Malta and the Ionian Islands, the Order consisted of the Sovereign and a Grand Master plus 7 Knights Grand Cross (GCMG), 12 Knights Commander (KCMG), and 24 Companions (CMG) who were, until 1832, Knights Companion. In the second half of the nineteenth century, the purpose of the Order was altered so as to reward services in the field of foreign and colonial affairs generally, and the numbers in each grade have been enlarged to 110 GCMG, 390 KCMG and 1775 CMG. Ladies have been admitted from 1965.

Knights Grand Cross wear the Mantle, Hat and Collar upon special occasions; normally they wear the Badge on the left hip suspended from the sash and the Breast Star. Knights Commander wear the Badge around the neck and the Breast Star. Companions wore the Badge on the left breast suspended from a ribbon but, since 1917, now wear it as a neck Badge.

The Badge of the Order is a white seven-armed cross surmounted by a crown and bearing on one side a representation of St. George and on the other St. Michael. From 1891, the insignia could be retained by relatives after death, but in 1948, the Collar was again required, together with the ceremonial items, to be returned.

Knight Grand Cross		Companion	
Collar Chain	£1,500	Breast badge (gold)	£750
Star	£600	Breast Badge (gilt)	£450
Sash Badge (gold)	£4,000	Neck Badge	£350
Sash Badge (gilt)	£800		

Knight Commander	
Star	£400
Neck Badge (gold)	£1,250
Neck Badge (gilt)	£450

Orders of Knighthood

7. THE MOST EXALTED ORDER OF THE STAR OF INDIA

Established by Queen Victoria in 1861, the Order originally consisted of the Sovereign, a Grand Master and 25 Knights (KSI). It was re-structured in 1866 into the familiar three grades of Knight Grand Commander (GCSI), Knight Commander (KCSI) and Companion (CSI). At the revision, the numbers of knights were fixed at 25, 50 and 100 respectively, but these limits were later extended. The Order was used to reward both high ranking British civil and military officers and Indian Princes and Chiefs exclusively for services to the Queen Empress in India.

Though there was a collar and mantle available for wear on special occasions, Knights Grand Commander usually wore the Badge from the sash and the Breast Star. Knights Commander wore the Badge from the neck and the Breast Star and Companions wore the Badge from a ribbon on the left breast, but were allowed to convert this to neck wear after 1917. Women were not normally admitted, but three escaped the net and became GSCI. Like other Orders associated with India, the Order of the Star of India was not awarded after 1948 and is thus obsolescent.

The insignia is among the most attractive in the British series, consisting of an onyx cameo of Queen Victoria's head surrounded by the motto in diamonds upon a light blue background. It was originally returnable, but the purchase of the Badge and Star has been permitted since 1947. The Collar still reverts after death.

Knight Grand Commander, Collar Chain (gold)	£35,000
Knight Grand Commander, Star & Sash Badge	£30,000
Knight Commander, Star & Neck Badge	£4,500
Companion Breast Badge	£2,500
Companion Neck Badge	£1,750

8. THE MOST EMINENT ORDER OF THE INDIAN EMPIRE

Instituted in 1877 to commemorate the assumption by Queen Victoria of the title of Empress of India, this Order was originally of one class only consisting of Companions plus the Sovereign and Grand Master. Members of the Council of the Governor General of India were admitted as ex-officio Companions. It was to be bestowed for meritorious services in India, but was seen as a junior alternative to the Order of the Star of India. In 1886 the Order was extended to two classes by the addition of Knights Commander of whom there were to be a maximum of 50. In the following year the Order was again re-organised into three classes: up to 25 Knights Grand Commander (GCIE), up to 50 Knights Commander (KCIE), and unlimited numbers of Companions (CIE). The last appointment made was in 1948, so the Order is now obsolescent.

Knights Grand Commander wear a Breast Star together with a collar composed of elephants, Lotus flowers, peacocks and Indian roses from which hangs the badge of the Order. When the collar was not worn, the badge was worn on the sash. Knights Commander wear a smaller badge from a two inch neck ribbon and a smaller star. Companions wore a still smaller breast badge suspended from a buckle, but were allowed to convert this to neck wear after 1917.

Until 1962, the insignia of GCIE and KCIE had to be returned at death, but thereafter only GCIE collars were returnable. Insignia of the higher grades is thus rare on the market and that of the lower grades not common.

Knight Grand Commander, Collar Chain	£15,000
Knight Grand Commander, Star & Sash Badge	£6,000
Knight Commander, Star & Neck Badge	£2,000
Companion ('India' on Petals)	£1,200
Companion Breast Badge	£500
Companion Neck Badge	£350

9. THE IMPERIAL ORDER OF THE CROWN OF INDIA

Instituted in 1877 on the same day of the Order of the Indian Empire, this Order was most unusual in that it was reserved exclusively for award to women, but only to "Princesses of Our Royal House and the Wives or other female relatives of Indian Princes and other to be by Us selected". It was therefore an essentially aristocratic Order and almost an Indian equivalent of the Order of Victoria and Albert. In one class only, the insignia of Members (CI) was the Royal and Imperial cypher of Queen Victoria in diamonds, pearls and turquoises set within an oval border and surmounted by the Imperial Crown. It was worn on the left shoulder from a bow.

Only about 120 members were appointed to this Order, the last in 1947, and the insignia was returnable after death. Examples which come on the market, mostly of ladies who died after 1947, are therefore extremely rare.

Breast Badge	£8,500

10. THE ROYAL VICTORIAN ORDER

Established by Queen Victoria in 1896, this Order broke new ground in three respects: it was the first to be organised into five rather than three classes; there was no numerical limit placed upon the top two and the Order was totally in the personal gift of the Sovereign without any reference to government ministers.

Though there is the usual mantle and Collar for ceremonial occasions, a Knight Grand Cross (GCVO) usually wears the Badge from the sash and the Breast Star. Knights Commander (KCVO) wear the Badge at the neck and the Breast Star. Commanders wear the neck Badge only and the members of the 4th and 5th class (MVO) wear the Badge from its ribbon on the left breast. In 1988 the designation Member 4th Class was changed to Lieutenant (LVO). Ladies have been admitted to the Order since 1936, as Dames Grand Cross and Dames Commander in the top two classes.

The Badge of the Order is a white cross of eight points with the Imperial monogram of Queen Victoria in the centre and the Imperial Crown above. The Badge of the 5th Class is in frosted silver rather than white. Lower awards to ladies are worn from a bow ribbon. The badges are numbered on the reverse and are returnable upon promotion in the Order.

	Gentlemen	Ladies
Knight Grand Cross Collar Chain	£7,500	£8,500
Knight Grand Cross Sash Badge & Breast Star	£850	£1,500
Knight Commander Neck Badge & Breast Star	£600	£950
Commander Neck Badge	£350	£500
Member 4th Class Breast Badge	£200	£350
Member 5th Class Breast Badge	£150	£300

10a. THE ROYAL VICTORIAN CHAIN

Though parts of the insignia of this award are identical with items in the Victorian Order, there is really no connection between the two. The Chain is simply an additional gift available to the Sovereign which is used to honour mostly foreign Royalty. The male insignia consists of the badge of the Royal Victorian Order pendant from a collar worn in the usual fashion, and the ladies' insignia is a similar badge with miniature chain worn from a shoulder bow. In view of the limited number awarded and the status of the recipients, neither versions is likely to appear on the market.

10b. THE ROYAL VICTORIAN MEDAL

The Royal Victorian medal is a lower grade alternative to the Order for award to those who have rendered personal service to the Sovereign. In the Royal Household it is usually given to servants such as footmen and house-maids. In the services and police, it is given to those of non-commissioned rank, and is a standard award to bearers at royal funerals etc. Foreign recipients have a white stripe down the centre of the ribbon, which is otherwise identical to the Order.

	Silver-gilt	Silver	Bronze
Victoria	*	£120	£85
Edward VII	*	£120	£85
George V	£150	£100	£75
Edward VIII	*	£2,500	*
George VI	£150	£90	£750
Elizabeth II	£150	£120	£100

11. THE ORDER OF MERIT

Instituted in 1902, this Order consists of the Sovereign and a maximum of 24 Members in one class only. In addition, 10 honorary awards have so far been given. It is open to those who have rendered exceptionally meritorious service in the military or towards the advancement of Art, Literature or Science. It confers no title, but members may use the postnominal letters OM.

The insignia consists of a neck badge only in the form of a red and blue enamelled Cross, military recipients having crossed swords between the arms.

An extremely high standard has been maintained in nominations to this Order and its ranks, not yet exceeding a total of 160, have comprised some of the foremost names in art and science. Five women have been admitted, including Florence Nightingale in 1907 and, most recently, Margaret Thatcher.

The insignia of such a prestigious Order is naturally very rare on the market, particularly the military version. It is likely to become more so as all those appointed after 1991 have to return the insignia upon death.

Edward VII	Mil. £5,500	Civil £3,000
George V	Mil. £6,000	Civil £3,000
George VI	Mil. £6,000	Civil £3,500
Elizabeth II	Mil. £7,000	Civil £2,000

12. THE MOST EXCELLENT ORDER OF THE BRITISH EMPIRE

Founded by George V in 1917 as a means of rewarding civilian and military services given during the First World War, this Order has developed into a general purpose national Order awarded to a wide variety of people for almost any type of public service. Women have been eligible for all grades from the outset. In 1918 the Order was separated into military and civil divisions, the only difference being the design of the ribbon.

Though there is the usual collar and mantle for special occasions, Knights and Dames Grand Cross (GBE) usually wear the Badge hanging from a sash and the Breast Star. Knights Commander (KBE) wear the Breast Star and the Badge at the neck, and Dames Commander (DBE) wear the Breast Star and the Badge hanging from a breast ribbon bow. Male Commanders wear the Badge at the neck and women (CBE) wear it on the breast bow. Officers (OBE) and Members (MBE) wear it on the left breast, women from a ribbon bow.

THE MOST EXCELLENT ORDER OF THE BRITISH EMPIRE *continued*.

The insignia is a cross patonce with a central medallion showing a seated figure of Britannia inside a red-enamelled circle bearing the motto 'For God and Empire'. The badges of the first three classes are of silver-gilt enamelled pearl grey. The fourth class is totally in silver-gilt and the fifth in silver. The ribbon is purple, with the military division having a central red stripe.

In 1937, a number of changes were made to the insignia. The central medallion was altered to show the conjoined busts of King George V and Queen Mary and the rays of the Breast Star were altered from a fluted to a chipped appearance. The ribbon was changed to pink with dove grey edges, the military division showing an additional centre stripe of grey.

From 1957 until 1974, it was possible for the Order to be awarded for gallantry. In such cases a small emblem of crossed silver oak leaves was worn on the ribbon. Those subsequently awarded the Order in the normal way could wear both sets of insignia.

All awards of the Order are published in the London Gazette and, for the 1914-18 War period, *Burke's Handbook to the Order of the British Empire*, 1921, gives many mini-biographies and has recently been reprinted by the London Stamp Exchange.

	1st Type	2nd Type
Men		
GBE Collar	£5,000	£5,000
GBE Badge and Star	£800	£1,000
KBE Badge and Star	£350	£375
CBE Neck Badge	£145	£125
OBE Breast Badge	£55	£65
MBE Breast Badge	£55	£55
Women		
GBE (smaller) Collar	£6,000	£6,000
GBE Badge and (smaller) Star	£1,250	£1,250
DBE Badge and Star	£350	£400
CBE Badge on bow	£145	£175
OBE Breast Badge on bow	£55	£65
MBE Breast Badge on bow	£55	£55

12a. THE MEDAL OF THE ORDER OF THE BRITISH EMPIRE

Partially in the fulfilment of vague promises which had earlier been made regarding a medal for war workers, but also as a lower grade award for those not of the 'officer' class, the Medal of the Order of the British Empire was also established in 1917 in a single division, but changed into military and civil divisions in 1918. It was widely used to reward gallant or meritorious service by police, firemen, civilians, industrial workers and military personnel not in the front line. About 2,000 awards were made before the Medal was discontinued in 1922 when the British Empire Medals for Meritorious Service and Gallantry were introduced.

Worn from a purple ribbon with an additional red central stripe in the military division, the small silver medal bears on the obverse a seated figure of Britannia and on the reverse the Royal and Imperial cypher. It was issued unnamed, but many privately engraved examples will be met with. All awards are published in the London Gazette, some with two-line citations.

Unnamed civil or military	£75
Military with accompanying named medals	£150
Civil with papers or named medals	£125

12b. THE MEDAL OF THE ORDER OF THE BRITISH EMPIRE FOR GALLANTRY

This was one of two new medals instituted in December 1922 when the first Medal of the Order was discontinued. It was awarded only for specific acts of gallantry and so became known as the Empire Gallantry Medal (EGM). Of silver, the obverse shows a seated figure of Britannia with the legend 'For God and the Empire'. Above the line of the exergue is the word 'For', and under the line 'Gallantry'. The reverse, of which there are two varieties, shows the Royal and Imperial cypher. After the death of George V, the cypher was changed to GRI and the words 'Instituted by King George V' added. The ribbon was 1¼ ins. wide, at first in plain purple for the civil division and with an additional central stripe of red for the military division. In common with the Order of the British Empire, the colours changed to rose pink and pearl grey in 1937.

In total there were 130 awards of this Medal; 64 in the civil division, 62 in the military division and 4 honorary awards to foreigners. All awards are published with citations in the London Gazette and a complete list may be found in *Heroic Endeavour* by D.V. Henderson, GM, published Hayward in 1988.

With the institution of the George Cross in 1940, the EGM became obsolete and living holders of the EGM awarded before the outbreak of war were required to surrender their medals in exchange for the George Cross. It is known, however, that some holders managed to retain their EGMs.

George V or George VI	£3,000

12c. THE MEDAL OF THE ORDER OF THE BRITISH EMPIRE FOR MERITORIOUS SERVICE

The second of the two new medals instituted in December 1922, when the first Medal of the Order was discontinued. Usually referred to as the British Empire Medal (BEM), it is widely awarded to persons who render meritorious service but are not of a high enough rank or social standing to be appointed to the Order. However, those subsequently appointed to any grade in the Order may wear both awards. Of silver, the obverse is the same as the EGM with the exception of the words in the exergue which read 'Meritorious Service'. The reverse, of which there are four varieties, shows the Royal and Imperial cypher. After the death of George V, the cypher was changed to GRI and the words 'Instituted by King George V' added. In 1948 the cypher was again changed to GR VI, and in 1952 it became EIIR. The ribbon was 1¼ ins. wide, at first in plain purple for the civil division and with an additional central stripe of red for the military division. In common with the Order of the British Empire, the colours changed to rose pink and pearl grey in 1937.

In 1941 provision was made for a bar to this Medal to be issued, but to date only about 25 of these have been awarded. As with the Order, during the period 1958 to 1974, the BEM could be awarded for gallantry, in which case crossed oak leaves were worn upon the ribbon. This provision became obsolete upon the institution of the Queen's Gallantry Medal.

The Medal is always issued named, often in engraved capitals, and all awards are published in the London Gazette. As of 1994 this Medal is no longer awarded in the United Kingdom.

	Military	Civil
George V	£145	£85
George VI 1st type	£80	£50
George VI 2nd type	£85	£60
EIIR	£100	£60
EIIR for Gallantry	£500	£300

13. THE ORDER OF THE COMPANIONS OF HONOUR

Established by George V in 1917 to consist of the Sovereign and a maximum of 50 members in one class only, but in 1943 the number of Companions was raised to 65. It is open to those who have rendered exceptionally conspicuous service of national importance and is used to reward those who have made outstanding contributions in Arts, Literature, Science, Politics, Industry and Religion. It confers no title, but Members may use the postnominal letters CH.

The insignia consists of a Neck Badge only in the form of an oval of blue enamel surrounding a gold rectangle bearing a representation of a mounted knight in armour by an oak tree, and surmounted by the Royal Crown. The Order has not been awarded in great numbers and is scarce on the market.

Gentlemen	£1,800
Ladies	£2,000

14. THE BARONET'S BADGE

The original version of this badge was instituted by a Royal Warrant in 1629, when Charles I authorised Baronets of Scotland to wear around their necks a tawny ribbon from which hung an oval of blue enamel bearing the motto 'Fax Mentis Honestae Gloria'. Within the oval was a white shield bearing the blue St. Andrew's Cross with a smaller shield bearing the lion of Scotland superimposed upon it. At this time, due to James I having given them a grant of land in the new world five years earlier, these Baronets were also referred to as Baronets of Nova Scotia.

Badges for the Baronets of England, Ireland, Great Britain and the United Kingdom were not authorised until 1929. They have a common centre of a white shield bearing the red hand of Ulster below a crown but the blue enamelled and gilt border differs in each case: England showing roses; Ireland showing shamrocks; Great Britain roses and thistles; and the United Kingdom all three devices.

Baronets of	Gold	Silver-gilt
Scotland (early versions)	£2,500	—
Scotland (late 19th & 20th century)	£2,000	£1,000
England	£950	£500
Ireland	£950	£500
Great britain	£950	£500
United Kingsom	£750	£400

15. THE KNIGHT BACHELOR'S BADGE

Until 1929, the holders of this honour had no means of showing their rank on formal occasions. In that year the King gave permission for a simple Badge to be worn on the left breast in the same manner as the star of an order. It consists of a red-enamelled oval upon which are depicted in gilt the emblems of knighthood, the belt, sword and spurs, the whole surrounded by a gilt border. The original version was some 3 x 2 inches, but it was reduced in size in 1933 and then further reduced and adapted for wear around the neck in 1974.

1st type Badge (1929)	£200
2nd type Badge (1933)	£180
3rd type (neck) Badge	£200

16. THE ORDER OF ST. JOHN OF JERUSALEM

Tracing its history back to the Knights Crusader of the Middle Ages, the Order of St. John was revived in Britain in the early part of the nineteenth century and incorporated by Royal Charter in 1888. The classes into which it is organised have varied throughout its history and more detailed information can be found in the book *The Insignia and Medals of the Grand Priory of the Most Venerable Order of the Hospital of St. John of Jerusalem* by C.W. Tozer, published Hayward in 1975. At present, the Order is divided into the usual five classes.

Bailiffs and Dames Grand Cross (GCStJ) wear the Badge from the sash and the Star on the left breast. Knights of Justice or Grace (KStJ) also wear the Star but have the Badge at the neck. Dames of Justice or Grace (DStJ) have the Star and the Badge on the left breast from a ribbon bow. Commanders (CStJ) omit the Breast Star. Officers (OStJ) have the Badge on the left breast from a straight or bow ribbon as do Serving Brother or Sisters.

The insignia of the Order is a true Maltese Cross enamelled white and set in either silver-gilt or silver. Between the angles, the cross is embellished with alternate lions and unicorns in the appropriate metal. Insignia of the 1st Class and of Knights and Dames of Justice is set in gold or silver-gilt and the Star is not embellished. Knights and Dames of Grace have their Stars embellished and all insignia set in silver. Officers and Serving Brothers and Sisters have their insignia set in silver. In the case of the 5th Class, the Badge is superimposed upon a circle of black enamel. During the period 1926-36, the Badges of Officers were made in frosted silver without enamel. The insignia of Serving Brother and Sister has recently changed to become an embellished Maltese Cross in white metal similar to the 1926-36 Officer pattern. Very early pieces may be found in gold and, since 1951, all silver insignia has been made in white metal.

Breast Stars are 3 ins. in diameter, Neck Badges 2¼ ins., and the Officer Brother and Commander Sister are of 1¾ ins. The Officer Sister Badge is only 1¼ ins. in diameter.

	Gold	Gilt or Silver	Base metal
GCStJ Badge and Star	£1,500	£800	*
GCStJ Badge and Star (Dame)	£1,500	£500	*
KStJ Justice Badge and Star	£750	£250	£150
DStJ Justice Badge and Star	£750	£250	£200
KStJ Grace Badge and Star	*	£250	£150
DStJ Grace Badge and Star	*	£250	£150
CStJ Brother	*	£125	£50
CStJ Sister	*	£30	£25
OStJ Brother	*	£30	£25
OStJ Sister	*	£35	£25
Serving Brother/Sister type 1		£45	£25
Skeletal type 2 (1940-47)		£30	*
3rd type plain cross		–	£25

Decorations

Following the drive of Prime Minister John Major towards a more 'Classless Society', some radical changes in the system of decorations took place in late 1993 and early 1994 which will result in some of those awards described in this section becoming obsolete. Though nothing has yet been properly published and no amendments have been made to the various Royal Warrants, it is understood that a Review Committee representing all three services has decided on the future structure of the service decorations. Briefly, the Victoria Cross will remain as the reward for first level gallantry and the mention in Despatches will continue as the fourth. A new second level decoration, probably called the Conspicuous Gallantry Cross will be instituted common to all three services and the third level will retain a rag-bag of individual service awards formerly given only to officers but now open to all ranks. This third level is likely to consist of the Distinguished Service Cross, the Military Cross and the Distinguished Flying and Air Force Crosses. At the time of writing, a DFC and an MC have already been awarded to non-commissioned officers. An ideal opportunity to get rid of the Distinguished Service Order, always an anomaly, has been missed and this has been retained for award in cases of great leadership. The result of this change is to make those decorations formerly awarded to non-commissioned officers and men obsolescent and the Conspicuous Gallantry Medal (Naval and Air Force), the Distinguished Service Medal, the Distinguished Conduct medal, the Military Medal, the Distinguished Flying Medal and the Air Force Medal will no longer be awarded. In due course this change will be reflected in the value of some decorations.

It is impossible to compile a price guide of gallantry medals in the same way as a guide to campaign or long service medals, as each award is different and the citation can make a great difference to the value and scarcity of a particular item. Many of the factors involved in valuing gallantry awards are held in common with other medals; rank, regiment, the theatre of war, and the rarity of the medal itself. The prices listed in the following pages are meant as a guide, and not as an exact valuation. For example, a single unnamed DFC is less expensive than one with a log book or some other substantial documentation, whilst a DFC with log book and an officially named medal might be expected to fetch a higher price than either of the two former categories.

Some specific categories of gallantry command far higher prices; either because they are rare issues, for example George the Fifth second type gallantry, or because of the theatre of award or battle, for example Jutland, the Somme, Arnhem and the Battle of Britain.

Therefore, this guide is designed to give a structure to the pricing of gallantry awards, although many awards may be sold for a higher price due to the abovementioned factors. Collecting gallantry awards is one of the most interesting areas in medal collecting, and this guide will provide a useful basis for collectors.

17. VICTORIA CROSS

During the Crimean War, there was a body of opinion that favoured the institution of a medal for acts of outstanding gallantry, and accordingly, in January 1856, Victoria signed a Royal Warrant creating the Victoria Cross. There are several books dealing with the institution of the VC, and several more list and detail all recipients of the Cross. A total of 1351 VCs have been awarded since 1856, plus three bars for a second award. Eight Crosses have been forfeited, the last in 1908. The VC is always named on the reverse, with the recipient's details on the reverse of the suspender bar, and the date of the act in the reverse centre. These details are engraved. All awarded are listed in the London Gazette, and all have citations. In addition, there is always a great deal of research relating to each recipient in newspapers, regimental histories and so on. The great majority of VCs—some 830— were awarded to the Army; the Royal Navy received 107 and the Royal Air Force 31. The balance is made up by Commonwealth and Imperial Forces, with 4 being awarded to civilians. It is impossible to price more than one VC in a single figure, as so much depends on the citation, action and regiment of the recipient. As a general guide, the minimum price for a VC with one or more officially named campaign medals would be £20,000.

Decorations

18. NEW ZEALAND CROSS

This rare award was instituted in New Zealand in 1869 to reward those who had distinguished themselves in the Maori Wars of the previous decade. The Victoria Cross could not be awarded to Colonial troops until 1867, and even then only when serving with Imperial troops. This vacuum was filled by the institution of the New Zealand Cross, which was awarded exclusively to New Zealand Colonial troops. It was awarded to just 23 men who had distinguished themselves against the Maoris. Due to complicated rules for the award and its unusual nature, awards were often made some time after the action for which the recipient had been recommended, and the last award was made in 1910. The Cross is named on the reverse with the recipient's name, rank and unit, and the date of the act of bravery. As so few recipients received the medal, much is known about most of them, and details of awards are given in the New Zealand Gazette.

£24,000

19. GEORGE CROSS

Instituted in September 1940 as a reward for heroism for civilians, both men and women, and to members of the Armed Forces in cases where a military award is not applicable. Awards were only to be made in instances where the most conspicuous courage was evident, with extreme danger to the recipient himself. There was also a provision in the Royal Warrant for living recipients of the Empire Gallantry Medal to exchange their original awards for the George Cross. between 1940 and 1947 some 105 GCs were awarded, with approximately 40 since the war. All issued crosses are engraved on the reverse with the recipient's name and the date of the London Gazette notification; if in the Armed Forces, the recipient's rank and unit is often added. Prices vary greatly depending on the specific details of the awards.

Service Award from 1940	from £5,000 to £20,000
Service Exchange Award	from £2,500 to £5,000
Civilian Award from 1940	from £2,750 to £5,000
Civilian Excgange Award	from £2,000 to £2,500

20. DISTINGUISHED SERVICE ORDER

The DSO was instituted in 1886 in order to fill a gap that had long existed in rewarding officers below the rank of major for distinguishing themselves on active service; previously the CB was the only possible award, and was very rarely issued to junior officers. The DSO was to be awarded to both the Army and Navy. The first issue of the DSO was in gold, and these were awarded between 1886 and 1890. After 1890 the award was issued in silver-gilt; the obverse has carried four variations of the crown in the centre, and there are six types of reverse – VR, EVIIR, GVR, GVIR first and second types and EIIR. The DSO has always been issued unnamed, although from about 1940 the year of award has been engraved on the reverse of the lower suspension bar. Approximately 150 of the gold VR types were issued. Some 1,150 silver-gilt VR awards were issued for the Boer War. It is not known exactly how many EVIIR types were issued, but they are rare. During the First World War approximately 9,000 DSOs were issued, with about 770 first bars and 75 second bars. There were also 7 DSOs with three bars.

DISTINGUISHED SERVICE ORDER *continued*

Between the wars some 160 DSO were awarded for various campaigns, with 16 first bars. In the Second World War some 4,900 DSOs were awarded, with 500 first bars, 59 second bars and 8 third bars. Since 1945 about 170 have been awarded with 20 first bars. There are generally no citations in the London Gazette for DSOs before 1914, though reference to dispatches and regimental histories may give a better picture of precisely why the award was made. In the First World War, many DSOs carry a specific citation, but there are periodic lists of recipients without citations. Since 1918 very few citations have been published and information must be sought away from the Gazette. Prices vary greatly depending on the citation and the theatre of award.

	Unnamed Single	Attributable Group
Victoria Gold	£2,000	£3,000
Victoria Silver Gilt	£700	£1,000
Edward VII	£1,400	£2,500
George V	£450	£650
George VI Type I	£600	£1,250
George VI Type II	£1,000	£2,500
Elizabeth II	£1,000	£2,500

21. IMPERIAL SERVICE ORDER AND MEDAL

Instituted by Edward VII in 1902, the Order recognises long and efficient service by both home and overseas civil servants. Recipients usually had to serve for 25 years at home, 20 years in India or 16 years in unhealthy climates. The Order consists of a Breast Badge in the form of a gold circular plaque bearing the Royal and Imperial cypher, surrounded by the inscription 'For Faithful Serrvice'. For male recipients the plaque is mounted on a seven point silver star surmounted by a crown. For women it is enclosed within a silver laurel wreath. The ribbon is watered red with a central light blue stripe, and women normally reveive the insignia on a bow. There is only the one class and the holders are known as Companions (ISO). Women were admitted from 1908 and, as only about 5 awards are made to them annually, the ladies' type badge is very scarce. It is understood that new dies showing a Queen's crown were made only within the last five years. As the Order is now to fall into disuse in the United Kingdom, following the egalitarian reforms of Prime Minister John Major, this version will be extremely rare. The medal was instituted at the same time as the Order for those manual grades of the service not eligible for the Order. At first the only difference between Order and Medal was the central plaque bearing the Royal cypher which was gold for the Order and silver for the Medal. However, in 1920, the design of the Medal was changed to become a circular silver medal bearing the head of the Sovereign on the obverse and a symbolic design on the reverse above the words 'For Faithful Service'. All medals are named and awards of the Order and Medal are published in the London Gazette.

		Order	Medal
Edward VII	Gentlemen	£100	£45
	Lady	£250	£125
George V	Gentlemen	£85	£40
	Lady	£200	£100
	Post 1920 medal	*	£8
George VI	Gentlemen	£100	£8
	Lady	£175	£8
Elizabeth	Gentlemen	£125	£8
	Lady	£150	£8

22. INDIAN ORDER OF MERIT

Originally known simply as the Order of Merit, this award was created by the Honourable East India Company in 1837, making it the oldest in this catalogue. However, it did not become an official British award until the take over of India by the Crown after the Mutiny in 1857. The word 'Indian' was added in 1902 when the British Order of Merit was introduced.

Instituted in three classes, it could be awarded to all ranks for conspicuous gallantry in the field and possession entitled the holders to higher pensions on retirement. In 1902 a civil division was also introduced. When Indian troops became eligible for the award of the Victoria Cross in 1911, the military first class was abolished and the remaining classes renumbered. The civil division was reduced to a single class in 1939 and the military followed suit in 1944.

The design of the award is a simple eight pointed star in gold or silver with a central enamelled circle bearing crossed swords and the legend 'Reward of Valor', 'Reward of Gallantry'. or 'For Bravery'. The ribbon of the military division is dark blue with crimson edges, and that of the civil division the reverse. After 1915, awards are published in the London Gazette.

Military Division
1837-1911:	1st class in gold	£1,500
	2nd class in silver with gold centre	£650
	3rd class in silver	£120
1912-1939:	1st class in silver with gold centre with reverse engraved 1st class	£900
	2nd class in silver, reverse engraved 2nd class	£150
1939-1945:	1st class Reward of Gallantry	Rare
	2nd class Reward of Gallantry	£220
1945-1947:	Single class	£1,000

Civil Division
1902-1939:	1st class—none awarded	*
	2nd class—none awarded	*
	3rd class	£1,000
1939-1947:	Single class	£1,000

23. ROYAL RED CROSS

This decoration, to reward cases of special devotion in nursing the sick and wounded of the army and navy, was instituted in 1883 and was, until 1976, limited to females including foreign subjects. In November 1915, a second class award known as the Associate of the Royal Red Cross was introduced and in December 1917, a bar to the first class was instituted. The bar is not available for the second class award, promotion to first class being the normal route upwards. In 1920 a new provision allowing for the award of the decoration for 'some very exceptional act of bravery and devotion at her post of duty' was introduced.

Apart from the initial 31 awards, which are believed to be of gold, the first class is a silver-gilt cross patee with the centre of each arm enamelled crimson. Upon the four arms are the words FAITH HOPE CHARITY 1883. In the centre is the bust of the Sovereign. The reverse is plain except for the central medallion which bears the appropriate Royal and Imperial cypher. The second class decoration is similar but of silver enamelled red. The words FAITH HOPE CHARITY and the date of foundation appear on the reverse. From 1938 both classes have the year of award engraved on the reverse lower arm. The ribbon for both classes is the same, dark blue with red edges. Though it is always issued in bow form, the decoration may be worn from a straight ribbon when mounted with other medals.

All awards, except those honorary ones to foreigners, are published in the London Gazette. There are no citations. Since its institution only about 1.850 of the first class have been awarded and about 100 bars. About 6,600 of the second class have been issued.

	1st class (RRC)	2nd class (ARRC)
Queen Victoria Gold	£1,000	*
Queen Victoria	£400	*
Queen Victoria with Bar	£750	*
Edward VII	£600	*
George V	£150	£60
George V with Bar	£450	*
George VI first type	£220	£100
George VI	£250	£120
Elizabeth II	£250	£100

24. DISTINGUISHED SERVICE CROSS

Instituted in June 1901 as a reward for Warrant and Subordinate Officers of the Royal Navy, as these ranks were not eligible to receive the DSO. Originally called the Conspicuous Service Cross. Only eight CSCs were awarded for China and South Africa, including three to Gunners (warrant rank) and five to Midshipmen (subordinate rank). The CSC is thus excessively rare. In October 1914 there were two major changes to the CSC: firstly it was renamed the Distinguished Service Cross, and secondly the rules on eligibility were changed so that officers below the rank of Lieutenant-Commander could receive it. In 1931 the Merchant Navy was made eligible for the DSC in certain circumstances. There are five types of obverse: EVIIR (on the CSC), GVR, GVIR first and second types, and EIIR. The reverse of the DSC is common to all issues, but from 1940 onwards the year of award was engraved on the lower limb. During the First World War approximately 1700 DSCs were awarded, with about 90 first bars and 10 second bars. Between the wars only 7 DSCs were awarded. In the Second World War some 4500 DSCs were awarded, with 430 first and 44 second bars. One medal was issued with three bars. A very small number of Army and RAF Officers received the DSC. Since 1945 some 90 DSCs have been awarded, with 15 first and 5 second bars. All recipients are listed in the London Gazette, but apart from some First World War awards, citations are not generally published in the Gazette. A complete roll of all

24. DISTINGUISHED SERVICE CROSS *continued*

recipients to 1938 can be found in *The Distinguished Service Cross* by W.H. Fevyer, published by the London Stamp Exchange in 1991.

	Unnamed Single	Attributable Group
Edward VII	£1,000	£5,000
George V	£350	£500
George VI Type 1	£350	£500
George VI Type 2	£700	£3,000
Elizabeth II	£800	£2,500

25. MILITARY CROSS

Instituted in December 1914 as a reward for gallantry for officers of the rank of Captain or below, and for warrant officers. Officers over the rank of Captain were eligible for the DSO. The reverse of the MC is common to all issues and is usually plain. From 1940 onwards the date of award was engraved on the lower limb of the reverse. There are four different obverse issues: GVR, GVIR first and second types, and EIIR. The MC was always issued unnamed, although some recipients had the reverse engraved privately. A bar was awarded for each further award of the Cross; there were four recipients of the MC and 3 bars in the First World War, with 170 2-bar awards and approximately 3000 first bars. Between 1914 and 1918 there were just over 37,000 awards of the MC. Between the wars there were about 350 awards for various campaigns, together with 30 first bars. In the Second World War some 10,000 Crosses and 500 first bars were awarded. Since 1945 about 600 Crosses and 28 bars have been awarded. All awards of the MC are listed in the London Gazette. A majority of awards for the First World War are accompanied by citations, but after 1920 few citations appear in the London Gazette. Prices vary depending on the regiment, citation and action.

	Unnamed Single	Attributable Group
George V	£225	£350
George VI 1st type	£275	£500
George VI 2nd type	£400	£1,000
Elizabeth II	£500	£2,000

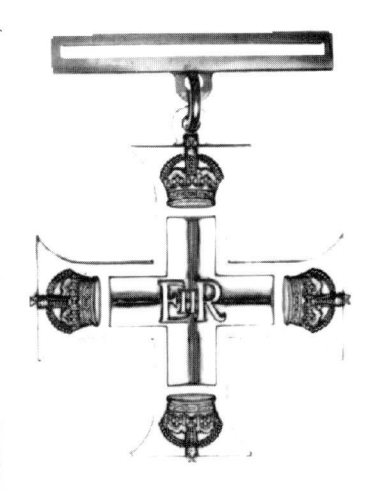

26. DISTINGUISHED FLYING CROSS

The DFC was instituted in 1918 as an award to officers and warrant officers who displayed courage or devotion to duty whilst flying in active operations. The design of the obverse is common to all issues, whilst the reverse centre has one of four cyphers: GVR, GVIR (first type GRI, second type GVIR), and EIIR. For services in the First World War there were awarded approximately 1,100 DFCs, with 70 first bars and 3 second bars. During the Second World War some 20,000 DFCs were awarded (making the DFC the commonest award for the war), with approximately 1500 first bars and 42 second bars. Between the wars about 130 DFCs were awarded, plus 20 first bars and 4 second bars. Since 1945 about 260 DFCs have been awarded, with 25 first bars and 3 second bars. Citations for a majority of awards are available, but difficulties are encountered in obtaining details for some First World War and post-1945 awards. The DFC is issued unnamed, but GVIR issues are usually found with the year of issue engraved on the reverse of the bottom limb.

	Unnamed Single	Attributable Awards
George V	£500	£800
George VI 1st type	£350	£550
George VI 2nd type	£700	£1,000
Elizabeth II	£750	£1,750

27. AIR FORCE CROSS

Instituted in June 1918, the AFC was awarded to officers and warrant officers for courage or devotion to duty whilst flying, though not in active operations against the enemy. From 1938 the year of issue was engraved on the reverse lower arm of the Cross. though usually issued unnamed, there is now provision for engraving the recipient's name on the reverse when awarded for gallantry. There are four varieties: GVR, GVIR first and second types, and EIIR. Approximately 680 were awarded for the First World War, and 2,000 for the Second World War. 160 were awarded between the wars, and approximately 2,000 have been awarded since the Second World War. Some first bars were issued, and there have been about 20 awards of a second bar. Generally there are no specific citations in the London Gazette, although some Gazette entries give some indication of the nature of the recipient's services.

	Unnamed Single	Attributable Awards
George V	£500	£850
George VI Type 1	£400	£600
George VI Type 2	£600	£1,000
Elizabeth II	£500	£850

28. THE ORDER OF BRITISH INDIA

This Order was established in 1837 by the Hon. East India Company, in two classes, to reward long and faithful service by Indian Officers. Members of the first class received the title of 'Sirdar Bahadoor', and those of the second class, that of 'Bahadoor'.

The badge of the first class consists of a gold star of eight radiated points upon which is a central medallion showing a gold lion on a light blue enamel ground, within a dark blue border bearing the title of the Order, the whole surmounted by a crown. The badge of the second class is similar but slightly smaller, has no crown and the centre is enamelled entirely in dark blue. Both classes were worn at the neck suspended from a ribbon that was originally light blue, but changed in 1838 to crimson. The design of the first class was changed slightly in 1939 when the whole centre was enamelled in light blue. When the ribbon only was worn on undress uniform the classes were differentiated by two narrow light blue stripes for the first class, and a single central stripe for the second class. It was not until 1945 that these ribbons were worn with the insignia.

1st Class first type 1837-1939	£450
1st class second type 1939-47	£450
2nd class 1939-47	£350

29. ORDER OF BURMA

This Order was established in 1940 to reward long, faithful and honourable service in the Burma Army, Burma Frontier Force and Burma Military Police. In 1945, the conditions of award were altered to include meritorious service or conspicuous bravery. The Order became defunct in 1948 when Burma became independent, and only 24 awards are known to have been made.

Worn at the neck, the badge was a gold-rayed circle with a central medallion showing a blue peacock within a border bearing the title and a crown above. The ribbon was dark green with pale edges.

£

30. KAISAR-I-HIND

Instituted by Queen Victoria in 1900 for any persons, without distinction of race, occupation, position or sex who distinguished themselves by important and useful service in the advancement of the public interest in India. The first class, in gold, was awarded by the Sovereign upon the recommendation of the Secretary of State for India; the second class, in silver, was awarded by the Viceroy and the third class in bronze, introduced in the reign of George V, was also awarded by the Viceroy. A dated bar was available for further service. The award became obsolete in 1947.

The award is an oval badge measuring 1.75 by 1.375 inches. The obverse shows the Imperial cypher within an ornamental band, surmounted by the Imperial Crown. The reverse has the legend KAISAR-I-HIND on a scroll against a floral background, around which is a band carrying the words FOR PUBLIC SERVICE IN INDIA. The decoration is attached to its ribbon by a horizontal wire loop brooch attached to the top of the crown by a link. There is a top ribbon suspender bar carrying a floral design, without which the decoration is not complete. The ribbon is plain blue, ladies receiving their awards on a bow. Awards are normally published in the London Gazette, but a far more convenient and complete listing will be found in the annual issues of the *Indian Office List*.

	1st class (gold)	2nd class (silver)	3rd class (bronze)
Queen Victoria	£550	£170	*
Edward VII	£600	£180	*
George V 1st type	£450	£120	*
George V 2nd solid type	£550	£120	£100
George VI	£550	£120	£100

31. ALBERT MEDAL

Instituted in 1866 for heroic actions in saving life at sea, when the rescuer's own life was at risk. the medal was to be awarded in two classes – First Class (Gold) and Second Class (Bronze). The recipient was to be recommended to the Queen by the President of the Board of Trade. In 1877 the award of the medal was extended to cover awards for saving life on land; the two classes were kept for this issue, but the anchor on the obverse is omitted and the enamelling is in crimson, as opposed to blue enamel on the maritime issue. The medal is engraved on the reverse in various styles, and includes details of the recipient, the act of bravery and the date. Up to 1970, 69 gold and 491 bronze medals have been awarded in all. Citations are usually given in the London Gazette, and records are kept of awards by the Board of Trade. Awards to military personnel tend to fetch higher prices than those to civilians. A complete list of recipients can be found in *For Heroic Endeavour*, by D.V. Henderson, published Hayward in 1988.

	Civilian Award	Service Award
Gold Sea	£3,500	£4,000
Gold Land	£3,000	£3,500
Bronze Sea	£2,200	£3,000
Bronze Land	£1,800	£2,200

32. DISTINGUISHED CONDUCT MEDAL

Instituted in 1854 to recognise "distinguished, gallant and good conduct" by troops in the Crimea. At first intended to be issued on a quota basis for each regiment, due to the fixed amount of money available for the accompanying annuity. There are eight issues, all having a common reverse: VR, EVIIR, GVR, GVR crowned head, GVIR first and second types, EIIR first and second types. All issued DCMs are named, and there are a variety of types of naming: however, virtually all awards since 1914 are impressed. Two types of second award bars have been issued, the first type has the date of the second award on it, with the second type bearing laurel leaves. The early dated bars are rare. DCMs have been issued for almost every campaign in which the Army has participated; nearly 25,000 were issued for the First World War, but only 1900 for the Second World war. Apart from the two wars and the Boer and Crimean Wars, few DCMs have been issued for any one campaign. There are generally no citations in the London gazette for DCMs before 1914, and reference must be made to Regimental Histories and other works in order to find the details of the services of the recipient. After 1914, most DCMs appear in the London gazette with a citation, although there are periodic lists of recipients which do not include citations. Between the wars there are generally no citations in the Gazette, and since 1939 DCM awards in the gazette do not carry citations. Full details of all awards for the period until 1914 can be found in the book *The Distinguished Conduct Medal* by P.E. Abbott, published Hayward, and recently revised. Awards made during the First World War can be confirmed in a similar work by R.W. Walker, though citations are not given.

Victoria (Crimea)	from £600
Victoria (Small Wars)	from £1,000
Victoria (Boer War)	£600
Edward VII (Boer War)	£600
Edward VII (Small Wars)	from £1,000
George V	£300
George V (Crowned Head)	£3,000
George VI (Ind. Imp.)	£1,500
George VI (2nd type)	£1,500
Elizabeth II (1st type)	£5,000
Elizabeth II (2nd type)	£4,500

33. DISTINGUISHED CONDUCT MEDAL (COLONIAL AND DOMINION)

Instituted in 1894 to reward members of the Colonial Forces in the same way as Imperial troops. The medal is similar to the British DCM, but has the Colony over the top of the reverse inscription. Four types are known: Canada, Natal, King's African Rifles and West African Frontier Force. The Canadian issue is extremely rare, only one being known. The Natal issue comprises perhaps ten medals; nine for the Natal Rebellion 1906, and one known for the Boer War. The KAR issue was awarded up to 1942, with approximately 180 medals and 7 bars awarded. The WAFF issue ran to about 85 medals and 6 bars. In 1942 it was decided to replace the KAR and WAFF issues with the Imperial. These awards, which are all rare, are usually in the London Gazette but are often not differentiated from normal DCMs. The KAR history and East African Gazettes can provide information of the two African issues.

Natal	£1,850
Canada	£3,000
KAR (GVR)	£500
WAFF (GVR)	£550

34. CONSPICUOUS GALLANTRY MEDAL (ROYAL NAVY AND ROYAL AIR FORCE)

Instituted in 1855 as a reward for gallantry for the Royal Navy and Royal Marines, and intended to be a counterpart to the DCM for the Army. The first issue was made to ten recipients for gallantry in the Baltic and Crimea. These medals had the date '1848' on the obverse under the Queen's bust; in order to save money, the MSM die was used, with the wording on the reverse removed and 'Conspicuous Gallantry' engraved in the reverse centre. The naming was in engraved serif capitals. After a lull of some 18 years, the medal was re-instituted in 1874 with a batch of awards for Ashantee. From this date the medal was issued with the following obverses: Victoria (without date), EVIIR, GVR and GVIR. About 50 of the second Victorian issue were awarded, with 2 EVIIR medals, 110 GVR issues, and 72 GVIR issues. Only one second award bar has been awarded. In 1942 the award of CGM was extended to the RAF to recognise gallantry whilst flying in operations against the enemy. 103 CGMs (Flying) were awarded for the Second World War, and one has been awarded for Vietnam. From 1901, nearly all CGMs have citations, although before this date information on acts of gallantry varies somewhat.

Naval Issues	
Victoria 1st Issue '1848' Type	£3,500
Victoria 2nd Issue	£3,000
Edward VII	£6,000
George V	£1,800
George VI	£3,000
Elizabeth II	Rare
RAF Issues	
George VI	£3,000
Elizabeth II	Rare

35. GEORGE MEDAL

Instituted in September 1940 to reward men and women for acts of 'great bravery'. The medal was mainly a civilian award, but military personnel were eligible for the award if their act of gallantry did not fall within the scope of a military award. A bar was to be issued for a further act of gallantry. The GM has one reverse common to all issues, although there are four obverse types: GVIR first and second types and EIIR first and second types. Since 1940, approximately 1900 GMs have been awarded. 1030 civilians, 150 Royal Navy, 455 Army, 200 Royal Air Force, and 45 Merchant Navy. Some 25 bars have been issued. All issued GMs are named by engraved capital letters in various styles, although some awards for the Second World War are impressed. All awards are listed in the London Gazette, with those to civilians usually having citations, as do some RN and RAF recipients. However, awards to the Army generally appear in the Gazette without a citation. Prices vary greatly depending on the precise nature of the award and the citation. Details of 1940-45 George Medals can be found in the book *The George Medal* by W.H. Feyer, published Spink, and a complete listing to date in *Dragons Can Be Defeated* by D.V. Henderson, published Spink.

	Civilian Award	Service Award
George VI	£500	£850
Elizabeth II	£700	£1,800

36. KING'S OR QUEEN'S POLICE MEDAL
KING'S POLICE AND FIRE SERVICES MEDAL

Instituted by Royal Warrant in 1909 as a reward to members of both the Police and Fire Services for courage and devotion to duty. In 1940 the title of the award was changed to the King's Police and Fire Services Medal but it reverted to the Queen's Police medal upon the institution of a separate award for the Fire Service in 1954. There is provision for bars to be issued for subsequent awards. There are six obverse types: EVIIR, GVR, GVR crowned head, GVIR first and second types and EIIR. There are four reverse types, the original having no wording to show the grade of service for which it was issued. In 1934 two new reverse types were substituted, bearing the words 'For Gallantry' or 'For Distinguished Service' in the exergue. In 1954 a new reverse die was cut with the words 'For Distinguished Police Service' within a border around the rim. Between 1909 and 1911 there were about 100 awards, no differentiation being made between gallantry or distinguished service. There were about 1900 awards of the GVR first type, this total including both gallantry and distinguished service. Other gallantry reverse awards were approximately 350 with the GVR crowned head obverse, about 440 with the first type GVIR and about 50 with the GVIR second type obverse. Only 23 awards for gallantry have been made with the EIIR obverse as against well over 1200 for distinguished service in the same period. There are approximately 53 first bars and but one second. Naming is in engraved seriffed capital letters with name, rank and service. All awards are published in the London Gazette but citations are rarely given though many are available in the Public Records Office. The ribbon was originally dark blue with narrow silver stripes at each edge, but in 1916 a further centre stripe of silver was added. From 1934 gallantry awards were distinguished by a thin stripe of red through the centre of each silver stripe.

Edward VII	£500
GVR Coinage Head	£150
GVR Crowned Head	£250
GVR Gallantry	£400
GVR Distinguished Service	£200
GVIR Gallantry	£500
GVIR Distinguished Service	£200
GVIR 2nd Type Gallantry	£600
GVIR 2nd Type Distinguished Service	£200
EIIR Gallantry	£700
EIIR Distinguished Service	£400

36a. QUEEN'S FIRE SERVICE MEDAL

Instituted by Royal Warrant of 19 May 1954 for award to the Fire Services which had previously participated in the award of the King's Police medal and King's Police and Fire Services medal. The reverse of the medal when given for gallantry is identical to that awarded to the Police. It can only be given posthumously and has not yet been awarded. When given for distinguished service it has the words 'For Distinguished Fire Service' within a border around the reverse rim. Awards are published in the London Gazette and the medal has its own ribbon of red with a narrow yellow stripe at each edge and in the centre. When awarded for gallantry the ribbon carries a thin stripe of blue in the centre of each yellow stripe.

EIIR Galantry	*
EIIR Distinguished Service	£200

37. EDWARD MEDAL (MINES)

Instituted in July 1907 to recognise gallant attempts to save life in mines and quarries anywhere in the Empire. Two classes were created: the First Class medal was in silver, and the Second Class was in bronze. The obverse bore the head of the reigning monarch, and the reverse was common to all issues. There are six obverse types: EVIIR, GVR, GVR crowned head, GVIR first and second types, and EIIR. All issued medals are engraved in upright serif capital letters, and issues from the 1930s onwards have in addition the date, and sometimes the place, also engraved on the rim. Only a very few – perhaps two – bars were awarded for a second act of gallantry. Approximate numbers issued: silver—77, bronze—318. All awards are notified in the London Gazette, and usually citations are given, the exception being some awards during the First World War. There are also files at the Home Office and Colonial Office which relate to many awards, and contain letters and accounts on which the award is based. The prices below are for each issue, the first figure being the First Class, and the second figure for the Second Class. A complete list of recipients can be found in *For Heroic Endeavour*, by D.V. Henderson, published Hayward in 1988.

	Silver Issue	Bronze Issue
Edward VII	£800	£500
George V 1st Type	£650	£400
George V 2nd Type	£1,000	£650
George VI 1st Type	£850	£600
George VI 2nd Type	£1,200	£900
Elizabeth II Both Types	Not Issued	£1,500

37a. EDWARD MEDAL (INDUSTRY)

Instituted in December 1909, and created alongside the Edward Medal (Mines). Awarded for acts of gallantry which occurred in an industrial context. As with the Mines issue, two classes were created: First Class (silver) and Second Class (bronze). The Obverse bore the head of the reigning monarch, of which the following six types were issued: EVIIR, GVR, GVR crowned head, GVIR first and second types, and EIIR. In addition, there were two reverse types issued: the first was issued 1910-11, and the second has been issued since 1912. All issued medals are engraved in upright serif capital letters, and issues from the 1930s onwards have in addition the date, and sometimes the place, also engraved on the rim. No second award bars were issued. Approximate numbers issued: silver—25, bronze—1163. All awards are notified in the London Gazette, and usually citations are given, the exception being some awards during the First World War. There are also files at the Home Office and Colonial Office which relate to many awards, and contain letters and accounts on which the award is based. The prices below are for each issue, the first figure being the First Class, and the second figure for the Second Class. A complete list of recipients can be found in *For Heroic Endeavour*, by D.V. Henderson, published Hayward in 1988.

	Silver Issue	Bronze Issue
Edward VII	£1,200	£900
George V 1st Type Obv. 1st Type Rev.	£1,200	£900
George V 1st Type Obv. 2nd Type Rev.	£800	£400
George V 2nd Type Obv. 2nd Type Rev.	£1,200	£800
George VI 1st Type	£1,200	£800
George VI 2nd Type	Not Awarded	£1,500
Elizabeth II Both Types	Not Awarded	£1,500

38. INDIAN DISTINGUISHED SERVICE MEDAL

Instituted in June 1907 as a reward for distinguished service for Indian officers, NCOs and men of the Indian Army. Whilst the reverse remained common to all issues, there were four obverse types EVIIR, GVR Kaisar-I-Hind, GVR crowned head, and GVIR. From 1917 onwards a second act of gallantry was recognised by the award of a bar. Issued IDSMs are named in a variety of styles, both impressed and engraved. Approximate numbers awarded: EVIIR – 140, GVR first type _ 3,200, GVR second type – 140, GVIR – 1,150. 25 bars were awarded for the First World War, and 10 for the Second World War. between the wars about 15 bars were issued. There are several sources in which notifications appear; many, but not all, IDSMs awarded for the First and Second World War appear in the London Gazette, but citations are not given. Indian Army Lists 1907-31 contain a roll of serving and retired recipients of the IDSM. Some notifications appear in the gazette of India, although no citations appear. Regimental histories often list awards, and sometimes give details.

Edward VII	£550
George V 1st Type	£100
George V 2nd Type	£300
George VI	£220

39. BURMA GALLANTRY MEDAL

Instituted in 1940, this medal was awarded to Governor's Commissioned Officers, NCOs and men of the Burma Forces (including Burma RNVR and Air Force), for acts of conspicuous gallantry in the performance of their duties. This award was intended for Burmese troops who showed gallantry short of that required for the VC, MC or Empire Gallantry Medal. The award also carried a payment of five rupees per month for life. Naming is apparently in engraved upright capitals. Some 200 of these medals were issued, with 3 bars awarded. The awards were published in the London Gazette 1942-47, usually without citation. The Burma Gazette lists the awards and gives some citations. Many of these awards were for operations behind Japanese lines. The bulk of awards were to the Burma Regiment and the Burma Rifles, with a small number being awarded to Signals, Service Corps, Intelligence Corps, and other supporting arms. Only one type of this medal was issued.

£2,500

40. DISTINGUISHED SERVICE MEDAL

Instituted in October 1914 to supplement the CGM, and was to be awarded for acts of bravery of a lesser degree than those eligible for the CGM. A bar was sanctioned in 1916 for those who received a second award of the medal. In the Second World War, eligibility was extended to Army and RAF personnel serving on board ship, and also to the Merchant and Dominion Navies. Whilst the reverse of the DSM is common to all issues, there are five obverses: GVR, GVIR first and second types, and EIIR first and second types. All issued DSMs are named, those for the First World War in impressed capitals and those for the Second World War in both impressed and engraved capitals. 4,100 DSMs were issued for the First World War, with 67 first bars and 2 second bars. ten DSMs were awarded between the wars. In the Second World War there were approximately 7,100 DSMs issued with 152 first bars and 3 second bars. One medal with three bars was also awarded. About 50 DSMs were issued 1940-45 to the Maritime Royal Artillery,

40. DISTINGUISHED SERVICE MEDAL *continued*

and 23 were awarded to the RAF. Since 1945 there have been about 50 DSMs awarded, with one first bar. All awards of the DSM are listed in the London Gazette, but in general there are few citations, except for the early part of the First World War. However, the 1914-18 awards often have the name of the ship and a date after the other naming details, and this is a useful starting point for research. Finding citations for 1939-45 awards is more difficult, but many do exist in Admiralty records. As with other awards, prices for DSMs awarded for famous actions – Jutland, Q-Ships, Russian Convoys, etc., are considerably higher. Price below for GVR is for groups with named medals. A roll of recipients of this medal by W.H. Fevyer has been published by J.B. Hayward and Son in two volumes covering the First and Second World War periods.

George V	£200
George VI (1st Type)	£220
George VI (2nd Type)	£1,250
Elizabeth II (1st Type)	£2,500
Elizabeth II (2nd Type)	£2,500

41. MILITARY MEDAL

Instituted in March 1916 as an award for NCOs and men of the Army for acts of bravery. Later extended to women who showed bravery under fire. There was also a provision for the award of a bar for each further act of bravery. In the First World War the MM was awarded to a few recipients from the Royal Navy and Royal Air Force. Some RAF personnel also received the award in the Second World War. There are six obverse types: GVR, GVR crowned head, GVIR first and second types, and EIIR first and second types. In addition, there are four different reverses in that each monarch had the relevant cypher in the reverse field. All MMs issued to British personnel are named, usually in impressed capitals, although some awards to Indian troops are engraved in plain capitals. During the First World War some 115,000 awards were made, with 5,800 first bars and 180 second bars. There was one award of the MM and three bars. Between the wars there were some 260 MMs for various campaigns. The Second World War saw the award of 15,000 MMs with 164 first and 2 second bars. Since 1945 about 700 awards have been made, plus 8 first bars. All issued MMs have a notification in the London Gazette, but only a very small number have citations in the Gazette. Citations for First World War awards are generally not available, although some details appear in Regimental Histories. Second World War awards often have citations from official sources. A complete roll of all post World War One recipients by Chris Bate and Martin Smith has recently been published and is currently available. It is understood that they are now working on a volume covering 1916-20.

George V Type I	£75
George V Crowned Head	£2,500
George VI Type I	£400
George VI Type II	£1,200
Elizabeth II	£1,400
George V Type I Awards to Women	£1,600

42. DISTINGUISHED FLYING MEDAL

The DFM was created at the same time as the DFC, and was awarded under the same general provisions as the DFC to reward NCOs and men for bravery whilst flying on operations against the enemy. All issued DFMs are named; the First World War awards were impressed in large serif capitals, and the Second World War awards were rather crudely engraved. there are five obverses issued on the DFM: GVR, GVR crowned head, GVIR first type, GVIR second type (from 1949), and EIIR. In addition there are two reverse types: the GVR issues have no date on the reverse, whilst the GVIR and EIIR issues have the date '1918' at the top of the reverse. Approximately 105 DFMs and two first award bars were issued for the First World War; between the wars some 80 medals and 2 first award bars were issued. In the Second World War, 6,600 DFMs were issued, with 60 first bars and 1 second bar. The recipient of the two-bar DFM also had the DSO and AFC. Since the Second World War approximately 100 DFMs have been issued. Availability of citations varies: about half of the First World War issues have citations in the London Gazette, whilst only a third of the inter-war awards have citations in the Gazette. There are a substantial number of citations for Second World War awards, but of those DFMs awarded since the war, only 10 have Gazette citations. A complete roll of all recipients of the Distinguished Flying medal by Ian Tavender has been published by Hayward and Son.

George V 1st Type	£750
George V 2nd Type	£2,500
George VI 1st Type	£500
George VI 2nd Type	£1,250
Elizabeth II	£1,500

43. AIR FORCE MEDAL

Instituted at the same time as the AFC, this medal was awarded to NCOs and men for courage or devotion to duty whilst flying., though not in active operations against the enemy. All awards to British personnel are named – in large serif capitals. (First World War), or in a rather crude engraved style (Second World War). There are five varieties: GVR, GVR crowned head, GVIR first and second types, and EIIR. In addition, the GVIR and EIIR issues have the date '1918' in the reverse left field. Approximately 120 medals and 2 bars were issued for the First World War, and 259 medals for the Second World War. Since 1946 nearly 400 medals have been awarded. Almost all AFMs are listed in the London Gazette without citation, and often it is necessary to undertake in-depth research to find the reason for the award. The AFM was occasionally awarded to Commonwealth Air Forces, and a few have been issued to the Army Air Corps.

George V 1st Type	£750
George V 2nd Type	£1,500
George VI 1st Type	£500
George VI 2nd Type	£800
Elizabeth II	£850

44. CONSTABULARY MEDAL (IRELAND)

Instituted in 1842 by the Irish (later Royal Irish) Constabulary as a reward for its Constable whose conduct was exemplary and who showed a high degree of "intelligence, tact or courage". The first medal was awarded in 1848 and the last in 1922 when the force was disbanded. At first, the suspender on the medal was the fixed bar type but this was later altered to a swivelling wire suspender. The obverse design varies, early issues having the female figure on the harp and the Queen's crown and later issues having the King's crown and a different type of harp which omits the figure. On the reverse is engraved the name and rank of the recipient with the date, and sometimes place, of award. Approximately 315 of these medals were awarded, the majority for the 1916 Easter Rising and the 1920 "Troubles". Seven men received a second award, either in the form of a second medal or a bar. recipients can be found in the Constabulary Lists and sometimes detail of award can be found in Irish newspapers. Price varies according to the date and detail of the award.

From £850

45. INDIAN POLICE MEDAL

Instituted in 1932 to fill a gap in rewards to the Indian Police and Fire Brigade. These services were entitled to the King's Police Medal, but the KPM was limited to a total of 50 awards per year to Indian recipients. It was to be awarded for "services of conspicuous merit". There was a provision for the award of a bar for a second award. In 1942 the Warrant was amended to limit the number of medals issued to 200 in any one year, except in unusual circumstances. There were two obverse types issued: GVR crowned head, and GVIR. There were in addition three types of reverse: from 1932 to 1945 all medals had a common reverse inscription 'For Distinguished Conduct', while after 1945 there were two types – 'For Gallantry' and 'For Meritorious Service'. All medals issued are named, usually in italic script. Some 1100 IPMs for Gallantry were awarded between 1932 and 1950, plus 21 bars. All these appear in the Gazette of India, where citations for most are shown.

George V	£300
George VI (Distinguished Conduct)	£300
George VI (For Gallantry)	£400
George VI (For Meritorious Service)	£300

46. BURMA POLICE MEDAL

Instituted in December 1937 on the separation of Burma from India. Awarded to members of the Burma Police and Fire Brigade for distinguished and meritorious conduct. The recommendation was to come via the Governor, and was to be awarded for individual acts of gallantry or for long service showing "ability and merit". Only one issue of this medal – the GVIR type – is to be found, with one type of reverse. There was a provision for a bar to be awarded, but none were issued. A total of only 141 medals were awarded, including 53 for gallantry and 80 for meritorious service, plus 8 awards which were unclassified. The awards were published in the Burma Gazette, the great majority with citations.

Award For Gallantry	£800
Award for Meritorious Service	£500

47. COLONIAL POLICE MEDAL FOR GALLANTRY (POLICE)

Instituted in May 1938 as a reward for members of the Colonial Police Forces for distinguished conduct. Provision was made for a bar to be issued for a second award. The medal could be issued to all ranks of the police in any Colony or Territory of the Empire. Awards for conspicuous gallantry were to be made as soon as possible after the act of bravery. The number to be issued in any year could not exceed 150, except in unusual circumstances. There were four obverse types issued: GVIR first and second types and EIIR first and second types. There was only one type of reverse common to all issues. Naming was in one of several types of engraving, all medals being named. In all, approximately 450 CPMs for gallantry were awarded, together with 9 bars for a second award. All awards of this medal are notified in the London Gazette, though no citations are shown. Colonial Gazettes are the best source of information, and often give citations. Prices depend on the force to which the recipient belonged and the details of the award.

George VI (First Type)	£265
George VI (Second Type)	£275
Elizabeth II (First Type)	£340
Elizabeth II (Second Type)	£320

48. COLONIAL POLICE MEDAL FOR GALLANTRY (FIRE BRIGADE)

Instituted in May 1938 as a reward for members of Colonial Fire Brigades Forces for distinguished conduct. Provision was made for a bar to be issued for a second award. The medal could be issued to all ranks in the Colonial Fire Brigades in any Colony or Territory of the Empire. Awards for conspicuous gallantry were to be made as soon as possible after the act of bravery. The number to be issued in any year was very limited. There were four obverse types issued: GVIR first and second types and EIIR first and second types. There was only one type of reverse common to all issues. Naming was in one of several types of engraving, all medals being named. In all, only 12 CPMs for gallantry were awarded to Fire Brigades. All awards of this medal are notified in the London Gazette, though no citations are shown. Colonial Gazettes are the best source of information, and often give citations.

George VI (First Type)	£1,500
George VI (Second Type)	£1,300
Elizabeth II (First Type)	£650
Elizabeth II (Second Type)	£600

49. QUEEN'S GALLANTRY MEDAL

Instituted 20 June 1974 for exemplary acts of bravery. Made of silver with the crowned Effigy of the Queen and on the reverse a design of Laurel leaves and the words "The Queen's Gallantry Medal", surmounted by the crown. All persons both civil and military are eligible for this Award, and those awarded the medal may place the letters "Q.G.M." after their name. This medal is also awarded posthumously. The ribbon is 1¼ inches wide of dark blue with a central vertical stripe of pearl grey bearing a narrow stripe of rose pink at the centre. When a second award is made a bar is worn attached to the ribbon. When the ribbon alone is worn, a silver rosette is added to it. All the awards are gazetted, together with any citation. The naming is impressed with the name and the forces detail of the recipient.

Civilian Awards	£600
Military Awards	£1,250

50. ALLIED SUBJECTS MEDAL

The medal (never formally given a name) originated in proposals early in 1919 to recognise the services of Allied subjects who had assisted British prisoners of war or evadees during the First World War. A year was spent in argument between the War Office and the Foreign Office while the first design, by the famous illustrator Edmund Dulac, was rejected. But eventually a consolidated list of names was forwarded to the King by the Foreign Office on 12 November 1920 and further awards were made in 1921 and 1922. The medal was struck in silver and bronze. The obverse has the sovereign's head and the reverse shows the figure of humanity standing over a steel-helmeted British soldier offering him a cup of water, with ruins of war in the background. The ribbon is red with a light blue centre flanked by stripes of yellow, black and white and the suspender is the same as the Victory Medal. The names of recipients were not gazetted and the medals were issued unnamed; but details appear in the list of November 1920, in a supplementary list of 8 October 1921 and a few scattered references at the Public Record Office. A total of 134 silver and 574 bronze awards were made, these figures including 56 and 247 respectively to women. Nearly all the recipients were French or Belgian.

Silver	£800
Bronze	£300

51. KING'S MEDAL FOR COURAGE IN THE CAUSE OF FREEDOM

Instituted by a Royal Warrant of 23 August 1945 to recognise acts of courage by foreign civilians or members of foreign armed forces in the furtherance of the interests of the British Commonwealth in the Allied cause during the war, without distinction of rank or status. It was particularly intended for those who had helped British escapees in occupied territories. Both males and females were eligible and in the case of armed forces personnel a recommendation for special services outside the scope of normal military duties (e.g. clandestine operations) was required. The medal is silver, on the obverse the crowned effigy of George VI and on the reverse the title within a chain. The ribbon is white edged with red stripes and in the centre two dark blue stripes. It was issued unnamed and awards were not gazetted. Approximately 3,200 awards were made, beginning in 1947.

£400

52. KING'S MEDAL FOR SERVICE IN THE CAUSE OF FREEDOM

The medal was instituted at the same time as the King's Medal for Courage, but was limited to foreign civilians who had assisted the Allied cause in a variety of ways (e.g. Winthrop Aldrich for outstanding work as national president of the British War Relief Society in the USA). The obverse is identical and the reverse shows a knight in armour carrying a broken lance and receiving sustenance from an allegorical female figure. The ribbon is white with a central red stripe flanked on each side by dark blue stripes. Approximately 2,490 awards were made.

£200

53. SEA GALLANTRY MEDAL

This medal, the only gallantry award sanctioned by Act of Parliament, was instituted in the Merchant Shipping Act of 1854. The Act mentioned the provision of money as a reward for preserving life at sea, and in 1855 the Board of Trade approved the award of silver and bronze medals for gallantry in this field. The first (Victorian) issue of this medal was known as the "Board of Trade Medal for Saving Life". It was a large piece, without suspension; there were two types – the 'Gallantry' type (where the recipient risked his own life) and the 'Humanity' type, where the recipient's life was not in danger. The former had the word 'gallantry' mentioned on the obverse, whereas the latter did not. In 1903 Edward VII ordered that the medal should be reduced in size and be designed for wearing, bringing it into line with other gallantry awards. This smaller style of medal was issued in six types: EVIIR first and second types, GVR, GVIR first and second types, and EIIR. The reverse was common to all types. Naming is engraved, with details of the recipient, ship and the date. The following numbers issued are approximate, the first being for silver awards, the second figure for bronze awards; VR–500/650; EVIIR first (large) type–19/33; EVIIR second (small) type–70/78; GVR–385/370; GVIR first type–7/13; GVIR second type–none/6; EIIR–18/8. Lists of recipients appear in the London Gazette from 1926, mostly with citations. However, other sources exist from which details of most awards before 1926 can be extracted.

	SILVER	BRONZE
Victoria large (2.25ins)		
Gallantry	£350	£200
Humanity	Rare	Rare
Edward VII large (2.25ins)		
Gallantry	£950	£650
Edward VII Medal (1.27ins)		
First type small issue	£550	£500
Second type small issue	£400	£350
George V		
Awards to Army	£500	£500
George VI		
First type	£700	£650
Second type		£800
Elizabeth II	£700	£750

Campaign Medals

The field of campaign medals is so wide and varied that no book of this nature can do more than give a general guide to prices, nor can it possibly cover every combination of medal, clasp, recipient and regiment or ship which usually determines the value of a medal. The pages which follow are designed to catalogue those medals which exist and to give each an approximate price level and some general detail regarding issue and scope. Where no recent example of a price is known, an estimate based on the factors above has been given. Where a single price has been given for any item, it may be assumed to refer to an award in VF or better condition to a British other rank or rating in a regiment or ship which received the award as a unit. Where possible, values for army, navy, native and colonial units have been given separately.

Prices given are meant only as a guide to current value. Actual price charged by a dealer may be more or less than this and will vary according to the importance placed by the dealer on such things as clasps, rarity and unit. Those readers intending to sell medals should also remember that a dealer is in business to make a living and will therefore pay a lower price than listed when buying for stock. This price is, on average, two thirds of his selling price, but a dealer will often pay more for an interesting item which he knows will sell quickly. Conversely, a very low price may be offered for items which are "run-of-the-mill" or to less popular units.

It is important to remember that medals to officers, casualties, and recipients in regiments or ships not entitled to the medal as a whole (odd men) are usually valued above the average price quoted in the following pages. A more detailed explanation is given below.

Lastly, in the field of medal collecting, there are few 'absolutes'; most general statements can be countered by at least one exception. Every attempt has been made to make the statements in the following pages as accurate as they can be, and up-to-date information has been included where possible. Readers must bear in mind, however, the earlier comment on exceptions and take this into account, particularly where naming styles and numbers issued are commented upon.

HOW TO VALUE A MEDAL

Condition. Medal collectors do not pay the same attention to condition as do coin collectors, and few will concern themselves too much whether a medal is actually 'good VF' or 'nearly EF'. Large, obvious cuts or bruises will detract from the value of a medal, but a small edge knock is not usually remarked upon. Evidence of plugging at 180° or elsewhere is usually a sign that the medal has been brooched or made into a menu holder and the suspender and clasp are therefore not original. This will affect value. Collectors should also try to avoid the purchase of groups, usually to Guardsmen, where one side of the medal has been worn flat from polishing, and also those to cavalrymen characterised by severe bruising and cutting. Collectors should not forget, however, that some medals such as the Afghan Medal and the Egypt Medal are usually found in a pitted state due to the proximity of the Star.

Rarity. The rarity of any particular medal will depend, not only on the actual number issued, but also on the number and type of clasps attached to it and the rank, appointment and unit of the recipient. These areas are discussed more fully below. Medals awarded to women usually command a premium over those awarded to men.

Clasps. This aspect will require a great deal of study by the collector. Some clasps are rare in themselves and will always command a high price, such as the 'Defence of Legations' clasp to the China 1900 Medal. Others though common, are rare to one particular unit or service. Multi clasp medals are usually valued higher than a single clasp medal, but some common clasps are rare as a single.

Unit. Usually whole regiments were present at major engagements: at others only a few odd men from a unit were accidentally present as specialists, officers' servants, etc. In the latter case, a regimental collector will pay an enhanced price for an example where his unit was not 'regimentally entitled'. Often, a particular regiment will play a prominent or crucial part in a particular battle and awards to the unit are therefore more sought after than those who were not so favoured, the outstanding example here being medals to those who charged with the Light Brigade or at Omdurman. Some units are more popular than others and medals to large Corps such as the Royal Engineers and Army Service Corps, for instance, are not usually valued at the same level as those to a line regiment. Medals to Cavalrymen usually command a small premium over those to infantrymen.

Rank of Recipient. Medals to officers are valued more highly than those to other ranks or ratings and these, in turn, are valued more highly than those to native troops. The reason for this is based upon research potential. Though it is true that officers' medals are scarcer than those to rankers, it is also true that an officer may be researched through the army lists and regimental histories and some kind of picture built up about his career. There is a chance that this can be done with other ranks, particular those who served to pension, but most researchers will give you only a one in four chance of success With native troops there is no chance of finding any personal detail about the recipient nor, in some cases, any detail about the part played by his unit.

Personal Details. Medals or groups to recipients who show a potential for research are more attractive to the collector than those without. Awards to famous or notorious personalities will be popular as will those where a background story can be constructed.

Casualties. The fact of a man being wounded or killed in a particular action almost always increases the value of a medal or group. There is constant debate among collectors and in the columns of the medal magazines about the propriety of those who collect only casualties, but the popularity of medals to casualties cannot be denied.

Groups of Medals. Groups of medals to a single recipient tend to be preferred by collectors to single items, though there is a strong market for the latter. Most groups will command a premium over the combined value of the constituent parts as showing the complete service history of a man or woman. They should therefore never be broken up. Occasionally, however, if the combination of medals or the unit of the recipient is not of particular interest, the value may be only 'break-up'.

In the last analysis, the value of anything is the maximum that someone can be persuaded to pay for it, and there can be no doubt that the best way of fixing this amount is through a study of the prices paid at auction. There are four major auction houses in London which either specialise in medals or have specialist medal departments and any new collectors would be foolish to ignore the trends and levels which are revealed by a survey of the catalogues of at least a couple of these. Recent experience at auction, together with a considered assessment of the lists of leading dealers have informed the values which are given in the following pages. They are believed to be a fair reflection of the current state of the market.

54. MEDAL FOR THE CAPTURE OF LOUISBOURG 1758

Awarded to certain participants in the capture of Louisbourg, Canada, from the French on 27th July, 1758. The criterion used for distribution is not known but was presumably distinguished service in the battle.

| Gold | £12,500 | Silver | £2,200 | Bronze | £750 |

55. DEFENCE OF GIBRALTER MEDALS 1779-83

These two medals were presented by Generals Picton and Eliott at their own expense to certain troops in their commands for services during the Franco-Spanish siege of 1779-83. Picton's medal, which is of silver and has a diameter of 2.25", is the commonest of the two. The obverse depicts a view of Gibraltar with a legend and the date '13th September 1782' - the date on which the great naval assault on the rock took place. The reverse contains a long inscription. Eliott's medal was only issued to Hanoverian troops under his command. The reverse has the names of four officers, with 'Bruderschaft' around these, and the name of the designer, Pingo, at the bottom. The obverse shows a view of Gibraltar with an inscription and the same date as on Picton's medal. The award was of silver and had a diameter of 1.95". Both medals were issued unnamed, and are found with a variety of types of mounting.

| Picton's Medal | £550 |
| Eliott's Medal | £450 |

56. DECCAN MEDAL 1778-84

This scarce medal, the first issued by the East India Company, was awarded to officers, NCOs and men of the Bengal Army for services in Gujerat in 1778-84 and the Carnatic 1780-84. The award was struck in two sizes; those with a diameter of 1.6" were issued in gold and silver to officers, whilst those with a diameter of 1.25" were issued in silver only to NCOs and men. The obverse shows the seated figure of Britannia holding a wreath. In the background is a fort and the Union Jack. The reverse has a Persian inscription. The medal, which was struck by private contractors in Calcutta, has a milled edge and was issued unnamed. The award was suspended by a loop and yellow cord.

1.6" (gold)	£4,500
1.6" (silver)	£650
1.25" (silver)	£350

57. MYSORE MEDAL 1790-92

This award was issued in gold and silver to native troops who served under Lords Abercromby and Cornwallis during the campaign against Tippoo Sahib in 1790-92. The medal was issued in two sizes; the 1.7" diameter issue was struck in gold for subadars and in silver for jemadars, whilst NCOs and men received the smaller (1.5" diameter) medal in silver. Various strikings are known of both issues, being differentiated by the number of cannonballs on the obverse - two, five or seven. Copies of this medal are known. The obverse depicts a sepoy holding a flag in each hand, with the fort of Seringapatam in the background. The reverse contains an inscription in English, surrounded by a wreath and a Persian inscription. The award was worn around the neck by a cord, which passed through a ring attached to the medal. Designed and struck in India, the medals were issued unnamed.

1.7" (gold)	£4,500
1.7" (silver)	£650
1.5" (silver)	£350

58. CEYLON MEDAL

This medal was issued by the East India Company for services during the capture of the island from the Dutch. Two gold medals were issued to officers and 121 silver medals to natives, all recipients being in the Bengal Artillery. The obverse has an English inscription and the reverse a Persian inscription. This very rare medal was issued unnamed, and is suspended from a cord which is passed through a ring attached to the medal.

Gold	£8,000
Silver	£750

59. DAVISON'S NILE MEDAL 1798

This medal was issued to commemorate Nelson's victory off Egypt on 1st August 1798 by Alexander Davison, his prize agent. The obverse depicts the figure of Peace with an inscription, and the reverse shows the fleet in Aboukir Bay with an inscription. The suspension was by a loop fixed to the medal and a dark blue ribbon. The award, designed by Kuchler, was issued in gold to the most senior officers, in silver to junior officers, bronze-gilt to petty officers, and in bronze to ratings. On the edge is inscribed 'A tribute of regard from Alexr. Davison Esq., St. James's Square.' Most examples encountered are unnamed as issued, although the recipient occasionally had his name or initials engraved on the reverse. It was not until 50 years later that official government recognition was given to the survivors in the grant of a clasp on the Naval General Service Medal of 1793-1840.

Gold	£6,000
Silver	£450
Bronze-gilt	£200
Bronze	£100

60. SERINGAPATAM MEDAL 1799

This medal was issued in 1808, but was not allowed to be worn until 1815. Awarded without suspension, various types of suspender were fitted by recipients. The obverse depicts the British lion fighting a tiger with the date '4th May 1799' in the exergue, whilst the reverse shows the storming of Seringapatam.

There are two major types of this medal - the British striking and the Calcutta striking. There were five different types of the former striking and two of the latter. The British issue has a diameter of 1.9", the Calcutta issue being 1.8" The medal, designed by Kuchler, was issued in gold (113), silver-gilt (185), silver (3,600), bronze (5,000) and pewter (45,000), depending on the rank of the recipient. The latter issue was to Indian troops. Issued unnamed, the award is sometimes found privately named by the recipient. The ribbon is usually of pale orange, but the medal is sometimes found suspended by a yellow cord. The number of regiments that received the medal were: cavalry - 2 British; infantry - 9 British and 21 Indian. In addition, detachments of artillery and engineers received the award. Although there is no medal roll as such, a prize-money roll exists which lists most European recipients. Examples of this medal should be studied carefully, as copies exist.

	Gold	Silver-gilt	Silver	Bronze	Pewter
British Medals	£3,500	£400	£350	£150	£130
Calcutta Medals	£3,500	*	£250	*	*

61. EARL ST. VINCENT'S MEDAL 1800

This rare medal, issued in gold and silver, was awarded by Earl St. Vincent to the crew of his ship, the 'Ville de Paris' for remaining loyal during the 1797 mutinies in the Royal Navy. The obverse shows the Earl in uniform with an inscription, whilst the reverse depicts a sailor and a marine with a motto. The awards, which are 1.85" in diameter, were only given to petty officers and ratings. Most examples encountered are in silver, although a few gold awards are known.

Gold	£4,000
Silver	£500

62. HONOURABLE EAST INDIA COMPANY'S EGYPT MEDAL 1801

This medal, issued in both gold and silver, was awarded for services which were later recognised by the award of a clasp on the Military General Service Medal of 1793-1814, although no recipient could have both awards. The medal was issued to the troops of a division which came from India to Egypt under General Baird. Both British and Indian troops received the award, of which 16 gold and 2,200 silver issues were struck. The obverse of the medal, which has a diameter of 1.9", depicts a sepoy holding a Union Jack, with a Persian inscription in the exergue. The reverse shows a ship and the Pyramids. Struck at the Calcutta Mint, the award is suspended by a loop and cord. Later strikings are known in bronze and bronze-gilt.

Gold	£6,500
Silver	£600

63. SULTAN'S MEDAL FOR EGYPT 1801

This medal, issued in gold and silver, was awarded by Sultan Selim for services during the campaign against the French in Egypt between March and September 1801. The obverse shows a crescent and an eight-pointed star, whilst the reverse has a Turkish inscription and date. The gold medals were awarded to officers only, and are found in four sizes – 2.1", 1.9", 1.7" and 1.4". In addition, some gold awards to senior officers were studded with jewels. The silver awards were issued to NCOs and are only found with a 1.4" diameter. Those gold awards with jewels were suspended by an orange ribbon and loop, whilst other awards had a chain and hook attachment. The awards were very thin and were issued unnamed.

Gold 2.1"	£2,500
Gold 1.9"	£1,200
Gold 1.7"	£800
Gold 1.4"	£500
Silver 1.4"	£500

64. BOULTON'S TRAFALGAR MEDAL 1805

This medal, designed by Kuchler, was paid for and issued by Matthew Boulton, a Birmingham manufacturer. It was awarded to survivors of the battle of Trafalgar on 21st October, 1805. The obverse contains a bust of Nelson and an inscription, whilst the reverse contains a battle scene and an inscription. The medal was awarded in gold, silver, bronze-gilt, bronze and white metal, depending on the rank of the recipient. The award was issued unnamed, the edge being inscribed 'From M. Boulton to the Heroes of Trafalgar'. The medal is 1.9" in diameter.

Gold	£9,500
Silver	£750
Bronze-Gilt	£500
Bronze	£200
White Metal	£150

65. DAVISON'S TRAFALGAR MEDAL 1805

This medal is somewhat similar to Davison's Nile Medal of 1798, in that it was issued for Nelson's victory of 21st October 1805 by his prize-agent, Alexander Davison. The medal, which is of pewter and often has a copper ring, was issued to ratings present at the battle. The obverse shows the bust of Nelson with a Latin inscription, the reverse showing a man-of-war and an English inscription. The award has a diameter of 2.1", and is suspended from a dark blue ribbon by a ring. It was issued unnamed.

£600	

66. MEDAL FOR THE CAPTURE OF RODRIGUES, ISLE OF BOURBON AND ISLE OF FRANCE 1809-10

This medal, issued in gold and silver, was awarded by the East India Company for the capture of three islands between July 1809 and December 1810. The recipients were all native troops in the Bengal and Bombay armies, and although British troops took part in the operations they did not receive a medal. The first island, Rodrigues, was occupied in July 1809, only about 200 native troops being present. The Isle of Bourbon was taken in July 1810 after an earlier, smaller British force had been driven out; three regiments of native infantry were present during these operations. In December 1810, a force 10,000 strong under General Abercromby captured Isle de France, now Mauritius, which had been used as a pirate base. About 50 gold and 2,200 silver medals were issued. The obverse depicts a sepoy in front of a cannon holding the Union Jack, whilst the reverse has a Persian inscription surrounded by a wreath and an inscription in English. The award, which was struck at the Calcutta Mint, was suspended by a cord, and had a diameter of 1.9".

Gold	£5,000
Silver	£600

67. BAGUR AND PALAMOS MEDAL 1810

This medal was issued by the Spanish government to the crews of three British ships, the 'Ajax', 'Cambrian' and 'Kent' for services in 1810. The obverse depicts the shields of Britain and Spain, whilst the obverse bears an inscription. Eight gold medals were issued to officers and 600 in silver to ratings. This medal is unusual in that it was awarded in part for a serious reverse, the small British force being driven back to their ships by the enemy at Palamos. These medals are very rare, and are occasionally seen named in script on the reverse with either the full name or the initials of the recipient. The name of the ship on which the recipient served is also found on the reverse. The ribbon is of red with yellow edges.

Gold	£3,750
Silver	£500

68. JAVA MEDAL 1811

This medal, struck at the Calcutta Mint, was awarded for services in the same campaign as the clasp for 'Java' on the Military General Service Medal 1793- 1814. Whilst the latter medal was issued 38 years later to troops in the British Army, the Company's medal was issued soon after the campaign. 130 gold and 6,300 silver medals were issued, 750 Europeans receiving the medal. The gold issues were awarded to the senior officers of the Company who were present. The obverse depicts the attack on Fort Cornelis during the campaign, and the reverse has English and Persian inscriptions. The suspension is by a ring and cord.

Gold	£5,000
Silver	£500

69. NEPAUL MEDAL 1814-16

This rare medal, of which about 350 were awarded, was sanctioned by the East India Company in March 1816. The award was issued only to those native troops who had shown zeal and courage during the campaign, other troops - British and Indian - having to wait nearly 35 years for a medal, the Army of India Medal of 1799-1826 with the appropriate clasp. The medal was issued in silver from the Calcutta Mint, and was unnamed. The obverse depicts hill stockades and a field gun, whilst the reverse has a Persian inscription. The medal, which has a diameter of 2", was suspended by a cord which passed through a loop attached to the award.

£500

70. BURMA MEDAL 1824-26

This medal was sanctioned by the East India Company in April 1826, and was awarded to native officers and men in the Company's service. The fighting, for which the clasp 'Ava' was issued to European troops on the Army of India Medal 1799-1826, lasted from April 1824 to February 1826. The war was caused by troubles on the Indo~Burmese frontier. As well as several major actions around Rangoon, many small skirmishes were fought elsewhere. 750 gold medals were issued to native officers and 24,000 silver medals to native troops. The obverse shows the British Lion overcoming the Burmese elephant, the reverse depicting the storming of Rangoon and the Irrawady Flotilla. The medal has a diameter of 1.5", and is suspended by a ring and steel clip or a straight suspender and steel clip. The ribbon is of crimson with blue edges. No clasps were issued, and the medal was issued unnamed.

Gold	£1,800
Silver	£400

71. COORG MEDAL 1837

This very scarce medal was sanctioned in August 1837 for award to native troops who remained loyal during the Canara rebellion in April of that year. The obverse shows a Coorg and has a Canarese inscription around the edge whilst the reverse has war trophies and an inscription in English. The award is large, being nearly 2 inches in diameter and of varying thickness which leads to weight differences. Awards to officers were given suspended from a chain whilst those to other ranks were suspended from a cord. There are 44 gold medals which differ in weight and the attachment of a chain. 14 were issued with a chain, of which 2 were of heavier weight than the others: the remaining 30 had no chain and 10 of these were of lighter weight than the others. There were 200 issued in silver. Occasionally copper versions of this award are met with but these are specimen strikings.

Gold	£4,500
Silver	£550

72. NAVAL GOLD MEDAL 1795-1815

This very rare award was instituted in 1795 and abolished in 1815, and was awarded to Admirals and Captains who were present at certain naval engagements during the Napoleonic Wars. The actions for which these medals were issued were also commemorated by clasps on the Naval General Service Medal of 1793-1840. The obverse depicts Victory crowning Britannia on the prow of a galley, the Union Jack being in the background. The reverse contains the name of the recipient and the action for which the medal was awarded. The medal, issued in gold only, was issued in two sizes; 2" diameter for Admirals and 1.3" diameter for Captains. The large medals were worn around the neck and the small medals were worn from a buttonhole on the left side, being suspended by a straight gold wire attachment and ribbon. Only 22 large and 117 small medals were issued, mostly for fleet actions such as Trafalgar, Camperdown and the Glorious First of June. The ribbon is white, with dark blue edges. Due to the rarity of this award, it is difficult to give a general valuation, but the figures below may be regarded as a minimum.

Large Medal	From £30,000
Small Medal	From £12,000

73. NAVAL GENERAL SERVICE MEDAL 1793-1840

This medal, sanctioned in 1848 and issued in 1849, was awarded for a very wide range of naval actions between 1793 and 1840. Due to the belated nature of the award, and the fact that it was only issued to those survivors who claimed it, the medal is scarce and many of the clasps are very rare indeed, often less than 30 being issued. The obverse has the familiar Wyon bust of Queen Victoria with '1848' at the bottom, whilst the reverse shows Britannia on a seahorse. The suspension is plain and swivelling. In all, 231 different clasps were sanctioned, the largest number by far on any campaign medal, of which seven were not issued due to the lack of claimants. There were two types of clasp; 176 were awarded for 'ship' or 'fleet' actions, and usually bear the name of the ship or battle together with the date of the action. The second type of clasp, of which 55 were awarded, was the 'boat service' type. These were awards to men who went out from their vessel in ship's boats, either making up raiding parties ashore or boarding parties at sea. Most of these are very scarce indeed, and have a standard clasp, in that 'Boat Service' is in the centre of the clasp, separating the date from the year. The clasps are narrow and very similar to those on the Military General Service Medal of 1793-1814. Whilst most examples encountered have one clasp, the maximum number on one medal is seven, of which three are known. In all, some 21,000 medals and 24,000 clasps are known to have been issued. Careful research must be undertaken with some awards, as the rolls are not always complete or accurate, and reference must be made to other records to confirm the medal. The naming is always in impressed Roman capitals, the ranks of officers and warrant officers being shown, those awards to ratings bearing the recipients' name only. The ribbon is white with blue edges. Particularly sought-after are those awards for well-known actions, especially Trafalgar and the awards for actions off North America. Due to the impossibility of pricing all the clasps, a selection of clasps has been listed below, giving an approximate guide to prices. The figure in brackets shows the number of clasps awarded.
A complete roll of recipients of this medal has been published by the author, Capt. K.J. Douglas-Morris, and is obtainable from The Naval & Military Press.

73. NAVAL GENERAL SERVICE MEDAL *continued*

1 June 1794 (540)	£550
14 March 1795 (97)	£800
23 June 1795 (200)	£650
St. Vincent (348)	£500
Camperdown (298)	£500
Isle of St. Marcou 1798 (3)	£2,000
Lion 15 July 1798 (23)	£950
Nile (326)	£550
12 October 1798 (78)	£850
Acre 30 May 1799 (51)	£750
Egypt (618)	£350
Copenhagen 1801	£550
Gut of Gibralter 12 July 1801 (144)	£550
Acheron 3 February 1805 (2)	£2,000
Trafalgar (1,613)	£1,000
4 November 1805 (296)	£550
St. Domingo (396)	£350
Amazon 13 March 1806 (30)	£800
Curacao 1 January 1807 (62)	£650
Hydra 6 August 1807 (12)	£1,200
Comus 15 August 1807 (10)	£1,300
Stately 22 March 1808 (31)	£875
Redwing 7 May 1808 (7)	£1,500
Seahorse wh badere Zaffere (32)	£1,200
Martinique (486)	£300
Basque Roads 1809 (529)	£475
Pompee 17 June 1809 (47)	£1,100
Guadaloupe (483)	£300
Lissa (124)	£485
Java (665)	£300
Victorious with Rivoli (67)	£750
St. Sebastian (293)	£350
Shannon wh Chesapeake (42)	£2,500
Gluckstadt 5 January 1814 (44)	£850
Gaieta 24 July 1815 (89)	£550
Algiers (1,328)	£320
Navarino (1,142)	£350
Syria (6,978)	£200
BOAT SERVICE BARS	
16 July 1806 (52)	£700
1 November 1809 (110)	£550
28 June 1810 (26)	£800
29 September 1812 (25)	£825
April and May 1813 (57)	£1,400
2 May 1813 (48)	£720
8 April 1814 (24)	£2,000
24 May 1814 (12)	£900
14 December 1814 (205)	£850

The 'Pompee' clasp has been priced as a three clasp medal.

74. ARMY GOLD CROSS 1806-14

These magnificent awards, the most desirable in the campaign series, were issued to field and general officers for services in the Peninsular Wars. Whereas such officers who served at three or less actions received the gold medal with or without clasps, the cross was awarded for four or more actions. The cross is of the pattee design and is 1.5" in diameter. Both obverse and reverse are similar, with each arm bearing the name of an action in which the recipient served. The edge of each arm has a laurel wreath design. The suspension is by an ornate ring which connects to a plain ring, the latter swivelling from a straight suspender. The clasps on this award are similar to those on the gold medals. The naming is by large engraved capitals on the edge of each arm. Some 163 crosses were awarded, and in addition 237 clasps were issued. The maximum number of clasps on one cross is nine, commemorating thirteen actions in all; not surprisingly, this was awarded to the Duke of Wellington. These awards are very rare, the recipients usually being senior officers who played an important part in the war. Most examples seen on the market are accompanied by at least one other medal or order. Due to the rarity of this award, it is very difficult to put an exact value on the cross, and the price below is a guide to the minimum price for an award.

Cross without clasp	£10,000

75. ARMY GOLD MEDAL 1806-1814

These medals, sanctioned in 1810, were generally awarded to officers of the rank of major and above for services during the Peninsular War. The obverse depicts a seated figure of Britannia holding a laurel wreath and palm branch, together with a shield. The name of the battle for which the medal was awarded is engraved in the centre of the reverse and is surrounded by a wreath of laurels. Those nine awards for the battle of Barrosa have the name embossed on the reverse. There were two types of the medal; the large (2.1") medal for generals, and the small (1.3") medal for ranks down to and including major. The design on both sizes is identical. The clasps, of which the maximum on one medal was two, have embossed lettering surrounded by a wreath. The medals were designed to be worn from a buttonhole, the large awards being suspended by a ring and the small awards by a straight suspender. Some of the small medals are found named to Captains, usually those who commanded their regiments in the absence of senior officers. 88 large and 596 small medals were issued, with a total of 43 and 237 clasps respectively. Recipients of this medal could not receive a clasp for the same action on the Military General Service Medal in addition. The naming is engraved around the edge, and the ribbon is of crimson with blue edges.

Large medal without clasp	From £12,000
Small medal without clasp	From £3,800

76. MILITARY GENERAL SERVICE MEDAL 1793-1814

This medal, sanctioned in 1847 and issued in 1848, was awarded for services during the Napoleonic Wars 1801-14. It had been planned to award the medal for battles and campaigns as far back as 1793, but such was the time lapse that very few claimants would have come forward, and therefore the first clasp awarded was that for 'Egypt', for the campaign of 1801. Some 25,000 medals were issued with an almost infinite variety of the 29 clasps issued, the maximum on one medal being fifteen. The great variety of clasps and regiments found on this medal make it one of the most interesting of all campaign awards. The time lapse between the actual battles and the issue of the medal meant that only a small number of survivors from each regiment lived to receive the award. In addition, there were survivors who did not know about or could not claim the medal. Most of the clasps were awarded for services during the Peninsular War of 1811-14, although six clasps were issued for the Peninsula War of 1808-09. In addition, there were three clasps for services in Canada, two for services in the West Indies, and one each for Egypt (1801), Maida (southern Italy 1806), and Java (1811). The obverse is the usual Wyon head of Victoria, with the date '1848' at the foot, whilst the reverse depicts Victoria placing a laurel wreath on Wellington as he kneels before her; there is also an inscription, and the British Lion is represented. The clasps were struck in groups of three where applicable, and then rivetted together. The suspension is by a straight, swivelling suspension. The naming is always in impressed Roman capitals. There are too many rarities to detail both in terms of the clasps and the regiments, but it should be borne in mind that only about 10% of those who fought in these battles and campaigns lived to receive the medal, and that, when the number that have been lost, destroyed or placed in museums is taken into account, this medal can be described as scarce and a considerable number of issues as rare. The most up-to-date roll currently in print is by A.L.T. Mullen and published by The Naval & Military Press. The ribbon is of crimson with blue edges. Prices below for single clasps are for the commonest regiments, and those for multi-clasp awards are for the commonest clasps.

Albuhera	£380	Roleia	£600
Badajoz	£350	Sahagun	£700
Barrosa	£350	Sahagun & Benevente	£425
Benevente	£5,500	St. Sebastian	£350
Busaco	£350	Salamanca	£300
Chateauguay	£1,500	Talavera	£320
Chrystler's Farm	£1,800	Toulouse	£300
Ciudad Rodrigo	£350	Vimiera	£400
Corunna	£350	Vittoria	£250
Egypt	£370	Two clasps	£300
Fort Detroit	£1,600	Three clasps	£300
Fuented D'Onor	£320	Four clasps	£400
Guadaloupe	£380	Five clasps	£450
Java	£380	Six clasps	£500
Maida	£400	Seven clasps	£600
Martinique	£350	Eight clasps	£700
Nive	£320	Nine clasps	£850
Nivelle	£300	Ten clasps	£1,000
Orthes	£300	Eleven clasps	£1,400
Pyrenees	£300	Twelve or more clasps	£2,000

77. WATERLOO MEDAL

This medal was the first award issued to all ranks, and set a precedent for the issue of campaign medals. It was awarded to all those who served at the battles of Ligny, (Quatre Bras and Waterloo 16th-18th June 1815. The battle is well-known, and a wealth of literature on the subject is available. The most sought-after awards are, as usual, those to officers and to casualties. In addition, medals to cavalry regiments are popular, especially those to the 2nd Dragoons (Royal Scots Greys), who made a famous charge during the battle. Awards to members of Colville's Division, who remained in reserve during the battle, are less popular; the Division consisted of the 35th, 54th, 59th and 91st Foot. Some 39,000 of these medals were issued, although this is misleading, as very few of this number. still exist. 6,000 were issued to Cavalry; 4,000 to Guards; 16,000 to Line Regiments; and 5,000 to Artillery. In addition, there was the usual contingent of supply personnel, and a 6,500 strong contingent of the King's German Legion. This latter group played an important part in the battle and suffered high casualties, and their medals are somewhat underestimated. The medal itself was always issued in silver, and is unusual in that the head of the Prince Regent is shown, whilst all other campaign awards show the head of the relevant king or queen. The reverse depicts the figure of Victory, another facet which was incorporated in many future issues; the award was designed by a member of the Wyon family, who were to figure very largely in the design of campaign medals for the rest of the century. Originally, the suspension was by a steel clip and ring, but as this was unattractive and prone to rust, many recipients had suspenders fitted privately. The naming is always in large impressed Roman capitals, with stars at the beginning and end of the naming to free up any free space. The ribbon is of crimson, with blue edges.

There is a complete roll of recipients of this medal which is obtainable from The Naval & Military Press.

Household Cavalry	£650
Heavy Dragoons	£450
(Scots Greys) 2nd or R.N.B. Dragoons	£1,000
Hussars and Light Cavalry	£450
Royal Artillery	£450
Foot Guards	£450
27th, 28th, 42nd, 44th, 73rd, 79th, 92nd Foot	£600
Other Foot Regiments	£450
General Colville Reserve Division 35th, 54th, 59th, 91st, Foot	£380
King's German Legion	£400

78. THE BRUNSWICK MEDAL FOR WATERLOO

A medal was also issued by the Prince Regent to the troops of Duke Frederick William of Brunswick who fought at the Actions of Quatre Bras, where the Duke was killed, and Waterloo.

The medal is of bronze and shows the head of Duke Frederick William facing left and wearing a cap, with the legend 'Friedrich Wilhelm Hertzog'. The reverse shows a wreath of oak and laurel around the inscription 'Braunschweig Seinen Kriegern Quatrebras und Waterloo'. The ribbon is 1½, ins. wide of yellow with light blue stripes near each edge.

Bronze	£200

79. THE HANOVERIAN MEDAL FOR WATERLOO

This medal was instituted by the Prince Regent for award to survivors from Hanover. From the time of George I until 1837, the Kings of England were also Electors of Hanover.

The silver medal shows on the obverse the head of the Prince Regent with the date 1815 underneath and the legend 'Georg Prinz Regent'. The reverse shows a military trophy below the inscription 'Hannoverscher Tapferkeit'. Below is 'Waterloo Jun XVIII'. Suspension is by a ring as with the British version and the ribbon is similar but the edges are of much lighter blue.

Silver	£200

80. THE NASSAU MEDAL FOR WATERLOO

Distributed on 23rd December, 1815 by Frederick Duke of Nassau to all his troops who had been present at the battle. The silver medal is smaller than the others at just over one inch diameter and shows the head of the Duke facing right. The reverse shows a figure of Victory crowning a soldier above the date Den 18 Juni 1815 in the exergue. Suspension is by means of a ring through which passes the ribbon of dark blue edged yellow.

Silver	£180

81. THE SAXE-GOTHA-ALTENBURG MEDAL FOR 1814-1815

A larger medal of 1.6 inches diameter which was awarded in gilt to officers and bronze to other ranks of the Saxe-Gotha-Altenburg Foreign Legion. The obverse shows a Crown surrounded by the words 'im Kampfe Fuer das Recht'. The reverse shows a five-petalled rose surrounded by a complicated design. Around the edge of the medal is the name of the Duchy and the dates MDCCCXIV and MDCCCXV.

Suspension is by means of a ring through which passes the ribbon of green with black edges and gold horizontal stripes.

Gilt	£300
Bronze	£200

82. ARMY OF INDIA MEDAL 1799-1826

This medal, authorised in March 1851, was issued to the survivors of various battles and campaigns in India between 1803 and 1826. The fact that survivors only could receive the medal, coupled with the 48year gap between the first action and the award of the medal, meant that very few medals were issued. The medal itself is very scarce, and most of the clasps can be considered rare. The medal was issued in silver only, and was not awarded without at least one clasp. On multi-clasped medals, the correct order of award is that the last clasp earned is nearest the medal, and thus clasps should be read downwards. There are two reverse types, the long-hyphen and the short-hyphen, but these do not lead to any appreciable variation in price. In all twenty-one clasps were issued for various campaigns. These were: the Second Mahratta War 1803-4, the Nepal War 1814-16, the Third Mahratta War 1817-18, the Burmese War 1824-26, and the Siege of Bhurtpoor 1825-26. The clasps for the two Mahratta Wars are the most rare and interesting, those for 1803-04 commemorating some of Wellington's early victories. Clasps for both these wars are rare to Europeans. In fact, only the last two clasps awarded are seen regularly on the market. An example of the distortion caused by the lapse between the battles and the awards of medals is that of the 'Corygaum' clasp; this was issued to only 4 Europeans, the survivors of just 600 men who defeated three enemy divisions. Many varying clasp combinations exist, any medal with more than one clasp being rare. The naming is usually in one of two types, either impressed capitals for Europeans or running script for native troops, although impressed medals have been seen to the latter. Published rolls exist for European recipients. The ribbon is of plain light blue. Prices below are for the single clasps, or with other clasps where commoner, to Europeans, the number of whom received the medal is in brackets.

There is a complete roll of recipients of this medal which is obtainable from The Naval & Military Press.

Allighur (66)	£2,500
Battle of Delhi (40)	£3,000
Assye (87)	£2,500
Asseerghur (48)	£2,800
Laswarree (100)	£1,000
Argaum (126)	£2,500
Gawilghur (110)	£2,500
Defence of Delhi (5)	£12,000
Battle of Deig (47)	£3,000
Capture of Deig (103)	£2,000
Nepaul (505)	£450
Kirkee (5)	£12,000
Poona (75)	£900
Kirkee and Poona (88)	£850
Seetabuldee (2)	£15,000
Nagpore (155)	£650
Seetabuldee & Nagpore (21)	£8,000
Maheidpoor (75)	£850
Corygaum (4)	£12,000
Ava (2,325)	£300
Bhurtpoor (1.059)	£350

Medals with more than two clasps are very scarce.

Approx. No. Issued		
	3 clasps	150
	4 clasps	23
	5 clasps	10
	6 clasps	2
	7 clasps	1

83. GHUZNEE MEDAL 1839

This was only the second campaign medal to be issued to British troops, the first being the Waterloo Medal of 1815. The medal was awarded to both British and Indian troops who were present at the storming of and fighting around the fortress of Ghuznee 21st to 23rd July 1839. The British force had entered Afghanistan to reinstate Shah Soojah-ool-Mook, considered to be pro-British, who had been dethroned and exiled by the Persians. During the advance on Kabul, the Bombay Column stormed Ghuznee, and this effectively ended the resistance to Shah Soojah. The latter, as a mark of appreciation, ordered this medal to be struck and issued to all those who had been present at Ghuznee; he died before this task was completed, and so the Government of India bore the cost. It is interesting to note that, after a lapse of 24 years, medals began to be awarded again at the instigation of the ruler of Afghanistan, and not by the British government. It was struck in silver only and was issued unnamed, although it is often found named by the recipient on the reverse field or on the edge in various styles of engraving. Although no official clasps were issued, unofficial types are sometimes seen. Five British regiments - two cavalry and three infantry - were present, as well as a number of Europeans serving with the forces of the East India Company. The ribbon is half crimson and half green, the latter being worn on the recipients' left. Prize money was awarded for the capture of the fortress, and in effect this is the relevant medal roll. The so-called "tall towers" version of this medal is a contemporary tailors' copy.

Engraved to British Troops	£280
Engraved to Indian Troops	£175
Unnamed	£175

84. THE ST. JEAN D'ACRE 1840

In 1840 a three hour bombardment by a combined British, Austrian and Turkish fleet under the command of Sir Charles Napier succeeded in recapturing for the Turks the city of Acre. Though in Palestine, this was part of the Turkish Empire but had been occupied by the Egyptians for eight years. This medal was issued to participants by the Sultan of Turkey to commemorate the battle and was given in gold to naval captains and field officers, in silver to other officers and in copper to other ranks and ratings. The obverse shows a fortress flying the Turkish flag and six stars above. Below is a Turkish inscription. The reverse shows the cypher of the Sultan surrounded by laurel branches. The ribbon is red with white edges and suspension is by a double ring. Some eight years later, this action was also commemorated by the issue of the clasp 'Syria' to the newly instituted Naval General Service Medal. Any medal bearing this clasp should therefore be accompanied by a St. Jean d'Acre medal of the correct type.

Gold	£600
Silver	£100
Bronze	£65

85. CANDAHAR-GHUZNEE-CABUL MEDAL 1841-42

Sanctioned by a General Order in October 1842, this award was issued for services during the First Afghan War. There are four main types of this medal, with in addition two great rarities. The main types are identical except for the reverse inscription, which shows the battle or battles in which the recipient participated. These types are: 'Candahar' (May 1842); 'Cabul' (15th September 1842); 'Ghuznee and Cabul'; 'Candahar, Ghuznee, Cabul'. In addition to these, two rare types are known. Firstly, medals with the obverse legend 'Victoria Regina' instead of the usual 'Victoria Vindex' and secondly, the 'Cabvl' reverse instead of 'Cabul', fifteen of which were issued. The ribbon is of a rainbow pattern of red, white, yellow, white and blue. The suspension is straight and of steel, and is attached to the medal by a steel clip. The naming is engraved script or impressed Roman capitals. Whilst none of these medals is common, those for 'Candahar' and 'Ghuznee and Cabul' are very scarce. The two rarities mentioned above are only occasionally seen. The medal was awarded for a series of battles and sieges during the war, the British suffering several reverses and heavy casualties. Some excellent and very dangerous copies of this medal with the Candahar and Cabul reverses have recently appeared on the market. Collectors should exercise extreme care when purchasing examples of this medal and be particularly wary of bargain offers.

	Imperial Regiments	Indian Units	Unnamed
Candahar	£450	£200	£200
Cabul	£220	£145	£140
Cabvl (15 issued)	£1,000	£600	£400
Ghunzee/Cabul	£400	£200	£200
Candahar/Ghunzee/Cabul	£300	£175	£175

86. JELLALABAD MEDALS 1842

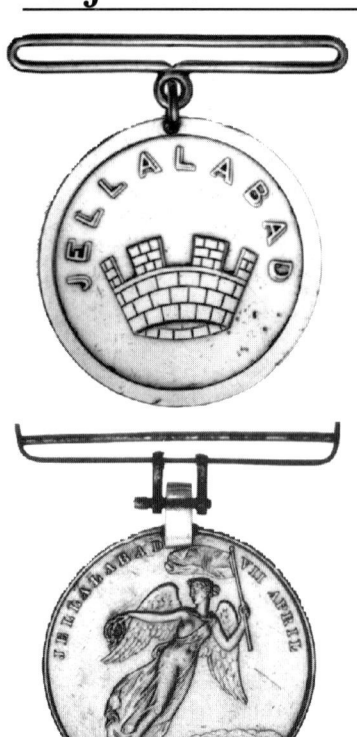

This medal was awarded to those who took part in the defence of Jellalabad between November 1841 and April 1842. The fighting was part of the First Afghan War, which began when the British envoy was murdered in Kabul and several British garrisons, including Jellalabad, were attacked. The garrison consisted of the 13th Foot, one regiment of Bengal NI, and several other detachments of Indian and loyal Afghan troops; in all about 2,600. The first ('Mural Crown') issue of this medal, minted in Calcutta, was thought to be too crude, and a second issue was minted in London. An exchange was offered to recipients, but only a handful received the second type, making it rarer than the first.

First Type

This type, known as the 'Mural Crown', had a crown and inscription on the obverse, with the date of the relief of the garrison on the reverse. The ribbon is of watered red, white, yellow, white and blue, and the suspension was straight and fixed to the rim. The award is found named in several styles, sometimes on the edge and sometimes on the obverse. Whilst examples are seen with engraved naming, those to the 13th Foot, named at the expense of the Commanding Officer, are usually impressed on the edge. The award, which is scarce, was issued in silver and without clasps.

Second Type

The second type, known as the 'Flying Victory', had the head of Queen Victoria on the obverse with the legend 'Victoria Vindex' or, rarely, 'Victoria Regina'. The reverse depicts the figure of Victory flying over the fort at Jellalabad. The ribbon is similar to that used on the first type, although the suspension is different, being straight with a steel clip and pin attachment. The naming on this type is usually by impressing on the edge.

	Imperial Regiments	Indian Units	Unnamed
1st Type	£450	£300	£150
2nd Type	£650	£375	£250

87. DEFENCE OF KELAT-I-GHILZIE MEDAL 1842

This medal, which was only issued in silver, was instituted by a General Order of October 1842. It was awarded to those who formed the garrison of the fort at Kelat-I-Ghilzie between February and May 1842. The fort, which was located between Kabul and Kandahar, was finally relieved on 26th May 1842 by General Nott. This medal is very rare, being awarded to only 50 or so Europeans and 900 native troops. Apart from 7 Staff Officers, the garrison consisted of: 4/2 Bengal Artillery (86); 43rd Bengal NI (250); and 3rd Shah Soojah's Infantry (570). This latter unit performed so well during the siege that it was taken into the Bengal Army as an infantry regiment. The straight suspension was of steel, with a metal clip. The naming was in engraved script. Due to the fact that the medal was issued to so few recipients, and considering that most of the medals issued to the native troops have been lost or destroyed, this medal is one of the rarest of all campaign awards. The ribbon is of a rainbow pattern of watered red, yellow, white and blue.

Europeans	£4000
Natives	£1,500
Unnamed	£850

88. CHINA MEDAL 1840-42

This medal, suggested by the East India Company and issued by the British government, was awarded to those who took part in the First China War of 1840-42. The war was caused by the insistence of British merchants that they should have a monopoly over opium imports from India. Attacks began on British nationals and their property, and in August 1839 the British seized Hong Kong. A protracted war followed, and after various naval and land engagements the Chinese sued for peace, which lasted until 1857. The obverse of the medal has the Wyon bust of Queen Victoria, whilst the reverse depicts military trophies under a palm tree with an inscription, and 'China 1842' in the exergue. The suspender is thick and straight, and is fixed directly onto the medal. No clasps were issued, and the naming is in large, deeply-impressed Roman capitals, any spare space on the rim being filled in with stars as on the Waterloo Medal of 1815. The approximate number of units present is: five companies of Artillery, four companies of Sappers and Miners, five British and nine Indian Infantry regiments. In addition, some 50 British and Indian ships were present during the operations. The ribbon is of crimson with yellow edges.

Royal Navy	£220
Indian & Bengal Marine Ships	£300
Imperial Army	£220
Indian Infantry	£300

89. CHINA 1842 - ORIGINAL DESIGN

The original reverse design of this medal was not eventually used as it was thought to be somewhat too provocative. Occasional examples do appear on the market from time to time, however.
The design shows the British Lion trampling a dragon, representing China, underfoot beneath the words 'Armis Exposcere Pacem', with 'Nanking, 1842' in the exergue. Suspension is usually by a steel clip and bar.

	£1,000

90. SCINDE MEDAL 1843

This medal was sanctioned in September 1843, and was issued in silver only. Although all medals have one common obverse, there are three differing reverses showing which of the two main battles the recipient fought in. The 'Meeanee' reverse is very scarce, whilst the other two are commoner. The campaign was undertaken to punish the Amirs of Scinde for attacks on British convoys to and from Afghanistan. The two major battles - Meeanee and Hyderabad - saw the complete rout of the enemy, and British troops then withdrew. These medals are particularly sought-after to recipients in the 22nd Foot, the only British regiment present, and to men of the Indus Flotilla. The 22nd Foot especially distinguished themselves during the campaign, and their commanding officer, disliking the steel suspenders issued with the medal, had them replaced with silver suspenders for his men at his own expense. The medal was issued without clasps and the naming is generally in large, thick lettering. Medal rolls exist for the 22nd Foot and the Indus Flotilla. The ribbon is of watered red, white, yellow, white and blue.

Meeanee	£800
Hyderabad	£550
Meeanee and Hyderabad	£350

91. GWALIOR STAR 1843

This unusual award, of which two types were issued, was sanctioned in January 1844 for services against the Mahrattas in December 1843. After various troubles on the Mahratta border, two columns entered the hostile state. In two battles on the same day - 29th December 1843 - the British forces inflicted crushing defeats on the Maahrattas. This was one of the shortest of the many campaigns to India, but the cost to the British was substantial, as casualties were quite high. The award, in the shape of a star, was made from the bronze of captured guns and is of a unique design. The obverse of this six-pointed star has, in the centre, an identical but much smaller star in silver; on the latter is the name of the battle in which the recipient fought, either 'Maharajpoor' or 'Punniar'. The reverse is plain except for the naming, which is almost always in running script and is arranged in several lines. When issued, these awards were designed to be worn from a buttonhole, and therefore had brass hooks screwed onto the reverse centre. However, most recipients converted their stars in various ways to accommodate the ribbon, and therefore a variety of types of suspension are found. As the force at Punniar was the smaller of the two, the star for this action is the scarcer. The ribbon is of watered red, white, yellow, white and blue,

Maharajpoor Star	£250
Punniar Star	£300

92. SUTLEJ MEDAL 1845-46

This medal, sanctioned in 1846, was the first campaign award issued to all ranks with clasps, although clasps had been awarded on the Gold Crosses and Medals issued to officers for the Peninsular Wars. The basic design of this medal set a precedent in campaign awards that has been generally adhered to ever since. Another unusual facet to this medal is that the name of the first battle at which the recipient was present is found at the bottom of the reverse; thus medals with one clasp are found to recipients who were at two actions, and so on. Those who were at all four battles for which clasps were awarded could only receive three clasps, and no clasp was issued for 'Moodkee', it being the first battle of the campaign. The 1845-46 Sikh War was a difficult one, as the Sikh army was well-trained and armed. As a result, British casualties at the four actions were heavy. However, the campaign was short and concentrated, lasting only three months, and the Sikhs returned for a further conflict with the British two years later (see Punjab Medal 1848-49). The medal is found named in two main styles; to British troops, in thin, upright impressed capitals, a rather distinctive style notable for the use of colons instead of full stops; and to Indian troops in engraved running script. The most sought-after medals in the series are those with three clasps to British troops, and medals for 'Aliwal' to the 16th Lancers, who made a famous charge at the battle. Medals to British recipients can almost always be verified. The ribbon is of dark blue with crimson edges.

Moodkee reverse	£140
Ferozeshuhur reverse	£140
Aliwal Reverse	£130
Sobraon reverse	£120
Moodkee with three clasps	£450
Moodkee with two clasps	£250
Moodkee with one clasp	£200
Ferozeshuhur with two clasps	£250
Ferozeshuhur with one clasp	£200
Aliwal with one clasp	£200
16th Lancers killed at "Aliwal"	£350

93. PUNJAB MEDAL 1848-49

Sanctioned in April 1849, this medal was awarded to all those who served in the Punjab between September 1848 and March 1849. Issued in silver only, it was awarded with and without clasps, there being three clasps, commemorating two battles and a siege. The obverse design was the familiar 'Wyon Head', and the reverse depicts General Gilbert receiving the Sikh surrender. The campaign was the third and final undertaken against the Sikhs; despite being defeated in 1845-46, the Sikhs continued to pose a threat to British interests in northern India, and when the British Resident was killed at Mooltan in 1848, war was declared. Whilst one column besieged Mooltan, another fought a bitter battle at Chilianwala, after which elements of both forces joined together and marched to Goojerat, where the Sikh army was destroyed. It is interesting to note that, despite three bitter campaigns against' the British, the Sikhs became the staunchest allies of the British in India, and Sikh troops remained loyal during the Mutiny of 1857. Approximate figures for the issue of clasps are: Mooltan - 2,900 to Europeans and 16,000 to Indian troops; Chilianwala - 4,300 and 16,000; Goojerat - 6,200 and 27,000. Despite the large number awarded to natives, very few remain on the market, the majority having been lost or melted down. Medals to native troops are thus scarcer than to European recipients. Due to the dates on which the operations took place, and the distances involved, it is impossible to find the first two clasps together on one medal. The most sought-after medals in the series are those to the 24th Foot who were present at Chilianwala, where half the regiment became casualties.

93. PUNJAB MEDAL 1848-49 *continued*

Medals to the Indus Flotilla are also very rare. Medals to European recipients are usually named in impressed capitals, and those to native troops are impressed in an uneven style or engraved in running script. The ribbon is of dark blue, with yellow edges.

No clasp	£90
Mooltan	£150
Chilianwala	£160
Goojerat	£150
Mooltan & Goojerat	£150
Chilianwala & Goojerat	£150
24th Foot killed at Chilianwala	£350

94. SOUTH AFRICA MEDAL 1834-53

This medal, sanctioned in November 1854, was awarded for services during three campaigns in South Africa in 1834-35, 1846-47 and 1850-53. It was awarded to approximately 9,500 survivors in both the Army and Navy, but was not issued to the next of kin. The area of operations in the campaigns was the eastern part of Cape Colony, and heavy fighting took place with the Kaffirs, particularly during the latter war. The obverse depicts the Wyon bust of Queen Victoria, whilst the reverse depicts a lion drinking by a protea bush with the date '1853' in the exergue. No clasps were issued, and reference to the rolls alone gives an indication of which campaign or campaigns the recipient served in. Almost all the recipients were British troops, although 650 were issued to Naval personnel on five ships. Only a few local troops and officers in native levies received the award. The suspension is ornamental and swivelling. The naming is always by impressed Roman capitals, no ship being shown on those medals to Naval recipients. An excellent and virtually complete roll has been compiled by Gordon Everson.

The ribbon is of orange with two wide and two narrow dark blue stripes.

Army recipient	£220
Naval recipient	£240
Colonial	£200

95. SIR HARRY SMITH'S MEDAL FOR GALLANTRY 1851

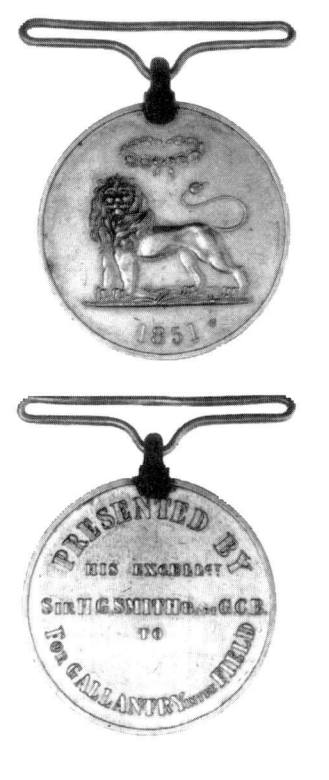

Approximately thirty medals are believed to have been awarded. When the Eighth Kaffir War started in December 1850, Sir Harry Smith was Governor and Commander-in-Chief at the Cape. Early in the campaign he was blockaded in Fort Cox, inland from Kingwilliamstown, by Gaikas under Chief Sandilli. Attempts to relieve the Fort were unsuccessful and the future of the beleaguered garrison appeared none too rosy. But there were wider issues than the survival of the garrison itself. The war had just started, and the fact that the Governor was being cooped up by 'the uncivilised Kaffirs' was adversely affecting the Colony's morale and could only result in the defection of additional tribes. Sir Harry therefore decided to make a break for it, and escorted by about 250 men of the Cape Mounted Riflemen (a unit which at that time was predominantly Cape Coloured), succeeded in getting through the Kaffir lines, and reached Kingwilliamstown in safety. The story goes that he was so impressed by the showing of the C.M.R. on his side, and by other feats of the Cape Colonial troops during the campaign, that before he was replaced by Sir George Cathcart in April, 1852, he decided to show his high regard for the men under his command by awarding a special medal.

Unnamed	£1,500
Named	£2,500

96. INDIA GENERAL SERVICE MEDAL 1854-95

This medal, instituted in 1854, covers a very long span of time and many campaigns, 23 clasps being issued in all, 17 of which were for services on the northern frontiers of India, where fighting was almost continual. The remaining clasps were issued for services during expeditions to nearby countries - Persia, Malaya and Burma. Very few pitched battles are commemorated by this medal, but none of the clasps were earned easily, as skirmishes were frequent and casualties often quite high. In addition, most of the expeditions were undertaken in very difficult terrain against determined and often fanatical resistance from tribesmen. Whilst some of the clasps are quite common, others are very scarce and some rare. The three rarest clasps in the series are 'Kachin Hills 1892-93', 'Hunza 1891' and 'Chin Hills 1892-93'. The medals were issued in silver to British and Indian troops, although from 1885 onwards bronze awards were issued to native transport personnel and followers. Medals with three or more clasps are very scarce. Whilst awards to British troops are more desirable than those to their Indian counterparts, the latter troops bore the brunt of the fighting on more than one occasion, and their medals give ample scope for an interesting and inexpensive collection. The obverse is the standard Wyon design of the bust of Queen Victoria, whilst the reverse depicts Victory crowning a seated warrior. There are several types of naming; engraved running script is the most commonly found to both British and Indian troops, although some of the earlier clasps to British troops are found impressed in Roman capitals. The ribbon is of red with two dark blue stripes.

96. INDIA GENERAL SERVICE MEDAL 1854-95 *continued*

	British	Bronze	Indian
Pegu	£75	—	—
Persia	£85	—	£55
North West Frontier	£75	—	£50
Umbeyla	£100	—	£55
Bhootan	£80	—	£50
Looshai	£175	—	£70
Perak	£80	—	£70
Jowaki 1877-8	£80	—	£55
Naga 1879-80	£350	—	£130
Burma 1885-7	£50	£50	£35
Sikkim 1888	£120	£100	£50
Hazara 1888	£75	£80	£50
Burma 1887-89	£50	£55	£35
Chin Lushai 1889-90	£90	£100	£40
Lushai 1889-90	£200	£250	£100
Samana 1891	£85	£75	£50
Hazara 1891	£75	£45	£40
N.E. Frontier 1891	£100	£95	£40
Hunza 1891	£2,000	£400	£20
Burma 1899-92	£75	£60	£45
Chin Hills 1892-93	£300	£350	£125
Kachin Hills 1892-93	£500	£850	£250
Waziristan 1894-95	£100	£80	£45

97. BALTIC MEDAL 1854-55

This medal, sanctioned in April 1856, was awarded almost exclusively to the Royal Navy and Royal Marines. It was issued for services with the fleet in the Baltic between March 1854 and August 1855 in operations against the Russians, and was awarded concurrently with the Crimea Medal of 1854-56. Over 100 vessels of various sizes took part in the operations, which included attacks on Kronstadt, Bomarsund, Kola, Petropaulovski, Sveaborg and Helsinki. The obverse is the familiar 'Wyon Head', whilst the reverse depicts Britannia with the forts of Sveaborg and Bomarsund in the background. The medal was only issued in silver, and no clasps were issued. It is usually found unnamed as issued, although 100 men of the Royal Sappers and Miners received medals impressed in the same style as the Crimea Medal of 1854-56. Some examples are found with engraved naming, carried out privately by the recipient. The ribbon is of yellow, with light blue edges.

Unnamed	£60
Officially impressed to R.E. Sappers & Miners	£600

98. CRIMEA MEDAL 1854-56

The war commemorated by this medal is most important, as it was the only war fought by Britain against a modern European power between 1815 and 1914. The war proved that, although the British Army was well-suited to Colonial warfare, there were serious deficiencies, particularly in generalship and in supply organisation, during a war with a modernising enemy. However, the war was redeemed by the fine fighting of junior officers and men; the battle of Inkermann is a classic example of this. The medal was awarded to 275,000 men of the Army and Navy who served in the Crimea 1854-56 alongside the French and Turkish forces. There were a number of causes of the war, the main one being British fears of Russian expansion through the Dardanelles into the eastern Mediterranean. The expedition landed in the Crimea in September 1854, and four days later stormed the Russian position at the Alma River. After a severe battle, the Russians retreated into Sebastopol, but the Allies allowed them to escape. The British set up camp at Balaklava, where on 25th October 1854 they were attacked by the Russians; the ensuing battle is famous for the Charge of the Light and Heavy Brigades, and the action fought by the 93rd Highlanders. Ten days later a battle was fought at Inkermann, in which troops took part in hand-to-hand fighting for many hours, both sides suffering very heavy casualties. There followed a long, ten-month siege, during which there were several major assaults on Sebastopol. Eventually the city fell, and the Allies withdrew their troops.

The medal is found both with and without clasps; five clasps were awarded in all, including one which was issued to the Royal Navy for services in the Sea of Azoff during the war. This is very scarce, particularly on an officially-named medal. Excepting this latter clasp, any combination of clasps is possible, although most have the clasp for 'Sebastopol'. Due to the confusing issue of this award, clasps are found in the wrong order and with unofficial rivets, but as rolls exist for virtually all recipients the awards can be checked. The unnamed Crimea medal is sometimes found with additional clasps not mentioned above, such as 'Traktir', 'Mamelon Vert', 'Malakoff, 'Mer d'Azof' and 'Kinburn'. These are unofficial clasps which were manufactured in France for wear on those medals which were presented to the French army. Those medals awarded to the Navy are often found unnamed, whilst those to Army recipients are found either engraved in large capitals, officially impressed or 'regimentally' impressed in a rather crude style. The most preferred style is of course the officially-impressed type. Some 2,250 Naval awards were officially impressed, and these are much sought-after. Other issues in the series that are particularly sought-after are medals to participants in the two cavalry charges at Balaklava; the 93rd Foot at the same action; and Naval medals if impressed or with the clasp 'Azoff'. Officially-impressed issues in good condition are quite scarce. All prices below are for officially-impressed medals.

No clasp	£65
Alma	£150
Balaklava	£200
Inkermann	£140
Sebastopol	£85
Azoff (RN) Unnamed	£100
Two clasps	£160
Three clasps	£250
Four clasps	£400
Balaklava (93rd Foot)	£500
Balaklava (Heavy Bde)	£600
Balaklava (Light Bde proven 'Charger')	£2,500

99. TURKISH CRIMEA MEDAL 1854-56

This medal was issued by the Sultan of Turkey to the armies of his allies for services in the Crimean War. There were three types - English, French and Sardinian - differentiated by the position of the flags on the obverse and the inscription in the obverse exergue. Regarding this latter feature, the English issue had 'Crimea 1855', the French issue 'La Crimee 1855', and the Sardinian issue 'La Crimea 1855'. However, it does not follow that British recipients received the appropriate issue, as the award of the medal was haphazard, and many of the British issues were lost in a shipwreck. The most common type found with the British Crimea Medal of 1854-56 is the Sardinian issue. The obverse on all types shows a cannon, with varying arrangements of the flags depending on the issue, whilst the reverse shows the Sultan's cipher and the Mohammedan date 1271. The medal was, when issued, suspended by means of a ring, but many recipients had this replaced with various types of straight suspension. Whilst this award is almost always found with the British medal for the Crimea, a small number of British officers served with the Turkish forces along the Danube, and received the Turkish medal only. The ribbon is of crimson with green edges. The medal was issued unnamed and privately named specimens do not attract a premium.

English issue	£50
Sardinian issue	£40
French issue	£150

100. INDIAN MUTINY MEDAL 1857-59

This medal, the last issued by the East India Company, was awarded in 1859 to all those who served against the mutineers and rebels 1857-59. In 1868 the award was extended to those civilians who had borne arms or taken part in the fighting. Some 270,000 medals were awarded, and these are found with five different clasps, the maximum number being four on one medal, and without clasp. The causes of the Mutiny are complex and are shrouded in legend, but the main cause was the continuing spread of British control over northern India, in particular the annexation of Oudh in 1856. When the initial revolt began in May 1857, all those who had grievances against the British joined them, and a widespread revolt began. After several massacres of Europeans, particularly at Cawnpore and Delhi, the rebellion was put down without mercy. Delhi was taken by the rebels and was besieged by British and loyal Indian troops whilst at Lucknow a small British garrison was besieged by a large rebel force. The 'original defenders' were augmented by the First Relief Force which broke through to them, but it was not until 1858 that Lucknow and its surrounding area were cleared. The fact that three of the five clasps awarded were for operations at Lucknow demonstrates the fame of the siege and relief. The clasp for 'Central India' commemorates a larger number of battles, skirmishes and sieges across the northern part of India. Carried out in extreme heat, the troops formed into flying columns which became noted for their rapid marches over long distances. Although major operations ended in July 1858, medals without clasps are found to men who took part in further operations until July 1859. Particularly sought-after are medals to 'original defenders' at Lucknow, to those who were killed in the massacres, to the Bengal Artillery with four clasps, and those to the Naval Brigade (HMSs 'Pearl' and 'Shannon'). Clasps should read downwards. Medals to Europeans are almost always in impressed Roman capitals, those to Indian troops being in running engraved script or crude impressing. Rolls exist for almost all Europeans. The ribbon is of white with two red stripes.

100. INDIAN MUTINY MEDAL 1857-59 *continued*

No Clasp	£80
Delhi	£120
Defence of Lucknow 'original defender'	£500
Defence of Lucknow '1st Relief'	£275
Relief of Lucknow	£160
Lucknow	£125
Central India	£125
Two Clasps	£185
Three Clasps (9th Lancers)	£600
Four Clasps (Bengal HA)	£1,500
Cawnpore Casualty	£1,000
"Pearl" No Clasp	£450
"Shannon" No Clasp	£650

101. SECOND CHINA WAR MEDAL 1857-60

This medal was instituted in 1861, and was awarded to men of the Royal Navy and of the British and Indian armies for various operations in China between 1857 and 1860. Although the ostensible reason for the war was the ill-treatment by the Chinese of the crew of the 'Arrow' in October 1856, this was mainly an excuse to make efforts to capture more of the Chinese trade - particularly the lucrative opium traffic. This series of campaigns suffered greatly from the aftermath of the Crimean War and the Indian Mutiny, and resulted in great delays whilst troops were gathered in many scattered posts. In May 1857 the Chinese fleet was caught and destroyed in Fatshan Creek, and after a further delay Canton was besieged and captured in early 1858. This was followed in May 1858 by a naval attack on the Taku Forts, which surrendered. A peace treaty was signed in May 1858, but neither side trusted the other. When the British envoys' vessel was fired on by the Chinese, a major expedition of 13,000 men was assembled. After the capture of the Taku Forts in August 1860 the force moved inland and captured Pekin in November 1860. In all, six clasps were issued on this medal, although that for 'China 1842' is highly anomalous. It was decided that those who had the China Medal of 1842 should receive the appropriate clasps, but not the 1857 medal. However, the suspender of the 1842 medal was such that it was very difficult to affix clasps. Finally, the China 1842' clasp was issued to be affixed to the 1857 medal. About 100 of these clasps were issued. The clasps for 'Fatshan 1857' and 'Taku Forts 1858' were only awarded to Naval personnel, the others being awarded to naval and military personnel alike. The most sought-after medals in the series are those to the Ist Dragoon Guards, the only British cavalry present, whilst medals to the Indian Marine are very scarce. Medals to the Navy were issued unnamed; those to the Army and Indian Marine were impressed in Roman capitals, and most medals to Indian troops were engraved in running script. Rolls exist for most of the Army and Navy recipients. The ribbon is of red with yellow edges.

No Clasp (unnamed)	£50
China 1842 RN	£1,500
Fatshan 1857 (unnamed)	£75
Canton 1857 (Army)	£140
Taku Forts 1858 (unnamed)	£70
Taku Forts 1860 (Army)	£115
Pekin 1860 (Army)	£120
Taku Forts 1860 & Pekin 1860 (Army)	£170
Three Clasps (unnamed)	£120

102. NEW ZEALAND MEDAL 1845-47 AND 1860-66

This medal was awarded in 1869 to the survivors of those who fought in New Zealand in the two Maori Wars of 1845-47 and 1860-66. Naval and military personnel received the medal, as well as local militia troops. This medal is one of the most complicated of the campaign series, as there were 29 different reverse types - one undated, the others bearing differing dates showing when the recipient served in New Zealand. Because of these dates no clasps were issued. It should be noted that the dates on the reverse do not always indicate the years that the recipient took part in active operations, but rather the years he actually served in the country. Due to the differing reverses, it is often difficult to give exact figure for the number of one type awarded to a regiment. Both campaigns were the result of Maori resistance to the continuing encroachment of settlers in their lands. The first campaign in 1845-47 took the form of a number of small engagements, after which a truce was agreed. Medals for this campaign are scarce, as the numbers of troops engaged were small, and only survivors could claim the medal 23 years later. About 300 awards for this campaign were made to the Royal Navy, most of them with the appropriate dates on the reverse. Most awards to the Army for this campaign are undated. The second campaign in 1860-66 was more widespread, and the Maoris proved to be a formidable enemy with their knowledge of the bush and their well-fortified 'pahs'. British and Colonial casualties in this campaign were quite heavy, and did not always lead to victory. Medals to those who were present at the action at Gate Pah in April 1864 are much sought-after, as this battle was an unusual example of British troops breaking before natives. The medal is almost always impressed in Roman capitals when awarded to Army and Navy personnel, although some awards to local militia are found engraved. The ribbon is of blue, with a central orange-red stripe. Prices below for each date are those for the commonest regiment or ship entitled.

Undated (First War)	£200	1861-63	£2,500
Undated (Second War)	£130	1861-64	£250
1845-46	£220	1861-65	£2,500
1845-47	£285	1861-66	£145
1846-47	£305	1862-66	£2,500
1846	£550	1863	£435
1847	£420	1863-64	£175
1848	£2,500	1863-65	£190
1860	£520	1863-66	£165
1860-61	£180	1864	£195
1860-3	£1,600	1864-65	£165
1860-64	£180	1864-66	£150
1860-65	£190	1865	£290
1860-66	£190	1865-66	£150
1861	£1,850	1866	£165

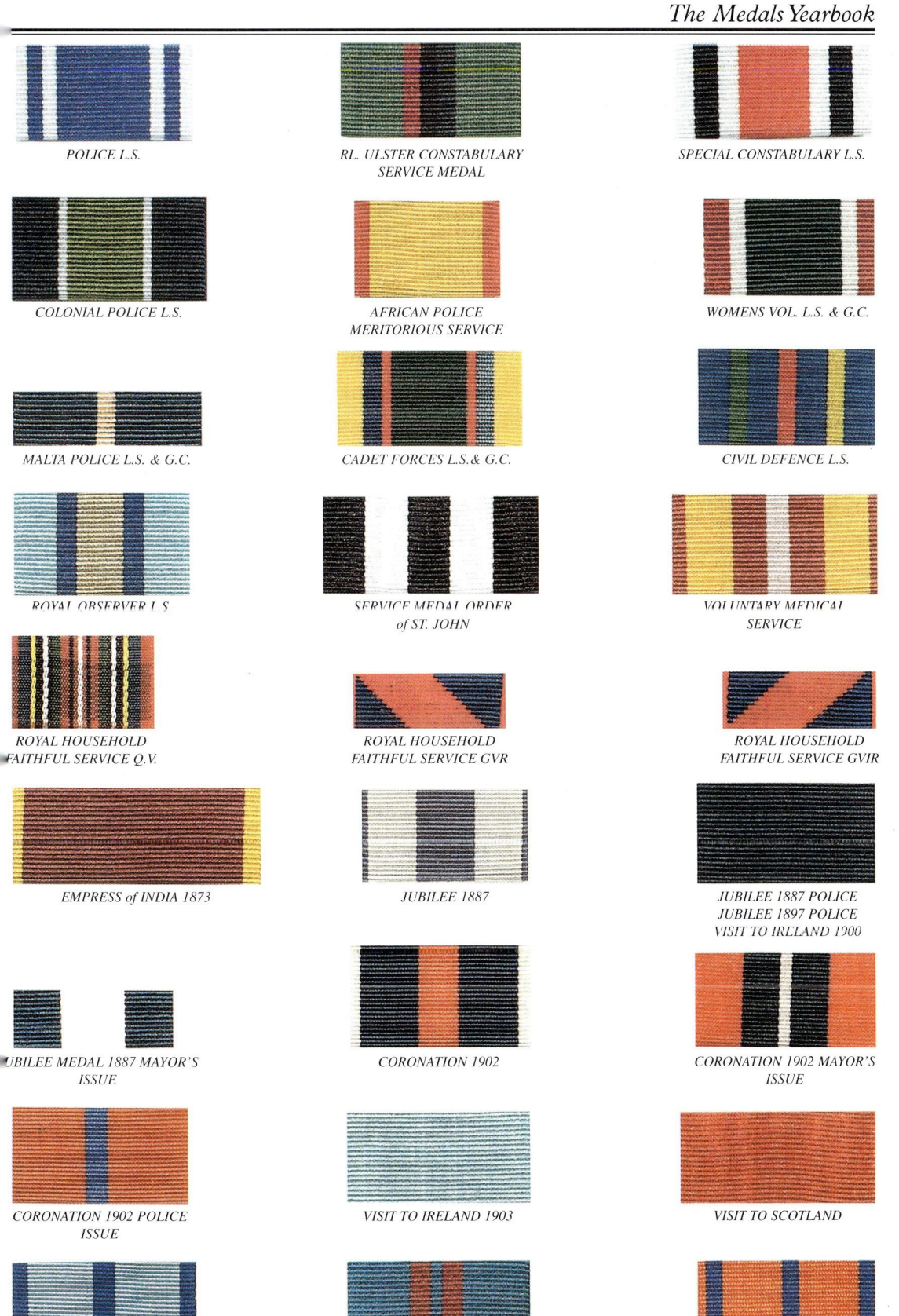

The Medals Yearbook

POLICE L.S.	RL. ULSTER CONSTABULARY SERVICE MEDAL	SPECIAL CONSTABULARY L.S.
COLONIAL POLICE L.S.	AFRICAN POLICE MERITORIOUS SERVICE	WOMENS VOL. L.S. & G.C.
MALTA POLICE L.S. & G.C.	CADET FORCES L.S. & G.C.	CIVIL DEFENCE L.S.
ROYAL OBSERVER L.S.	SERVICE MEDAL ORDER of ST. JOHN	VOLUNTARY MEDICAL SERVICE
ROYAL HOUSEHOLD FAITHFUL SERVICE Q.V.	ROYAL HOUSEHOLD FAITHFUL SERVICE GVR	ROYAL HOUSEHOLD FAITHFUL SERVICE GVIR
EMPRESS of INDIA 1873	JUBILEE 1887	JUBILEE 1887 POLICE JUBILEE 1897 POLICE VISIT TO IRELAND 1900
JUBILEE MEDAL 1887 MAYOR'S ISSUE	CORONATION 1902	CORONATION 1902 MAYOR'S ISSUE
CORONATION 1902 POLICE ISSUE	VISIT TO IRELAND 1903	VISIT TO SCOTLAND
DELHI DURBAR 1903	CORONATION MEDAL 1911 DELHI DURBAR 1911	CORONATION 1911 POLICE ISSUE

The Medals Yearbook

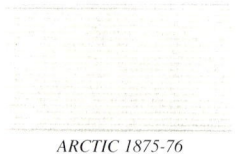

VISIT TO IRELAND 1911	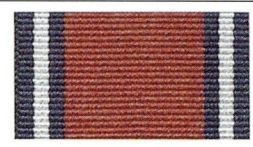 JUBILEE MEDAL 1935	 CORONATION MEDAL 1937
 CORONATION MEDAL 1953	 JUBILEE 1977	 ARMY BEST SHOT
 NAVAL GOOD SHOOTING	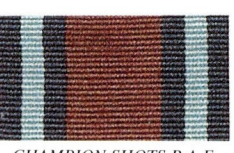 CHAMPION SHOTS R.A.F.	 ARCTIC 1818-55 POLAR MEDAL
ARCTIC 1875-76	 NAVAL ENGINEERS MEDAL 1842	 MALTA 50th ANNIVERSARY
 LIBERATION of KUWAIT	 VICTORIA CROSS / NEW ZEALAND CROSS	 GEORGE CROSS
 DISTINGUISHED SERVICE ORDER	 IMPERIAL SERVICE ORDER AND MEDAL	 INDIAN ORDER of MERIT
 ROYAL RED CROSS	 DISTINGUISHED SERVICE CROSS	 MILITARY CROSS
 DISTINGUISHED FLYING CROSS	 AIR FORCE CROSS	 THE KAISAR-I-HIND
 ALBERT MEDAL LAND 1ST CLASS	 ALBERT MEDAL SEA 1ST CLASS	 DISTINGUISHED CONDUCT MEDAL

The Medals Yearbook

- KAR & WAFF D.C.M.
- CONSPICUOUS GALLANTRY MEDAL ROYAL NAVY 
- CONSPICUOUS GALLANTRY MEDAL R.A.F. 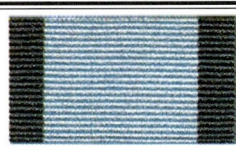
- GEORGE MEDAL
- KING/QUEENS POLICE MEDAL GALLANTRY 
- K.P.M./Q.P.M. DISTINGUISHED SERVICE 
- EDWARD MEDAL 
- BURMA GALLANTRY MEDAL 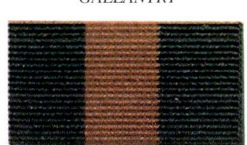
- INDIAN DISTINGUISHED SERVICE MEDAL 
- DISTINGUISHED SERVICE MEDAL 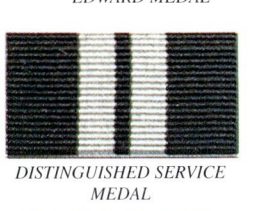
- MILITARY MEDAL 
- DISTINGUISHED FLYING MEDAL 
- AIR FORCE MEDAL 
- CONSTABULARY MEDAL (IRELAND) 
- INDIAN POLICE MEDAL GALLANTRY 
- INDIAN POLICE MEDAL MERITORIOUS SERVICE 
- BURMA POLICE MEDAL 
- COLONIAL POLICE MEDAL FOR GALLANTRY 
- CEYLON POLICE MEDAL FOR GALLANTRY
- COLONIAL POLICE MERITORIOUS SERVICE 
- QUEENS GALLANTRY MEDAL 
- ALLIED SUBJECTS MEDAL 
- 51 KINGS MEDAL FOR COURAGE 
- KINGS MEDAL FOR SERVICE 
- SEA GALLANTRY MEDAL
- EARLY CAMPAIGN CORD 
- BURMA MEDAL WATERLOO MEDAL

The Medals Yearbook

NAVAL GENERAL SERVICE 1793

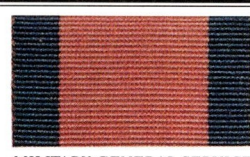

MILITARY GENERAL SERVICE 1793

ARMY OF INDIA MEDAL

GHUZNEE MEDAL

THE ST. JEAN D'ACRE

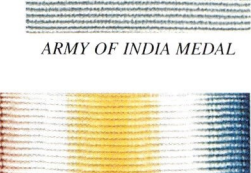

CANDAHAR-GHUZNEE-CABUL
JELLALABAD MEDALS
KELAT-I-GHILZIE MEDAL
SCINDE MEDAL
GWALIOR STAR

CHINA MEDAL 1842

SUTLEJ 1845
HARRY SMITH'S MEDAL FOR GALLANTRY

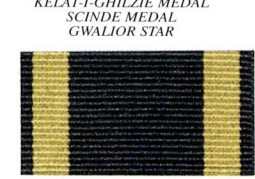

PUNJAB 1848

SOUTH AFRICA 1853

INDIA GENERAL SERVICE 1854

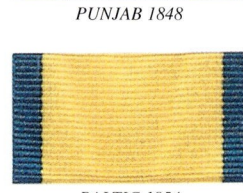

BALTIC 1854

CRIMEA 1854

TURKISH CRIMEA 1854

INDIAN MUTINY 1857

SECOND CHINA WAR 1857

NEW ZEALAND 1845 & 1860

ABYSSINIA 1867

CANADA GENERAL SERVICE 1866

ASHANTEE 1873
EAST & WEST AFRICA 1887

SOUTH AFRICA 1877

AFGHANISTAN 1878

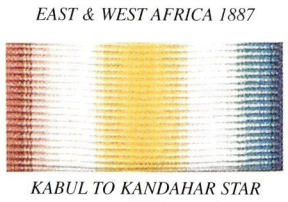

KABUL TO KANDAHAR STAR 1880

CAPE of GOOD HOPE G.S. 1880

EGYPT 1882

KHEDIVE'S STAR 1882

NORTH WEST CANADA 1885

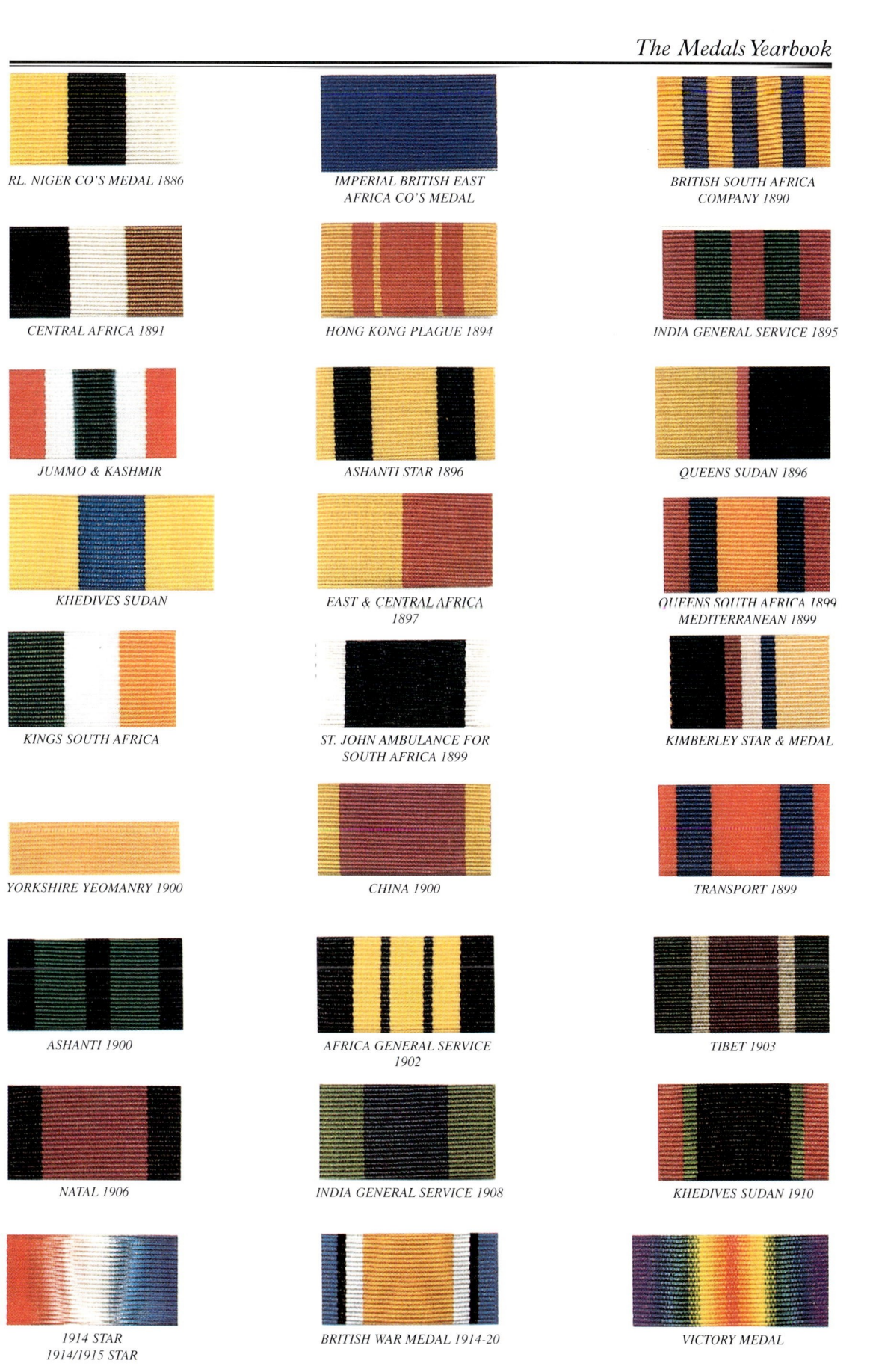

The Medals Yearbook

RL. NIGER CO'S MEDAL 1886	IMPERIAL BRITISH EAST AFRICA CO'S MEDAL	BRITISH SOUTH AFRICA COMPANY 1890
CENTRAL AFRICA 1891	HONG KONG PLAGUE 1894	INDIA GENERAL SERVICE 1895
JUMMO & KASHMIR	ASHANTI STAR 1896	QUEENS SUDAN 1896
KHEDIVES SUDAN	EAST & CENTRAL AFRICA 1897	QUEENS SOUTH AFRICA 1899 MEDITERRANEAN 1899
KINGS SOUTH AFRICA	ST. JOHN AMBULANCE FOR SOUTH AFRICA 1899	KIMBERLEY STAR & MEDAL
YORKSHIRE YEOMANRY 1900	CHINA 1900	TRANSPORT 1899
ASHANTI 1900	AFRICA GENERAL SERVICE 1902	TIBET 1903
NATAL 1906	INDIA GENERAL SERVICE 1908	KHEDIVES SUDAN 1910
1914 STAR 1914/1915 STAR	BRITISH WAR MEDAL 1914-20	VICTORY MEDAL

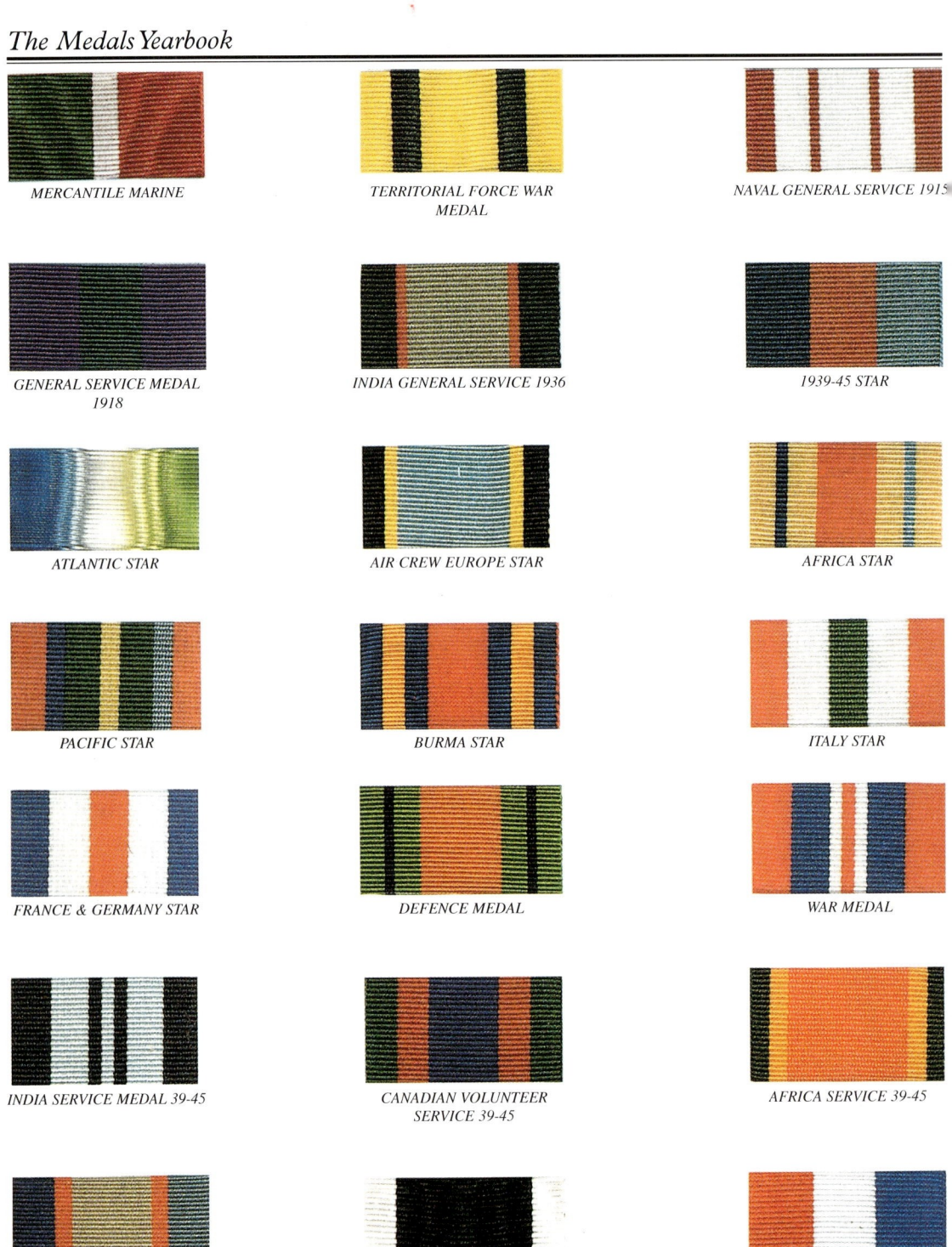

The Medals Yearbook

MERCANTILE MARINE	TERRITORIAL FORCE WAR MEDAL	NAVAL GENERAL SERVICE 1915
GENERAL SERVICE MEDAL 1918	INDIA GENERAL SERVICE 1936	1939-45 STAR
ATLANTIC STAR	AIR CREW EUROPE STAR	AFRICA STAR
PACIFIC STAR	BURMA STAR	ITALY STAR
FRANCE & GERMANY STAR	DEFENCE MEDAL	WAR MEDAL
INDIA SERVICE MEDAL 39-45	CANADIAN VOLUNTEER SERVICE 39-45	AFRICA SERVICE 39-45
AUSTRALIA SERVICE 39-45	NEW ZEALAND SERVICE 39-45	SOUTH AFRICA SERVICE 39-45
SOUTHERN RHODESIA SERVICE 39-45	KOREA 1950	UNITED NATIONS KOREA

The Medals Yearbook

SOUTH AFRICA KOREA

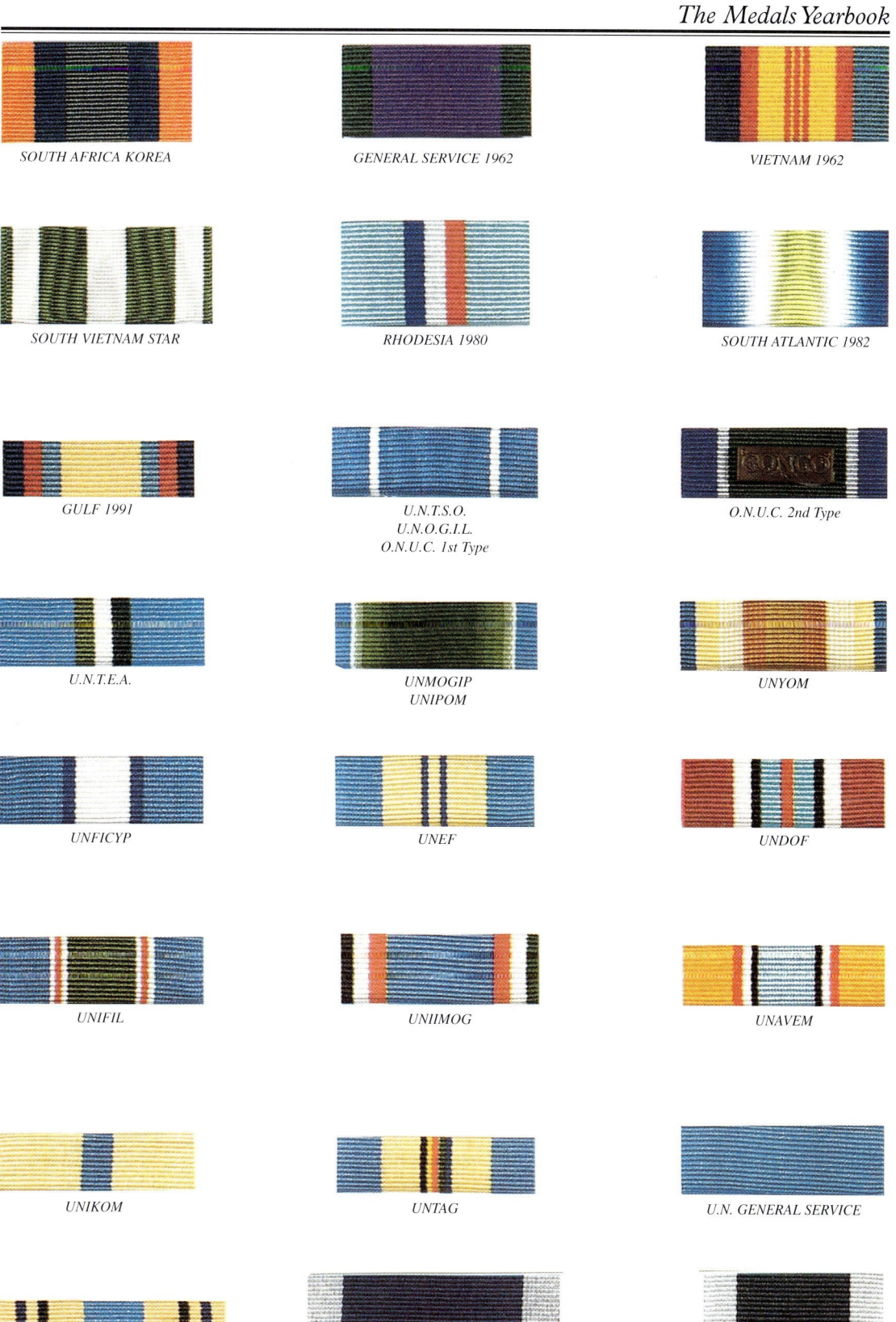

GENERAL SERVICE 1962

VIETNAM 1962

SOUTH VIETNAM STAR

RHODESIA 1980

SOUTH ATLANTIC 1982

GULF 1991

U.N.T.S.O.
U.N.O.G.I.L.
O.N.U.C. 1st Type

O.N.U.C. 2nd Type

U.N.T.E.A.

UNMOGIP
UNIPOM

UNYOM

UNFICYP

UNEF

UNDOF

UNIFIL

UNIIMOG

UNAVEM

UNIKOM

UNTAG

U.N. GENERAL SERVICE

UNEF 1956-67

ROYAL NAVY L.S. & G.C. WIDE

ROYAL NAVY L.S. & G.C. 1875

The Medals Yearbook

ROYAL NAVAL RESERVE DECORATION

ROYAL NAVAL RESERVE L.S. & G.C. 2nd Type
ROYAL NAVAL SICK BERTH Reserve 2nd Type

ROYAL NAVAL VOL DECORATION 2nd Type

R.N.V.R. L.S. & G.C. 2nd Type
R.N. WIRELESS AUXILIARY Res. L.S. & G.C.

ROYAL FLEET RESERVE L.S. & G.C.

ROCKET APPARATUS VOL. L.S.
COAST GUARD AUX. L.S.

MERITORIOUS SERVICE

ARMY L.S. & G.C. 1831-1916

ARMY L.S. & G.C. 1916-

VOLUNTEER DECORATION

VOLUNTEER FORCE L.S. & G.C.

TERRITORIAL DECORATION

TERRITORIAL FORCE EFFICIENCY

EFFICIENCY MEDAL

IMPERIAL YEOMANRY L.S. & G.C.

MILITIA L.S. & G.C.

SPECIAL RESERVE L.S. & G.C.

MERITORIOUS SERVICE

R.A.F. L.S. & G.C.

AIR EFFICIENCY AWARD

PERMANENT FORCES OF THE EMPIRE

CANADIAN FORCES DECORATION

103. ABYSSINIA MEDAL 1867-68

This medal, sanctioned in 1869 for the war against King Theodore of Abyssinia, is unique for two reasons. Firstly, the name and regiment of the recipient is embossed in the centre of the reverse, so that a separate die was needed for each medal; and secondly the ornate but weak suspension was not used again. The war was caused by the imprisonment of several British subjects by Theodore, and in January 1868 a punitive expedition began the long march of 300 miles to Magdala, the Abyssinian capital. After an arduous approach, the city was stormed in April 1868; Theodore committed suicide and the force was withdrawn. In all, some 14,000 medals were issued, of which 2,000 went to the Royal Navy. Though most of the latter were awarded for services off the Abyssinian coast, a small naval brigade of less than 100 men under Commander Fellowes accompanied the march to Magdala, where they used their rockets to good effect. Medals to men in this brigade are much sought-after, as are those to the 3rd Dragoon Guards, the only cavalry present. Awards to Indian troops are generally found named in running script in the centre of the reverse. Rolls exist for the British ships and regiments present. The ribbon, which is wider than the medal, is of red and white edges.

Army recipient	£175
Royal Navy recipient	£175
Indian recipient	£125
Naval (Rocket) Brigade	£275

104. CANADA GENERAL SERVICE MEDAL 1866-70

In 1899, an Army Order approved the issue of this medal by the Canadian Government. As with the Military General Service Medal of 1793-1814, the lapse of time between the campaign and the issue of the medal meant that only a portion of those troops engaged actually received the medal. The award was for services during several serious disturbances in Canada by the Fenians - sympathisers with Irish Nationalism - in Canada and the United States. The two 'Fenian Raid' clasps were awarded to troops who were engaged during the two raids from the United States. On both occasions the Fenians, led by John O'Neil, crossed the border into Canada and tried to incite a revolt against British rule. They were twice defeated by Imperial troops and Canadian Militia and pushed back across the border. The third clasp, that for 'Red River 1870'. which is much the rarest clasp on the medal, was awarded to troops under Colonel (later Field-Marshall) Wolseley; his force marched 1,100 miles to Manitoba, where rebels were occupying Fort Garry; they fled before the force arrived. Some 16,500 medals were issued in all, some 85 % of them to various units of the Canadian Militia, the remainder to Imperial troops. The medal was not issued without a clasp, and only 11 three clasp medals were issued. 1,400 medals were issued with two clasps. The total number of each clasp issued was approximately: 'Fenian Raid 1866' - 12,000; 'Fenian Raid 1870' - 5,600; 'Red River 1870' 450. Medals to Imperial troops are scarce, and although those to local Militia units are common overall, the great number of small units involved in the operations has meant that many regiments received very few medals. A few medals to the Royal Navy are occasionally found, usually with the first clasp; these are very scarce. There are several different styles of naming, both engraved and impressed, the commonest style being the 'Canadian' type of impressing in lower case letters. The ribbon is of red, with a central white stripe. Prices below are for recipients in Canadian Militia units.

Fenian Raid 1866	£120
Fenian Raid 1870	£140
Red River 1870	£450
Two Clasps FR 1866 & 1870	£200
Three Clasps	£2,800

105. ASHANTEE MEDAL 1873-74

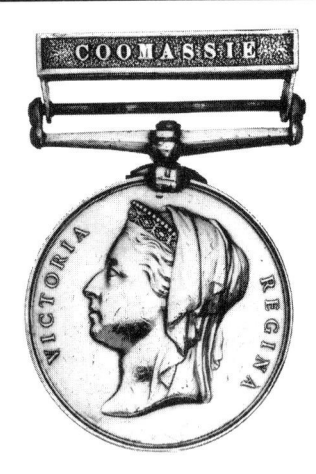

Sanctioned in June 1874, this medal was awarded to those who served under Wolseley in operations against King Kalkali in 187374. It was awarded in silver to combatant troops and in bronze to local transport personnel, although the latter issue is very rare. Both the obverse and reverse are identical to the East and West Africa Medal of 1887-1900, the only differences between the medals being the thickness and the naming. Recipients of this medal could not receive the later medal, merely adding the later clasps to this medal. Such issues are very rare. One clasp was issued for the 1873-74 campaign, and this was awarded to all those who served beyond the River Prah or who took part in the actions at Amoaful and Ardahsa. The campaign can be divided into two phases, the first taking place before the arrival of Wolseley and the main force. During this phase operations were undertaken by a small naval brigade (June and July 1873), the town of Chamah being shelled. After Wolseley arrived, the second phase - the steady advance inland towards Kumassi - was begun. Several major actions were fought, and the nature of the terrain and the determined Ashanti resistance made the campaign most difficult. In February 1874, the force entered Kumassi and Kalkali agreed to peace. About 3,500 men of the Royal Navy received the medal, only about 300 of these with a clasp. Apart from the usual contingent's of corps troops, three British regiments and two battalions of the West India Regiment received the medal, and as a rough guide slightly less than half the Army personnel received the clasp. Occasionally, medals are seen to natives in one of the tribal contingent's, such as the Kassoos and the Eliminas, or to Wood's and Russel's Regiments, which were locally-raised levies commanded by leading members of the Wolseley Ring. These medals are most interesting, and the recipients usually acted as scouts, seeing a great deal of action. Rolls exist for almost all the naval and military personnel who received the medal. The naming is in engraved Roman capitals, with '1873-74 or '73-74' after the other details, and was filled in in black. The ribbon is of yellow, with black edges and two thin black stripes towards the centre.

	Royal Navy	Army	Natives
No clasp	£100	£120	£75
Clasp Coomassie	£185	£225	£125

106. SOUTH AFRICA MEDAL 1877-79

Instituted in 1880, this medal is similar in many ways to the South Africa Medal of 183453. The main differences are in the naming, and in the reverse, at the foot of which this medal has a shield and assegais; and unlike the earlier medal, this issue was usually awarded with a clasp. It is most important to remember that although attention at the time and since has focused on the operations against the Zulus in 1879, there were other long and difficult campaigns against other tribes both in 1879 and in 1877-78. The campaigns for which this medal was awarded were: an expedition against the Galeka and Gaika tribes in 1877-78; fighting against the Griquas near Kimberley in 1878; and a campaign against the Basutos which ran concurrently with the Zulu War of 18'79. The reason for the latter overshadowing the other campaigns is that two important pitched battles were fought - Isandhlwana and Rorke's Drift - which are notable events in British military history. Medals to those present at these two actions are the most sought-after amongst the later Victorian campaign medals. The Zulus were decisively defeated at Ulundi in July 1879, after which there were a few smaller operations to subdue Zululand. The medal is found without a clasp to those who served in Natal during the war; those who entered Zululand or Basutoland in 1879, or the other native areas in 1877-78, received a clasp bearing the dates the recipient served. The clasp for '1877' is very rare, as few men served during that year only. The clasps '1877-8' and '1878-9' are

106. SOUTH AFRICA MEDAL 1877-79 *continued*

scarce, that for '1879' being the commonest. A wide and interesting range of local units, raised from settlers, received the medal, as well as Imperial troops and a strong contingent of the Royal Navy. The naming is almost always in engraved capitals, either upright or sloping. The ribbon is of yellow with four dark blue stripes.

	Royal Navy	Army	Colonial
No clasp	£120	£100	£90
1877	-	-	£1,200
1877-78	£350	£220	£165
1877-8-9	£380	£220	£165
1878		£250	£185
1878-9	£300	£250	£185
1879	£175	£200	£110
Killed at Isandhlwawa		-	£1,500
Present at Rorke's Drift		-	£7,500

107. AFGHANISTAN MEDAL 1878-80

This medal was issued to all those who took part in the operations in Afghanistan between 1878 and 1880. There were two distinct phases in the war, which was caused by British fears of Russian involvement in Afghan affairs. The first phase (1878-79) began when Shere Ali, the Afghan ruler, refused to accept a British Resident and signed a treaty with Russia. An ultimatum was sent to the Afghans, and when this was ignored three columns entered the country in November 1878. The Afghans were defeated at Ali Musjid and Peiwar Khotal, and as the British advanced, the Afghans sued for peace. The Amir accepted a Resident in return for a large annuity, and Major Cavagnari was sent to Kabul. However, in September 1879 Cavagnari and his escort were massacred and the war recommenced. There was considerably more fighting in the second phase than in the first. Roberts marched on Kabul, defeating the Afghans en route at Charasia, and reached the city in October 1879. A full-scale action took place, and the city fell. There was then a lull in the fighting until April 1880, when another large battle was fought at Ahmed Khel near Ghuznee. In July 1880, General Burrows was severely defeated at Maiwand, near Kandahar, the Horse Artillery and 66th Foot suffering heavily. The force withdrew into Kandahar where it was besieged by a large force. Roberts collected a force at Kabul and made his epic march to Kandahar, where, in a major battle on 1st September 1880, he soundly defeated the Afghans. Following this peace was agreed and the troops withdrew. A wide range of British and Indian troops were involved, all receiving the medal in silver; transport personnel and camp followers were awarded the medal in bronze. The maximum number of clasps issued on one medal was four, those with three and two clasps being fairly common. For British recipients, the medals were named in upright or sloping engraved capitals, whilst those to Indian recipients were usually engraved in running script. Rolls exist for most British recipients. Most sought-after in the series are four-clasped medals, and particularly medals to casualties at Maiwand in July 1880. The ribbon is of green, with crimson edges.

No Clasp (Silver)	£50	Kandahar	£100
Ali Musjid	£100	Two Clasps	£120
Peiwar Kotal	£100	Three Clasps	£180
Charasia	£100	Four Clasps	£450
Kabul	£100	66th Foot killed at Maiwand	£600
Ahmed Khel	£100	E/B RHA killed at Maiwand	£500

108. KABUL TO KANDAHAR STAR 1880

This bronze star, made from captured guns, was issued in conjunction with the Afghanistan Medal of 1878-80. It could not be awarded to anyone who did not have the British medal. The star is five-pointed, with the royal monogram on the obverse. The reverse has a hollow centre and is plain, except for the recipients' name and other details, which are arranged in a semi-circle around the top of the hollow. The award was given to all those troops - both British and Indian - who took part in the famous march made by Lord Roberts in August 1880. The force set out from Kabul, and marched 310 miles to the relief of Kandahar. The units that received the awards were: one British and three Indian cavalry regiments; three batteries of artillery; and four British and ten Indian infantry regiments, plus the usual ancillary detachments. The naming is usually in small, heavily-impressed capitals for British troops, and engraved running script for Indians. This award must be studied carefully, as good copies exist. The ribbon is of a rainbow pattern of red, white, yellow, white and blue.

British Recipient	£135
Indian Recipient	£90
Unnamed	£75

109. CAPE OF GOOD HOPE GENERAL SERVICE MEDAL 1880-97

This medal, which was issued in silver only, was instituted in 1881. Almost all of these medals were issued with one or more clasps, only about 10 being issued unclasped. The reverse design shows the arms of Cape Colony. Some 5,200 were issued in all for three risings, each commemorated by a clasp. That for 'Transkei', the rarest of the three, was awarded for operations during a small rising in Tembuland and Griqualand East in 1880-81. The clasp for 'Basutoland' was awarded for service in the more extensive operations in that area, several major engagements taking place. The last clasp, that for 'Bechuanaland', was awarded, after a lapse of 16 years from the first two clasps, for an uprising amongst several tribes. The fighting took place in 1896-97, and it was only by the employment of considerable forces that the natives were defeated. It is worth noting that, apart from 15 British troops, all the awards of this medal were to colonial units, many of which were small. The total issue for each clasp is approximately: 'Transkei' - 1,070; 'Basutoland' - 2,150; 'Bechuanaland' - 2,580. Only 23 medals were issued with all three clasps, and medals with two clasps are very scarce. A complete roll of recipients has recently been published. The naming is in thin, faint block capitals, and the ribbon is of dark blue with a central yellow stripe.

Transkei	£250
Basutoland	£145
Bechuanaland	£125
Two Clasps	£200
Three Clasps	£950

110. EGYPT MEDAL 1882-89

This medal was awarded for several campaigns in Egypt between the above dates. The medal remained a constant design with one exception, which is the date on the reverse; those who served in the 1882 campaign had the date '1882' at the bottom of the reverse, those medals issued for later campaigns having no date. The first campaign in Egypt was caused by the political chaos there and the resulting threat to the vital Suez Canal. A British Fleet arrived off Alexandria in July 1882, and after bombarding the city landed a strong force. In a campaign which became famous for its efficiency, the force defeated the Egyptians several times, the last action being at Tel-el-Kebir. After the war British troops remained in Egypt and on the Sudan coast to protect the Suez Canal. The second campaign took place in the eastern Sudan, where the Dervishes laid siege to Suakin, on the Red Sea coast. After advancing from the coast and winning actions at El-Teb and Tamaai, the British withdrew again to the coast. A third campaign took place in 1885, when the British belatedly decided to relieve General Gordon at Khartoum. A column advanced up the Nile, fighting numerous skirmishes and pitched battles at Abu Klea and Kirbekan, but was too late to help Gordon. At about the same time, fighting was going on again around Suakin, and an action was fought at Tofrek. The British withdrew again from the Sudan, although fighting continued along the Egyptian frontier, for which the medal without clasp was awarded. Late in the 1880's there were two further battles - at Gemaizah near Suakin and at Toski on the Egyptian frontier. This medal is usually in worse condition than other contemporary issues, as it was worn with the Khedive's Star, and consequently is found with contact marks. Many issues without clasps are also encountered, but often recipients of these saw some action. The maximum number of clasps on a medal is seven, of which one was awarded. None were issued with six clasps, and those with five clasps are very scarce. The clasps 'Abu Klea and 'Kirbekan' must be on a medal with the clasp 'The Nile 1884-5', and 'Tofrek' must accompany 'Suakin 1885'. The naming for British troops is usually in sloping engraved capitals, some medals to the Royal Navy being in tall, thin impressed capitals. Medals to Indian troops are usually found in engraved running script, whilst those to Egyptian and Sudanese troops are named in Arabic. Rolls exist for almost all British recipients, although the complicated nature of the RN rolls make close scrutiny advisable. The ribbon is of five equal stripes - three blue and two white.

No Clasp (dated)	£40
No Clasp (undated)	£45
Alexandria 11th July	£60
Tel-el-Kebir	£55
El-Teb	£100
Tamaai	£95
El-Teb-Tamaai	£70
Suakin 1884	£70
The Nile 1884-85	£70
The Nile 1884-85/Abu Klea	£300
The Nile 1884-85/Kirbekan	£225
Suakin 1885	£60
Suakin 1885/Tofrek	£125
Gemaizah	£95
Toski	£250
Two Clasps	£85
Three Clasps	£150
Four Clasps	£280
Five Clasps	£500
Medals to Canadian Boatmen	£750
Medals to New South Wales Units	£850

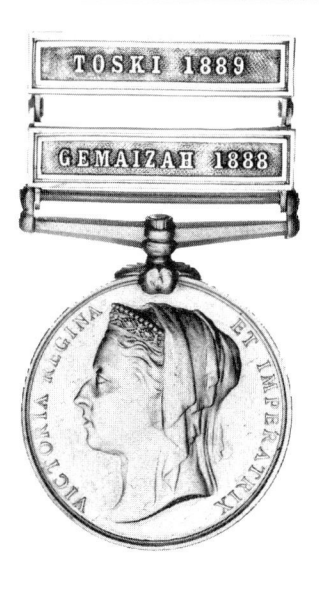

111. KHEDIVE'S STAR 1882-91

This medal was awarded by the Khedive of Egypt to all those who received the Egypt Medal of 1882-89. The award is of bronze and is in the form of a five-pointed star. The obverse centre depicts the Sphinx with pyramids in the background; in a circle around this is the word 'Egypt' with one of several different dates. The reverse is plain except for the Khedive's monogram in a raised circle. The suspension is by a straight bar, on which is a crescent and a star, which is attached to the award by a small ring. There are four types of this star, which was made by Jenkins of Birmingham; these are differentiated by the date on the obverse - 1882, 1884, 1884-6, and undated, according to the campaign in which the recipient served. The undated star was awarded for operations in 1887-89. One clasp was issued, being awarded to those who were present at the action of Tokar in February 1891. This clasp is of bronze and bears an Arabic inscription. Due to the design of this award and the fact that it was worn next to the Egypt Medal of 1882-89, the latter medal is often found to have been pitted by the star. The award is usually found unnamed, although a few were impressed on the reverse or engraved privately by the recipient. The ribbon is of dark blue.

1882 Star	£35
1884 Star	£45
1884-6 Star	£35
Undated Star	£60
Undated Star with Clasp 'Tokar'	£125

112. GENERAL GORDON'S STAR FOR THE SEIGE OF KHARTOUM

During the siege of Khartoum in 1884, General Gordon arranged for this unofficial medal to be cast, using, it is said, his own example of the Order of the Mejidieh as a base design. Very crudely cast in sand, these Stars were issued in pewter and silver. It is believed that some of them were later gilded.

Silver	£500
Pewter	£300

113. NORTH WEST CANADA MEDAL 1885

This medal, sanctioned by the Canadian Government in September 1885, was awarded to those who took part in the suppression of the rebellion of that year led by Louis Riel. The rising was caused by the continuing westward advance of settlers into the Indian lands in west and north-west Canada. Unrest amongst the Indians was channelled into a revolt by Riel, who had been prominent in the Fenian disturbances of 1866-70 (see Canada General Service Medal 1866-70). He set up a provisional government in the west, and the Government mobilised the Militia to put down the rebellion; apart from 16 British staff officers, all the recipients of this medal were members of the Canadian forces. The fighting lasted for just one month (April - May 1885), after which the defeated rebels were rounded up, Riel being captured and hanged. Some 5,600 medals were issued, about 1,750 being with the clasp 'Saskatchewan'; the award of the clasp was confined to those who had been in operations along the Saskatchewan and Fish rivers or at the action at Batoche. The majority of medals encountered are named in one of several styles of engraving; however, some are found unnamed, and those to the steamer 'Northcote' were impressed. A complete medal roll has recently been published. The ribbon is of blue-grey, with a red stripe near each edge.

No Clasp	£175
Saskatchewan	£380
Northcote	£750

114. ROYAL NIGER COMPANY'S MEDAL 1886-97

This medal, issued in silver to Europeans and bronze to natives, was awarded in 1899 by the Royal Niger Company. The obverse shows the head of Queen Victoria, whilst the reverse shows a field and a Latin motto. The silver issue, awarded to some 85 officers and NCOs in the Company's service, had the clasp 'Nigeria 1886-97'. These medals were named in impressed capitals. The bronze issue, awarded to some 250 natives in the Company's service, had the clasp 'Nigeria', and are found either impressed naming or with only the recipients' number stamped on the edge. Later specimens of these medals, taken from the original dies, exist but these are either unnamed or unnumbered. All the recipients were Company servants, usually in the Constabulary which took part in numerous small expeditions. The ribbon is of three equal stripes of yellow, black and white.

Silver issue - 'Nigeria 1886-97' - named	£1,000
Silver issue - 'Nigeria 1886-97' - unnamed specimen	£55
Bronze issue - 'Nigeria' - named/numbered	£350
Bronze issue - 'Nigeria' - named/numbered	£45

115. IMPERIAL BRITISH EAST AFRICA COMPANY'S MEDAL

The origin and purpose of this medal are very obscure, but it is thought to have been instituted by the Company as a bravery reward in about 1890. After the liquidation of the Company in 1895, it was mistakenly assumed that it had been a campaign award given for service in Witu 1890 and during the Ugandan Civil War 1890-91, and further issues were authorised by the Foreign Office.

The obverse shows the crowned, rayed sun emblem of the Company surrounded by the Company's title. Below is a scroll bearing the motto 'Light and Liberty' and below this an Arabic inscription 'The Reward of Bravery'. The reverse is plain except for a wreath. Early issues are thought to have been suspended from a scroll suspender and later issues from a ring. The ribbon was plain blue.

It is believed that fewer than 30 of these medals were awarded.

£500

116. BRITISH SOUTH AFRICA COMPANY MEDAL 1890-97

This medal was originally sanctioned by Queen Victoria in 1896, for issue to those troops who took part in the Matabeleland operations of 1893 and in Rhodesia in 1896. In 1897, the award of the medal was extended to those who fought in Mashonaland in 1897. The obverse of the medal has the crowned head of Queen Victoria and an inscription, whilst the reverse shows a speared lion and a mimosa bush, together with spears and a shield. At the top of the reverse is the name of the first campaign in which the recipient fought, with 'British South Africa Company' in the exergue. Those who fought in two or three of the campaigns added clasps to the medals, so that the maximum clasps for this issue was two. Some 30 years later, in 1927, the Rhodesian Government decided to issue this medal to those who had taken part in the occupation of Mashonaland in 1890 - although not one shot was fired during these operations - and a new issue was minted. This was identical to the 1893-97 issue, except that no campaign was shown on the reverse, service being recognised by the clasp 'Mashonaland 1890'. Those who had the first issue of the medal returned these and were issued with the new medal, thereby having a net gain of two clasps. It was therefore possible to have a medal with four clasps, and three such awards were made. In all, there were some 200 awards for the 1890 operations. 1,575 awards were made for the 1893 operations, and about 9,500 awards were made for operations in Rhodesia in 1896. The 1896-97 operations were extensive and involved large forces, many casualties being suffered. The medal, which was made in Birmingham, is suspended from a heavy, ornate suspender which has on it roses, leeks and shamrocks. The naming is in engraved capitals, either upright or sloping, or in large impressed capitals. Medals to Imperial troops are scarcer than those to local forces, as fewer of the former were engaged. The ribbon is of seven equal stripes - four yellow and three dark blue. Prices below are for awards to the commonest local units.

Mashonaland 1890	£650
Matabeleland 1893 No Clasp	£120
Matabeleland 1893 One Clasp	£170
Matabeleland 1893 Two Clasp	£350
Rhodesia 1896 No Clasp	£100
Rhodesia 1896 One Clasp	£160
Mashonaland 1897	£140

117. EAST AND WEST AFRICA MEDAL 1887-1900

This medal was awarded for various operations, mainly punitive expeditions, on or near the coasts of Africa. The medal is identical to the Ashantee Medal for 1873-74, except for being rather thinner and having different styles of naming. Twenty-two clasps were awarded for various small operations against local rulers; sometimes these were to rescue Europeans held hostage, and sometimes to halt inter-tribal fighting in British areas of influence. Due to the very difficult nature of the terrain, the Royal Navy were the mainstay of British power, operating easily on the coasts and up rivers into the interior. Sometimes a small naval brigade was landed to storm the local stronghold or tribal capital. The other main groups to receive the medal were Indian troops, who were employed in several expeditions in East Africa, and the West India Regiment, who were employed in the very difficult operations in West Africa; medals to the latter are somewhat underrated. Very few British army personnel received this medal, except for officers and NCO instructors attached to local forces. The vast majority of medals to all groups of recipients were issued in silver, although a few exist in bronze to transport and other auxiliary personnel. These latter are rare. Due to the number of clasps issued and the various regiments involved, there are a number of rarities in the series. Particularly rare are the following clasps to the Royal Navy: 'Liwondi 1893', 'Juba River 1893' and 'Lake Nyassa 1893'. Of the clasps mainly awarded to native troops, those for 'Niger 1897' and '1900' are rare. It should be noted that those who took part in the operations at M'wele in 1895-96 did not receive a clasp, but had 'M'wele 1895' or 'M'wele 1895-96' impressed on the edge of the medal. There are several styles of naming on this medal; WIR recipients usually had their medals engraved in sloping capitals, whilst medals to the Royal Navy are usually named in large impressed capitals. Some later clasps are found with naming in small impressed capitals, whilst those to Indian troops are engraved in running script. Rolls exist for the Royal Navy and West India Regiment but records concerning local native troops are scanty. The ribbon is similar to that on the Ashantee Medal of 1873-74.

	Royal Navy	Europeans	Natives
1887-8	£300	£200	£120
Witu 1890	£130	£200	£100
1891-2	£130	£150	£120
1892	£160	£140	£120
Witu August 1893	£160	*	£150
Liwondi 1893	£1,500	*	*
Juba River 1893	£1,500	*	*
Lake Nyassa 1893	£1,500	*	*
1893-94 (Colonial Steamer)	£200	*	£110
Gambia 1894	£130	*	£140
Benin River 1894	£150	*	£120
Brass River	£150	*	*
M'wele 1895-96	£100	£300	£75
1896-98	*	£300	£200
Niger 1897	*	£450	£200
Benin 1897	£90	£300	£100
Dawkita 1897		£10,000	£1,800
1897-98		£120	£100
1898	£700	£140	£130
Sierra Leone 1898-99	£120	£120	£100
1899	*	£320	£185
1900	*	£280	£175

118. HUNZA NAGAR BADGE 1891

A bronze rectangular badge of approximately two inches wide by one inch awarded by the Maharajah of Jummo and Kashmir to his troops who took part in the expedition to Hunza Nagar and received the India General Service Medal with bar Hunza 1891.

The front of the badge shows a hill fort with three figures in military attitudes in the foreground. At bottom right are the words 'Hunza Nagar 1891'. The reverse is plain apart from the name of the maker, Gurney and Son of London. As originally issued, the badge had a brooch fitting, but many were altered to enable them to be worn as medals.

Bronze	£500

119. CENTRAL AFRICA MEDAL 1891-98

This medal, first issued in 1895, was awarded for a number of small expeditions in Central Africa, in the area of what is now Uganda. In many ways similar to the East and West Africa Medal of 1887-1900, this medal has the same obverse and reverse as the latter. The first issue of the medal was in 1895, and this was awarded to those who took part in any of ten small expeditions against various tribes 1891-94. The usual causes of these expeditions were slave-trading or depredations against neighbouring tribes. The first issue had no clasp and a ring suspension. In 1899, the award of this medal with a clasp and straight suspender was sanctioned to those who took part in expeditions in 1894-98. This medal is rare, particularly when found with the clasp. No British regiments were entitled to this award, although a few officers and NCOs who were attached to local troops received the medal. The majority of recipients were Ugandan and Sudanese troops, and as the latter mutinied in 1898, few of their medals survive. Some medals are found impressed, others engraved in running script and others unnamed. The medal without clasp is found to Indian troops. The ribbon is of three equal stripes of black, white and brown, with the black on the wearers' right.

No Clasp Ring Suspender	£250
With Clasp Ring Suspender	£300
With Clasp Bar Suspender	£450
In Bronze	£1,500

120. HONG KONG PLAGUE MEDAL 1894

This medal, issued by the government of Hong Kong, was awarded to members of the Army and Navy, together with selected civilians, for services during the outbreak of bubonic plague in the colony between May and September 1894. The award was not allowed to be worn when in uniform. Similar in size to many other official campaign awards, the award was issued in gold to officers and senior civilians, and in silver for other recipients. About 45 of the former and 400 of the latter were issued. The obverse shows a man and a woman tending a plague victim, the man fending off an allegorical figure of Death. The reverse contains an inscription in raised lettering. The suspension is by a loop and ring. The main recipients of this award were 300 men of the Shropshire Light Infantry, with in addition a few awards to the Royal Navy and Royal Engineers. There were also awards to civilians, including policemen and nurses. The naming is in impressed capitals which are well-spaced, the recipients' number not being given. The ribbon is of red with yellow edges and two thin yellow stripes in the centre.

Gold	£2,500
Silver	£750

121. INDIA GENERAL SERVICE MEDAL 1895-1902

This medal, the second in the IGS series, was sanctioned in 1895, and was awarded in silver to British and Indian troops and in bronze to native transport personnel and followers. The first two clasps awarded relate to the siege of the fort at Chitral in 1895; the garrison were besieged by tribesmen for 7 weeks before being relieved by a substantial force. In July 1897 a rising began against the British on the North West Frontier which lasted for nearly a year and involved virtually every tribe in the area. All medals for this campaign have the clasp "Punjab Frontier 1897-98", with the following additional clasps where applicable: a clasp to members of the Tirah Expeditionary Force; to those who fought in the several Malakand battles; and to those who served on the Samana beyond Kohat. These latter clasps are very scarce, whilst the two former clasps are more common. The final clasp, awarded after the death of Queen Victoria, was on the Edward VII issue of this medal; the main differences from the first issue are the obverse bust, the lack of a date on the reverse, and the thickness of the medal. The difficult nature of the terrain and the fanatical disposition of the enemy made the 1897-98 campaign particularly hard, and casualties amongst British and Indian troops were quite high. Particularly sought after are medals to those who formed the Chitral garrison, which are rare. In addition, the Edward VII medal is scarce. Most medals are named in running script. The ribbon is of crimson with two dark green stripes.

	British Regiments	Indian	Natives
Defence of Chitral 1895		£600	£1,000
Relief of Chitral 1895	£50	£28	£45
Punjab Frontier 1897-98	£45	£25	£30
Punjab Frontier 1897-98 in pair with Malakand 1897		£45	£65
Punjab Frontier 1897-98 in pair with Samana 1897	£80	£45	£75
Punjab Frontier 1897-98 in pair with Tirah 1897-98	£60	£38	£50
Waziristan 1901-02		£85	£65

122. JUMMOO AND KASHMIR MEDAL 1895

This is the second medal awarded by the Maharajah of Jummoo and Kashmir to his own troops for service with Imperial forces, and was awarded to all those who took part in the Defence of Chitral. Of bronze, and also made by Gurney of London, the obverse shows a coat of arms with native supporters above a scroll and the words 'Jummoo and Kashmir'. The reverse shows a fortress with troops in the foreground. The medal is unusual in being kidney-shaped, and was not issued without the single bronze clasp "Chitral 1895" which appears similar in design to the clasp to the India General Service Medal of 1895. Suspension is from the usual scroll suspender and the ribbon is similar to that of the Italy Star, though watered and with a slightly wider green stripe. The medal is usually crudely impressed in block capitals, but is frequently found unnamed.

Named	£300
Unnamed	£200

123. ASHANTI STAR 1896

This star, the design of which is unique among campaign medals, was awarded for a short war in West Africa December 1895 to January 1896. It was issued in gun-metal only, without clasps and was unnamed. However, the Colonel of the West Yorkshire Regiment, the only British regiment present as a whole, bore the expense of naming the stars issued to the regiment. Other recipients had their awards privately engraved, often with just their regimental number and their regiment. Some 2,000 of these stars were issued to troops who served under Major-General Scott in operations against King Prempeh, who was ruling his subjects rather too harshly. The short campaign consisted of an advance inland on the Ashanti capital, which was occupied, after which the fighting stopped. Apart from the West Yorkshire Regiment, there was a composite battalion formed from detachments from eleven other regiments, each of which contributed about 25 men. In addition there were the usual contingents from the supporting corps. The ribbon is of yellow, with two black stripes. There is an excellent account of the Campaign including a complete roll by Ian McInnes and Mark Fraser, published by Picton Print.

Unnamed	£120
Named to West Yorks	£200

124. QUEEN'S SUDAN MEDAL 1896-98

This medal, sanctioned in 1899, was awarded to all those who took part in the reconquest of the Sudan between 1896 and 1898. It was awarded concurrently with the first clasps on the Khedive's Sudan Medal of 1896-1908, and recipients of the British medal also received the Egyptian medal, although the reverse is not necessarily true. The award was issued in silver to troops of the British, Indian and Egyptian armies, and in bronze to native transport personnel and followers. There are several types of naming, the commonest found to British troops being in sloping engraved capitals; others are seen impressed or unnamed. Those to Indian troops are often engraved in running script, whilst those to Egyptian troops are named in Arabic. Although most recipients received this award for services in 1898 and most are found with the Khedive's medal with clasps 'The Atbara' and 'Khartoum', some were awarded for the reconquest of Dongola province in 1896 and further actions in 1897. These earlier issues are very scarce, as few British troops were involved. Medals to the 21st Lancers, who made a famous charge at Omdurman, are much sought-after. Medal rolls exist for most of the British troops entitled to the medal. The ribbon is of half yellow and half black, with a thin red stripe down the centre. This is symbolic of the desert, the Dervish army and the British Army in between.

Prices are for named examples:	
Silver Issue (British)	£125
Silver 21st Lancers	£500
Bronze Issue	£175

125. KHEDIVE'S SUDAN MEDAL 1896-1908

This medal was sanctioned by the Khedive of Egypt in February 1897, and was awarded to those who took part in the reconquest of the Sudan in 1896-98, and for later operations in pacifying the southern part of the country. It was issued in silver to British, Indian, Egyptian and Sudanese troops, and in bronze to native transport personnel and followers. Fifteen clasps were issued, and the award is also found without clasps. This latter type was issued to those who served in the northern or eastern Sudan in 1896. The first two clasps were issued to those who took part in battles during the 1896 reconquest of Dongola, only one British battalion being present. There was another advance in 1897, for which a further two clasps were awarded. In 1898, there was a final advance on and battle near Khartoum, in which the Dervishes were defeated at Atbara and Omdurman. It was only during this campaign that British troops played a major part, one cavalry and seven infantry regiments being present. After the defeat of the Dervishes, British troops withdrew, and the task of pacifying the lawless south was undertaken by Egyptian and Sudanese troops commanded by a handful of British officers and NCOs; thus, medals with clasps after 1898 to British recipients are rare. A few medals are found to the Royal Navy, usually no clasp awards to 'Melita' and 'Scout' for operations in 1896. The obverse shows an Arabic inscription, whilst the reverse has a shield in the centre surrounded by various weapons; the medal is slightly larger than most British campaign medals. Examples are found both unnamed, and named in one of several styles, most of those to British troops being engraved. Those to Indian recipients are engraved in running script, whilst those to Egyptian and Sudanese troops are engraved in Arabic letters. The ribbon is of yellow with a central blue stripe, symbolic of the desert and the Nile. Prices below are for unnamed medals and those named to natives, except where otherwise stated.

No Clasp (silver)	£50
No Clasp (bronze)	£75
Firket	£65
Hafir	£65
Abu Hamed	£75
Sudan 1897	£75
The Atbara (British)	£50
Khartoum (British)	£50
Gedaref	£65
Gedid	£65
Sudan 1899	£65
Bahr-el-Ghazal 1900-02	£100
Jerok	£100
Nyam-Nyam	£100
Talodi	£100
Katfia	£100
Nyima	£100
Multi Clasp medals	
2 Clasps	£80
3 Clasps	£100
4 Clasps	£125
5 Clasps	£140
6 Clasps	£160
7 Clasps	£180
8 Clasps	£200

126. EAST AND CENTRAL AFRICA 1897-99

This medal was awarded for various operations in what is now Uganda and the southern Sudan between 1897 and 1899. The medal was issued in silver to combatants and, rarely, in bronze to native followers. The obverse depicts a half-length figure of Queen Victoria with an inscription, whilst the reverse shows Britannia holding a trident, an olive branch and a scroll, with the sun and the British lion included in the design. The suspension is by a plain, straight attachment. Four clasps were issued for various operations. The first, for "Lubwa's", was awarded for an expedition to quell a rebellion by Sudanese troops who were holding Fort Lubwas. After a battle in October 1897, the mutineers were pursued across the Nile and defeated again early in 1898. The clasp "Uganda 1897-98" was awarded for operations during a rising in that country, and that for "1898" was for an expedition against the Ogaden Somalis. The fourth clasp, "Uganda 1899" was for operations on the Nile. These medals are very scarce, and are particularly rare to European officers and NCOs. Most recipients were from locally-raised units or the Indian Army, and so many awards must have been lost or destroyed. The naming is in thin engraved capitals, and the ribbon is of half yellow and half red.

Prices are for medals named to natives.	
No Clasp	£225
Clasp Lubwa's	£350
2 Clasp	£275
Clasp Uganda 1897-98	£200
Clasp 1898 (Silver)	£225
Clasp 1898 (Bronze)	£500
Clasp Uganda 1899	£225

127. BRITISH NORTH BORNEO COMPANY'S MEDALS 1897-1937

Four different awards were issued by the Company, a Bravery Cross, two campaign medals and a General Service Medal. A considerable number of disturbances, some of which resulted in quite serious rebellions against the Company Administration, led to a series of small punitive actions undertaken by the Constabulary a force officered by Europeans. Between 1883 and 1916, this Force, which never involved more than about 150 men in action at any one time, dealt with 17 minor and 2 major disturbances.

The Bravery Cross, made by Joseph Moore Ltd. in Birmingham in 1890, was issued in silver and bronze. Total numbers made or issued are not known, but details of 5 silver and 4 bronze recipients are. It was suspended from a gold coloured ribbon.

The **first Campaign Medal** features on the obverse the Company's shield supported by a warrior on either side with the reverse showing the British lion and the Company flag. The suspension and clasps are of the scroll India General Service pattern. Three clasps were issued: "Punitive Expedition", "Punitive Expeditions" and "Rundum". The ribbon had a wide blue centre flanked by gold stripes and edged with maroon stripes. The award was given to those men who took part in any one of the nine actions which took place between 1883 and 1915, with those who took part in more than one receiving the plural clasp. The medal was manufactured by Spink and Son and their original issue for the **"Punitive Expedition"** clasp was 75 bronze and 13 silver, but a further 22 silver were later supplied. In 1906 the originally issued bronze medals were replaced with silver, but the originals do not seem to have been recalled as a number are known to exist. The original issue of the **"Punitive Expeditions"** plural clasp was 100 bronze and 18 silver. A further 12 silver were supplied in 1900 and in 1906 47 silver medals were issued to holders of the bronzes. The **Rundum** clasp was only issued in silver to 143 men, one of whom received the clasp only to add to

BRITISH NORTH BORNEO COMPANY'S MEDALS 1897-1937 *continued*

an Expedition medal and one the clasp only to add to an Expeditions medal. The **Tambunan Medal** was issued complete with a clasp bearing the name of the action. It features on the obverse the Company shield and the words 'British North Borneo 1900' and, on the reverse, the Company flag surrounded by the motto 'Pergo et Perago'. The India General Service pattern clasp was retained but the suspender through which passed the ribbon of yellow with a central green stripe, was now straight. A total of 8 silver and 125 bronze medals were issued. From 1906 the bronzes could be exchanged for silver. Though 22 more silver medals were supplied by Spink, the final number exchanged is not known.

The **General Service Medal** was issued in 1937 in silver only. On the obverse the usual shield of the Company is shown supported by warriors and, on the reverse, appeared the seated figure of Britannia. Suspension was by a ring through which passed the ribbon of half green and half yellow. A total of 44 medals were awarded, mostly to civilians.

Prices quoted are for single medals officially named to other ranks. Medals to Europeans and senior locally recruited officers and NCOs or for groups or pairs will fetch more. Copies of these medals are sometimes met with. They were struck by Spink on a thicker flan or have the letter S of Spink and Son missing.

	Named	Unnamed	Copy
Bravery Silver Cross	Not Known	£400	Not Known
Bravery Cross Bronze	Not Known	£175	Not Known
Punitive Expedition Silver	Rare	Rare	£75
Punitive Expedition Bronze	£600	£250	£75
Punitive Expeditions Silver	Rare	£400	£75
Punitive Expeditions Bronze	£600	£200	£75
Rundum	£680	£175	£75
Tambunan	Rare	£400	£75
General Service 1937	Rare	Not Known	£75

128. SULTAN OF ZANZIBAR'S MEDAL 1896

A silver medal, 1.4 inches in diameter which was awarded by Sultan Hamid bin Thwain of Zanzibar to local troops engaged in operations during the period 1893-6. The obverse of the medal shows the portrait of the Sultan surrounded by Arabic script. The reverse has the same inscription in four lines.

Suspension is by a straight suspender carrying a plain red ribbon and there were four clasps issued to this medal. Pumwani and Jongeni were given for the operations which led to the award of the East and West Africa Medal with clasp "Witu August 1893", and Takaungu and Mwele were given for the operations which led to the "Mwele 1895" or "Mwele 1895-6" inscription on the rim of the same medal.

Silver	£225

129. QUEEN'S SOUTH AFRICA MEDAL 1899-1902

This medal, the commonest in the Victorian series, was awarded for services during the Beer War of 1899-1902. It is a complex award, due to the 26 clasps issued and the hundreds of different units who served during the war. These factors, together with the comparatively low price of an average example, make the medal most collectable. The war, which lasted from October 1899 to May 1902, was one of the longest and most costly - both financially and in terms of casualties - between the Napoleonic Wars and the First World War. Very briefly, there were three phases of the war; the first, from October 1899 to February 1900, consisted of the Boer advance into Natal and Cape Colony, and the sieges of Kimberley, Ladysmith and Mafeking, together with the operations of the various British relieving forces. This first phase is marked by several large pitched battles such as Magersfontein and Spion Kop. The second phase, from February to July 1900, consisted of the British advances into the Boer republics and their annexation. At this point the war was thought to be over, but the third phase, which began in August 1900 and lasted for 20 months, was one of continued guerrilla warfare with numerous small but bitter engagements fought over a very wide area. Only when the British resorted to economic warfare - the destruction of crops and farms - did the Boers surrender. The medal itself was issued in silver to combatants; a very small number were issued in bronze to Indian transport personnel, and these latter are scarce. In all, about 178,000 medals were issued. The obverse shows the crowned head of Queen Victoria with an inscription, whilst the reverse has three different designs. The basic common design is of Britannia in the foreground holding a flag and laurel wreath, with in the background a body of troops and two ships. The words 'South Africa' appear at the top. The first type had, in addition to these features, the raised dates '1899-1900' in the reverse field; this type is very rare, only about 70 being issued, the majority being to Lord Strathcona's Horse. The second type has Britannia's hand pointing to the 'R' in the inscription, the third type having the hand pointing to the 'F'. The clasps are small and narrow, the maximum number of clasps on one medal being nine. Nineteen 'battle' clasps were issued, together with five 'state' and two 'date' clasps. There are many examples of desirable medals in the series, being sought-after due to clasps, regiment or participation in a famous action - for example, a casualty at Spion Kop. The suspender is straight and plain. Examples are seen without clasps to the Royal Navy, nurses and those who served on St. Helena. The naming is either impressed or engraved in various styles. The ribbon is of red, with two blue stripes and a broad orange central stripe. Due to the complexity of this award, it is impossible to price every variant of clasps, and the below prices are intended to give a general guide. Prices are for British infantry regiments except where otherwise stated.

There is a complete roll of all issues to the Royal Navy and Royal Marines compiled by W. H. Fevyer and J. W. Wilson. Certain combinations of bar are not possible, and collectors should study the full conditions of award to become familiar with these. Medals awarded to contingents from Canada, Australia and New Zealand command a considerable premium as do those to War Correspondents.

Nurses were not permitted to receive the bars to which their service entitled them and their medals usually sell at about £75 if impressed 'Nursing Sister'. Any other rank such as Matron or Miss will command a premium. Those named to nursing nuns seem to be sought after. Medals awarded to nurses which have had original naming erased and then been officially re-impressed are quite common and accepted by collectors, though they tend to fetch slightly less than a perfect example. Medals awarded to members of the St. John Ambulance Brigade should be accompanied by the bronze St. John Medal for South Africa.

129. QUEEN'S SOUTH AFRICA MEDAL 1899-1902 *continued*

No Clasp Medal to Royal Navy		£65
No Clasp Medal to Army		£30
No Clasp Medal in Bronze		£100

For multi-clasp medals add, to the base price of £20, the highest value clasp together with 50% of the value shown for each additional clasp.

State Clasp	Cape Colony	£5
	Natal	£25
	Rhodesia	£50
	Orange Free State	£5
	Transvaal	£5
Battle Clasp	Defence of Mafeking	£400
	Defence of Kimberley	£100
	Talana	£85
	Elandslaagte	£85
	Defence of Ladysmith	£35
	Belmont	£45
	Modder River	£45
	Tugela Heights	£25
	Releif of Kimberley	£25
	Paardeburg	£25
	Relief of Ladysmith	£25
	Driefontein	£40
	Wepener	£125
	Relief of Mafeking	£100
	Johannesburg	£5
	Laing's Nek	£25
	Diamond Hill	£25
	Wittebergen	£25
	Belfast	£25
Date Clasp	South Africa 1901	£8
	South Africa 1902	£8
	Medal with 'raised dates' from	£1,800

130. MEDITERRANEAN MEDAL 1899-1902

This medal is identical to the Queen's South Africa Medal of 1899-1902, except for the inscription 'Mediterranean' on the reverse in place of 'South Africa'. The medal was issued in silver only and without clasps, and is found with impressed or engraved naming in similar styles to the Queen's South Africa Medal of 1899-1902. On the outbreak of the Boer War in October 1899, many Regular battalions were withdrawn from the Mediterranean garrisons to join the fighting in South Africa. To replace these garrisons, eight Militia battalions were mobilised in the United Kingdom and were sent to the Mediterranean. Approximately 5,000 of these medals were issued, nearly all of them to Militia infantry. Rolls exist for the recipients of this medal. The ribbon is identical to that of the Queen's South Africa Medal of 1899-1902.

£125

131. THE KING'S SOUTH AFRICAN MEDAL

This medal, sanctioned in 1902, was awarded for services during the Boer War of 1899-1902. As no specific battle clasps were issued to the Queen's Medal after July 1900, this medal commemorates nearly two years of hard fighting in the guerrilla war which followed the official Boer surrenders of 1900. Although the actions of 1901 and 1902 were on a smaller scale, than those in 1899 and 1900, there were a number of bitter engagements and the British suffered severe casualties.

Struck in silver only, the medal shows on the obverse the bust of Edward VII with imperial titles and the reverse is identical to the second die of the Queen's Medal. The ribbon of three equal stripes of green, white and orange is attached by a straight suspender. It was awarded in addition to the Queen's medal and must always be accompanied by it.

It was given to all those troops - British and Imperial - who served in South Africa during the latter stages of the war and who had completed 18 months service prior to 31 May, 1902. Two clasps were issued, "South Africa 1901" and "South Africa 1902" but nurses were not permitted to receive these. The requirement for 18 months service prior to the end of the war means that a man must have arrived in South Africa in 1900 and would therefore automatically be entitled to both clasps. However, a few cases are known where a man served in South Africa in late 1899, throughout most of 1900 and was invalided home before 1901. If he subsequently returned in 1902 and managed to complete 18 months service, he could be awarded this medal with the single clasp "South Africa 1902". Verified single clasp medals are extremely rare.

Apart from this example, single King's South Africa medals do not arouse a great deal of interest as they must, of necessity, be part of a broken pair or group. Examples to nurses or Imperial units usually command a premium.

Single verified clasp	£100
Two clasps	£25
No clasp to a nurse	£75

132. SOUTH AFRICAN WAR MEDAL OF THE ORDER OF ST. JOHN OF JERUSALEM

This medal was instituted by the Chapter-General of the Order in November, 1900 for award to members of the St. John Ambulance Brigade who either went to South Africa or took an active part in the mobilisation, training or despatch of medical comforts. It was awarded to the next of kin of those who died on active service.

Of bronze, the medal shows on the obverse the head of Edward VII with titles surrounding. The reverse shows the arms of the Order superimposed upon the Cross of the Order. Above is the inscription 'South Africa 1899-1902' and below is a scroll bearing the mottoes of the Order. Surrounding the whole is the title of the Order in Latin. Suspension is by a straight bar and the ribbon is black with white edges. The number, rank, name and Corps of the recipient is engraved in block capitals around the rim.

Most, but not all of these medals, should be accompanied by a Queen's South Africa Medal. Conversely, any Q.S.A. to a St. John recipient must be accompanied by this medal.

Bronze	£125

Campaign Medals

133. THE KIMBERLEY STAR

This silver medal was presented to those who had defended the town during the siege which ended in February, 1900. It was an unofficial award and was not permitted to be worn in uniform.

The medal is in the form of a star of six points, each tipped with a ball, the centre medallion bearing the arms of the town and the words "Kimberley 1899-1900". The reverse is plain except for the inscription "Mayor's Siege Medal 1900". Suspension is by means of a small ring attached to a narrow straight suspender bearing scrolls. The one inch ribbon was of yellow and black, separated by a centre band of red, white and blue.

Those issues bearing the Birmingham hall-mark 'a' for 1900 are usually preferred by collectors as being part of the original striking. Approximately 11,000 were issued and two gold issues are known.

Silver 'a' hallmark	£125
Other	£95

134. THE KIMBERLEY MEDAL

Awarded for the same purpose as the Star, this silver medal bears on the obverse the figure of Victory above the Town Hall of Kimberley. On the reverse are two shields, bearing the words "Invested 15 Oct. 1899" and "Relieved 15 Feb. 1900". Above this is the Imperial crown and below the Royal cypher, all within the legend "To the Gallant Defenders of Kimberley". Suspension is by a ring and the same ribbon was used as for the Star. The medal is quite unofficial and not permitted to be worn in uniform.

Silver	£500

135. THE YORKSHIRE IMPERIAL YEOMANRY MEDAL

This locally produced, unofficial medal is frequently found accompanying South Africa Medals to the Yorkshire Imperial Yeomanry. Collectors tend to keep it with the recipients group, usually mounted at the end.

There are three versions. One bears the figure 3 in the centre below the three feathers of the Prince of Wales, and had dates of either 1900-1901 or 1901-1902, and the other and scarcest issue has the central figure 66. The other side is common to all three types and consists of a rose below a crown and the legend "A Tribute from Yorkshire". It is believed that the rose and crown were intended to be shown as the obverse, but collectors tend to mount this medal with the Battalion figure showing, for obvious reasons.

3rd Battalion dated 1900-1901	£75
3rd Battalion dated 1901-1902	£95
66th Battalion dated 1900-1901	£135

136. THE CAPE COPPER COMPANY'S MEDAL

Yet another unofficial medal issued in silver to officers and bronze to other ranks by the Cape Copper Company. Ltd., for the defence of the town of Ookiep, which was the centre of the Company's operations.

The obverse shows a miner, complete with shovel and pit truck, encircled by the words "The Cape Copper Company Limited 1888". The reverse has a 13 line inscription "Presented to the Officers, Non-Commissioned Officers and Men of the Garrison of Ookiep in Recognition of their defence of the Town under Lt. Col. Shelton, DSO, against a Greatly Superior Force of Boers April 4th to May 4th 1902".

The ribbon of dark brown with central green stripe hangs from a scroll suspender fixed directly to the top of the piece. Total issue is believed to be in the region of 900 and naming is usually by impressed capitals. There is a published medal roll.

Silver	£1,500
Bronze	£500

137. CHINA MEDAL 1900

This medal was sanctioned in 1901 and was awarded to those who served during the Boxer Rebellion of 1900. The campaign was caused by the Boxers, an anti-foreign movement who carried out a series of attacks on foreign missionaries, merchants and property. The Chinese government did little to remedy the situation, and in June 1900 issued an edict which amounted to support for the Boxers. The foreign legations in Pekin were besieged, and held out for three months despite having a small garrison. The British contingent in the legation guard comprised 82 members of the Royal Marines, and their medals are much sought-after. An international relief force was organised by seven nations, and in June 1900 the Taku Forts were captured. The force then moved on Pekin, which was relieved in August. Peace was concluded in January 1901. The obverse of the medal has the head of Queen Victoria and an inscription, whilst the reverse is similar to that of the China Medal of 1857-60, with the addition of the date '1900'. Three clasps were issued, two being the maximum to one recipient; the clasp for "Taku Forts" is very scarce, only about 620 being issued, almost exclusively to the Royal Navy. Some 35 ships of the Royal Navy took part in the operations, together with several Indian Marine ships and an Australian contingent. Only one British battalion - the 2nd Royal Welsh Fusiliers - was present, the remainder of the force being composed of Indian troops. In addition, some locally-raised European volunteer regiments received the medal. There are three types of naming; small, impressed capitals for European troops; large, impressed capitals for naval recipients; and an engraved running script for Indian troops. The medal was issued in silver to combatants and in bronze to native transport personnel and followers. The ribbon is of crimson with yellow edges.

	Royal Navy	Army	Native
No clasp	£85	£85	£60
No clasp bronze	—	—	£60
1 clasp Taku Forts	£300	—	—
1 clasp Defence of Legations	£3,500	—	—
1 clasp relief of Pekin	£150	£250	£150
1 clasp relief of Pekin bronze	—	—	£150
2 clasps	£350	—	—

138. TRANSPORT MEDAL 1899-1902

This medal was sanctioned in 1903 to reward the Masters, Officers, Engineers, Pursers and Surgeons of the many merchant ships that were used to carry troops to the wars in South Africa and China. The reverse design of the medal shows HMS 'Ophir', and the Latin inscription reads "For services rendered in transporting troops by sea." Two clasps were issued, one for each of the campaigns for which the transports were used; the medal was not issued without a clasp. The "China 1900" clasp is very scarce. The medals are impressed in block capitals; although the initials and name only of the recipient are given, it is possible to check with the medal roll to determine their rank and ship. A total of 1,783 medals were issued, including 188 with two clasps. 1,272 medals with the clasp for "South Africa 1899- 1902" were issued, and 323 with that for "China 1900". The ribbon is of red, with two blue stripes.

South Africa 1899-1902	£250
China 1900	£400
Two Clasps	£480

139. ASHANTI MEDAL 1900

This very scarce medal, sanctioned in October 1901, was the first campaign medal issued with the obverse bust of Edward VII. It was issued in silver to combatants and in bronze to native transport personnel and followers. A clasp was issued to those who garrisoned Kumassi between April and July 1900, and to those in the relief forces under Willcocks and Burroughs. The campaign began when an attempt was made by the British to capture the 'Golden Stool', which was a symbol of authority amongst the natives. This was unsuccessful, and a rebellion began. The Governor was besieged in Kumassi with a small force. Despite three small columns breaking through and joining in the defence, the situation remained serious. It became necessary to evacuate Kumassi, and it was not until two larger columns joined them that the city was recaptured and the Ashanti defeated. The fighting was severe, and the sickness rate very high. This campaign, which was largely overshadowed by events in China and South Africa at the time, was important in that it showed that the native troops, with very few European officers and NCOs, could fight well in appaling conditions. The medals are usually named in small impressed capitals, but some to officers have been seen engraved in large sloping capitals. Some 3,500 troops - all native - served during the campaign and received the silver medal, but only 900 or so bronze medals were issued. Only 135 European officers and 35 European NCOs received the medal, together with a handful of civilians. The ribbon is of black, with two green stripes.

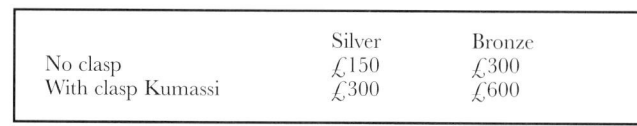

	Silver	Bronze
No clasp	£150	£300
With clasp Kumassi	£300	£600

140. AFRICA GENERAL SERVICE MEDAL 1902

Sanctioned in 1902, this medal replaced several other medals and had the effect of standardising awards for the various small expeditions in both east and west Africa. There were three obverse types – Edward VII (1902-10), George V (1910-20), and Elizabeth II (1952-56). It will be noticed that there is a large gap between the second and third types, the latter only being issued for operations during the Mau-Mau troubles in Kenya. The reverse design, which was standard throughout, shows Britannia holding a trident, palm branch and scroll, with the sun and the British lion in the background; the word 'Africa' appears in the exergue. In all, 45 different clasps were issued for many small campaigns of an almost continuous nature. Most of the operations in West Africa took place in Nigeria, as the clasps show. Operations in East Africa tended to be far inland, with four clasps for lengthy operations against the 'Mad Mullah' in Somaliland. With a few exceptions the clasps were mainly awarded to native troops, only a few British officers and NCOs on detachment receiving the medal. The only occasion on which a sizeable British force was deployed was during the Somaliland operations of 1902-04. Medals to combatants were in silver, and a few were awarded to native followers in bronze; these latter are now very scarce indeed. The medal was suspended from a plain, straight suspender. The naming is usually in small, impressed capitals, except for those to the Royal Navy, which are named in tall, thin impressed capitals. Most examples encountered have only one clasp, although medals with as many as seven clasps are known. The clasp "Jidballi" is always found with that for "Somaliland 1902-04". The ribbon is of yellow with black edges and two thin green stripes towards the centre. Prices below are for silver medals to native recipients.

There is a printed roll of Royal Navy recipients compiled by W. H. Fevyer and J. W. Wilson.

N. Nigeria	£145	East Africa 1915	£200
N. Nigeria 1902	£145	East Africa 1918	£185
N. Nigeria 1903	£130	West Africa 1906	£190
N. Nigeria 1903-04	£180	West Africa 1908	£240
N. Nigeria 1904	£170	West Africa 1909-10	£225
N. Nigeria 1906	£155	Somaliland 1901	£270
S. Nigeria	£200	Somaliland 1902-04 (RN)	£65
S. Nigeria 1902	£185	Somaliland 1908-10 (RN)	£80
S. Nigeria 1902-03	£185	Somaliland 1920	£180
S. Nigeria 1903	£175	Somaliland 1902-04 and	
S. Nigeria 1903-04	£200	Jidballi	£170
S. Nigeria 1904	£165	Uganda 1900	£225
S. Nigeria 1904-05	£205	B.C.A. 1899-1900	£225
S. Nigeria 1905	£350	Jubaland (RN)	£185
S. Nigeria 1905-06	£175	Jubaland (1917-18)	£210
Nigeria 1918	£150	Gambia	£150
East Africa 1902	£390	Aro 1901-02	£180
East Africa 1904	£225	Lango 1901	£265
East Africa 1905	£200	Kissi 1905	£265
East Africa 1906	£200	Nandi 1905-06	£180
East Africa 1913	£270	Shimber Berris 1914-15	£200
East Africa 1914	£260	Nyasaland 1915	£170
East Africa 1913-14	£180	Kenya	£30

141. TIBET MEDAL 1903-04

This medal was authorised in 1905, and was issued to those who were with the Tibet Mission at or beyond Silgari between December 1903 and September 1904. A clasp was issued to those who were at Gyantse between May and July 1904. Only one British battalion was present, the remainder of the force being made up of Indian troops, who received silver medals, and natives in various transport units, who received bronze medals. The major cause of the expedition was the British desire to extend their trade influence to the north of India and to counter growing Russian influence in Central Asia. Various patrols and missions had been attacked by the Tibetans, and this led to a punitive expedition. After several skirmishes and engagements, in which the Tibetans were easily defeated, a treaty was signed in the Potala at Lhasa, which is depicted on the reverse of the medal. Although the bronze issue without clasp is fairly common, other issues are scarce. The most popular in the series are the silver issues with clap to the Royal Fusiliers, the only British regiment present as a whole. About 850 silver medals were issued to British recipients, and about 2,500 to Indian troops. The ribbon is of green, with two white stripes and a broad maroon stripe in the centre. Rolls exist for most British recipients.

	Silver British Regiments	Silver Indian Regiments	Bronze
No clasp	£200	£140	£65
Clasp Gyantse	£400	£225	£150

142. NATAL MEDAL 1906

This medal, issued by the Natal Government, was awarded to those who took part in the operations against the Zulus in 1906. The medal itself is unusual in that the obverse head of Edward VII faces to the right instead of the left, the first medal to do so. The reverse design shows the figures of Natalia and Britannia. Some 10,000 of these medals were issued, about 2,000 being without clasp. The Natal Government refused the help of the Imperial Government in putting down the rebellion, and thus the medal was only awarded to Colonial troops. The rebellion began in February 1906, when the Zulus refused to pay hut tax and murdered two policemen. The authorities acted quickly and arrested several chiefs, and fines were imposed. The threatened rising seemed to have been averted, but in April 1906 Bambata led a serious rising, and Greytown and Eshowe were besieged by the rebels. Troops were quickly raised in the Transvaal and Natal, and several columns entered Zululand, pursuing the rebels into the forest. By early July the revolt had been crushed, and, as with the Riel Rebellion of 1885 in Canada, a colony had proved quite capable of defending itself without the use of Imperial troops. The medal was awarded to all those who served for twenty days or more during operations, whilst those who served for fifty days or more received the medal with clasp. This medal is named in thin block capitals to men and engraved in running script to officers. A complete medal roll has recently been published for this campaign. The ribbon is of crimson with black edges.

No clasp	£95
1906	£145

143. INDIA GENERAL SERVICE MEDAL 1908-35

This medal, the third in the IGS series, was issued for various campaigns before and after the First World War. There were three obverse types: Edward VII (1908-10); George V "Kaisar-I-Hind" (1910-30) and George V "Indiae Imp" (1930-35). The reverse depicts the fort at Jamrud in the Khyber Pass. All issues were of silver, except that the first two clasps- "NWF 1908" and "Abor 1911-12" - are found in bronze to native transport personnel and followers. Most of the 12 clasps issued were for services on the North West Frontier, except those for "Malabar 1921-22" and "Burma 1930-32". There are a multitude of combinations of clasps and regiments found on this medal. Whilst some of the clasps are common to both British and Indian troops, those for "Waziristan 1925" (issued to the RAF only) and "Mohmand 1933" (no British regiments present) are very scarce to European recipients. In addition, clasps for "NWF 1908" "Mahsud 1919-20" and "Malabar 1921-22" are scarce. Apart from medals with the first two clasps, which are named in running script, all other issues should be named in impressed capitals, those to Indian troops having rather larger lettering than those to British recipients. The medal was struck both at the Royal Mint and at the Calcutta Mint, the main difference between the two strikings being in the clasp fixing the suspension to the medal; the former is ornate and has shoulders, whilst the latter is plain. Those recipients who were mentioned in despatches after August 1920 were permitted to wear a bronze oakleaf emblem on the ribbon. The ribbon is of green, with a wide dark blue stripe in the centre. Readers who have an interest in this medal may like to acquire *The Story of the India General Service Medal 1908-1935* by Richard G. M. Styles. There is also a published roll of all awards to the Royal Air Force.

	British Regiments	RAF	Indian Units
North West Frontier 1908 silver	£50	*	£25
North West Frontier 1908 bronze	*	*	£65
Abor 1911-12 silver	*	*	£150
Abor 1911-12 bronze	*	*	£300
Afganistan N.W.F. 1919	£35	£100	*
Mahsud 1919-20	*	*	*
In combination with Waziristan 1919-21	£60	£120	£35
Malabar 1921-22	£80	*	£30
Waziristan 1921-24	£35	£80	£20
Waziristan 1925	*	£400	*
North West Frontier 1930-31	£35	£60	£20
Burma 1930-32	£45	£600	£25
Mohamand 1933	Rare	£200	£25
North West Frontier 1935	£35	£25	£20

144. KHEDIVE'S SUDAN MEDAL 1910

This very scarce medal was sanctioned by the Khedive in June 1911 to replace the Sudan Medal of 1896-1908. It was awarded for various small expeditions in the southern part of the country between 1910 and 1922 and one major revolt in 1916, 16 clasps in all being awarded. Each clasp had an inscription in both English and Arabic. The award was issued in silver both with and without clasp to combatant troops, and in bronze without clasp only to transport personnel and followers. There were two issues of this medal, the 1910 type and the 1918 type, differentiated by the obverse cipher and date. The reverse shows a lion standing by the Nile, with trees and the sun in the background. This medal is very scarce, and when it is encountered is usually either without clasp or with the clasp "Darfur 1916". The clasp "Fasher" is always found in conjunction with the clasp "Darfur 1916". These clasps were qualified for by a small number of Army and RAF personnel, whilst the other clasps were only issued to a few British officers attached to native troops. The majority of the recipients of this medal were Egyptian and Sudanese troops. Medals with two or more clasps are rare, as most of the expeditions were comprised of only 500 men or less. The medal is usually found unnamed, although some to British troops are found impressed in small capitals and a few others are found with Arabic naming. The ribbon is of black, with a thin red and green stripe at each side. Prices below are for unnamed and unattributable awards. Approximate numbers awarded to Europeans are in brackets.

No clasp (silver)	£140
No clasp (bronze)	£225
Atwot (25)	£180
S. Kordofan 1910	£180
Sudan 1912 (40)	£200
Zeraf 1913-14 (15)	£240
Mandal (25)	£240
Miri	£240
Mongalla 1915-16 (25)	£220
Dafur 1916 (250)	£220
Fasher (60)	£200
Lau Nuer (40)	£220
Nyima 1917-18 (75)	£190
Atwot 1918 (15)	£200
Garjak Nuer (35)	£200
Aliab Dinka (45)	£250
Nyala (25)	£250
Darfur 1921	£350

The First World War

It is necessary to say something about the possible combinations of medals which arise from the series instituted to reward service in this war.

The 1914 Star was awarded ONLY for service on land, within France and Belgium. It is scarce to naval units and must always be accompanied by the British War and Victory Medals. The 1914-15 Star was much more widely awarded, but must also be accompanied by the British War and Victory Medals. It was not awarded to the Merchant Navy. It was not possible to earn both Stars.

The British War Medal was awarded to all those who left their places of residence and rendered approved service overseas. It could thus be awarded on its own to those who served abroad, but not in a theatre of war, in Malta, Gibraltar or certain parts of India, for instance. It was also awarded to those who came from abroad and served in the United Kingdom. The Victory Medal was awarded to those who actually served on the establishment of a unit within a theatre of war. Thus, it was not awarded to those who entered a theatre of war as the result of a temporary attachment or draft conducting, for instance. It must always be accompanied by the British War medal.

The Territorial Force War Medal could only be awarded to those who left the United Kingdom, but did not receive either Star. It must be accompanied by the British War Medal but not necessarily by the Victory Medal. The Mercantile Marine War Medal was awarded only to those who had qualified for the British War Medal and must therefore be accompanied by it. Those whose service was totally in the Merchant Navy were not awarded the 1915 Star, but certain organisations such as the Merchant Fleet Auxiliary (MFA) could qualify for this medal and the 1914-15 Star. The Mercantile Marine pair commands a premium when awarded to a stewardess.

Particularly popular are 1914 Star groups to officers and to any of the small short-lived medical units such as the Women's Hospital Corps. Also in demand are medals to the Royal Naval Division and the other smaller naval units which served on shore. 1914-15 Star groups are not greatly sought after, though those to officers and nurses shown a small premium. The Territorial Force War Medal is particularly popular when awarded to nurses or members of the Royal Flying Corps or Royal Air Force.

Casualties are keenly collected, particularly for specific actions such as the first day of the Somme.

The medal rolls of the 1914 Star, 1914-15 Star, British War Medal, Victory Medal and Territorial Force War Medal awarded to personnel of the army and Royal Navy are now available in the Public Record Office, as are awards of the 1914 and 1914-15 Stars to the Royal Flying Corps. Rolls of awards to the Royal Air Force and Merchant Navy are not available.

Readers particularly interested in collecting the medals of this period should acquire *Collecting and Researching the Campaign Medals of the Great War* by H.J. Williamson.

145. 1914 STAR

This award was sanctioned in 1917 for members of the British Expeditionary Force for services during the first phase of the war. It was issued to those who served in France and Belgium between 5th August 1914 and 22nd November 1914. Most of the 378,000 recipients were military personnel belonging to the Regular Army or Territorial Force, although some naval units who served ashore received the award. In addition, a very small number of Australian and Canadian recipients were entitled to the award. The star is of bronze and has three points, the fourth ending in a crown and the suspension ring. There are two crossed swords incorporated in the design between these points. The obverse contains a scroll and the date '1914' in the centre, with 'Aug' above and 'Nov' below, the above all surrounded by a wreath. The reverse is plain and contains the recipients' number, rank, name and regiment in three lines of small impressed capitals. Recipients of this star who were under fire during the period were entitled to wear a bar, sanctioned in 1919, which was sewn onto the ribbon; this bar simply had the relevant qualifying dates on it. This award is incomplete without the British War Medal and Victory Medal, as these two awards were automatically issued to those with the star. The ribbon is of watered red, white and blue.

Star	£20
Star with verified bar	£35

146. 1914-15 STAR

This award is identical to the 1914 Star, except for the obverse centre, which has the date '1914-15' instead of '1914', and the two months are omitted. In all other respects the two awards are the same. The 1914-15 award was issued to all those who served in a theatre of war between 5th August 1914 and 31st December 1915, except those who already qualified for the 1914 Star by virtue of their service with the BEF. Thus a naval rating who was killed at sea in 1914 would receive the 1914-15 Star. The star was issued for services in France, the Dardanelles, East and West Africa, New Guinea, and several other small theatres of war. Due to the large number issued - 2,350,000 - the star is very common. It was issued to the three British services, various Commonwealth and Imperial forces, and various other recipients such as civilians attached to the forces. The ribbon is identical to that of the 1914 Star.

£10

147. BRITISH WAR MEDAL 1914-20

This medal, issued in both silver and bronze, was issued for services during the First World War. The basic qualification for the award was service in any of the three armed services, any Commonwealth or Imperial formation, or in certain recognised voluntary organisations. No clasps were issued, the medal applying to all theatres of war, including some categories of service in the United Kingdom. This award is usually found with the Victory Medal of 1914-18, but can be awarded singly. In all, some six and a half million were issued in silver, with some 110,000 in bronze to natives in various labour corps. The medal was issued for some operations after the 1918 Armistice, mainly for services in Russia and minesweeping operations. The obverse shows the coinage head of George V with an inscription, whilst the reverse depicts the mounted figure of St. George trampling the shield of the Central Powers.
The dates '1914' and '1918' also appear. The suspension is straight and non-

147. BRITISH WAR MEDAL 1914-29 *continued*

swivelling. All awards have impressed naming in small, block capitals of varying types; the regiment or corps is omitted from the naming on awards to Army officers. This is the most common silver medal in the British series, and as such its value is unfortunately dominated by the price of scrap silver. The ribbon is of a wide central orange stripe with, at each edge, narrow stripes of white, black and blue.

Silver	£8
Bronze	£50

148. VICTORY MEDAL 1914-19

This bronze medal was issued for services during the First World War. It was awarded to all those who received the 1914 or 1914-15 Star and to most of those who received the British War Medal of 1914-20; it could not be awarded alone. The main qualification for the award was any service in a theatre of war between 5th August 1914 and 11th November 1918. Most recipients were service personnel, including those from Commonwealth and Imperial services, although some civilians working in recognised voluntary organisations also received the award. Those who were mentioned in dispatches between August 1914 and August 1920 wore a bronze oakleaf on the ribbon. Some 5,750,000 medals were issued in all. The obverse depicts the winged figure of Victory holding a palm branch, whilst the reverse contains an inscription inside a wreath; those awards to South African recipients have this inscription in both English and Afrikaans. The naming is always impressed in one of several styles, the regimental details being omitted on those awards to Army officers. The suspension is by a loop attached to the medal and a ring, whilst the ribbon is of a double rainbow pattern of red, green, blue and violet.

Standard UK issue	£3
South African issue	£15

149. MERCANTILE MARINE MEDAL 1914-18

This medal, issued in bronze only, was awarded to officers and men of the Mercantile Marine, the British merchant fleet, for services during the First World War. Issued by the Board of Trade, the basic qualification for the award was one voyage on a merchant vessel through a zone of operations. The obverse shows the coinage head of George V and an inscription, being identical to the obverse of the British War Medal of 1914-20. The reverse depicts a steamship, a sailing ship and a sinking submarine, together with an inscription. The suspension is straight and does not swivel. The award is usually named in small impressed capitals, with only the name of the recipient shown; the first christian name being given in full. The medal is sometimes found in a group with a 1914-15 Star, the recipient having been attached to the Royal Navy at some stage during the early part of the war. Some 133,000 of these awards were issued. The ribbon is of green and red, with a thin white stripe in the centre.

£15

150. TERRITORIAL FORCE WAR MEDAL 1914-19

This medal, which was issued in bronze and without a clasp, was awarded only to members of the Territorial Force. To qualify, the recipient had to be a member of the TF on or before 30th September 1914, and had to have served outside the United Kingdom between 4th August 1914 and 11th November 1918. However, members of the TF who qualified for the 1914 or 1914-15 Stars were not eligible to receive the award, which was worn after the Victory Medal. Some 34,000 medals were issued, making it the scarcest award for the First World War. Many units received very few medals indeed. Particularly sought-after are awards to Yeomanry, Nursing Sisters and RFC/RAF. The medal is always named in small block capitals, and those to officers include the regiment or corps in the naming. The ribbon is of yellow with two green stripes.

Regiments	£75
R.A. or Corps	£40
Yeomanry	£120
R.F.C./R.A.F.	£150
Nursing Sisters	£125

151. BRONZE MEMORIAL PLAQUE

Issued to the next of kin of those members of His Majesty's Forces who lost their lives during World War One. Each plaque is named in raised capitals with the deceased Christian names and surname in full, but not his regiment or service. Of the 1,355,000 plaques distributed, approximately 600 were issued to women; these had the inscription "She Died for Freedom & Honour" in place of "He Died". A parchment scroll stating the deceased's name and regiment or services was issued with each plaque.

"He Died"	£20
"She Died"	£1,000
Parchment scroll	£15

152. NAVAL GENERAL SERVICE MEDAL 1915-62

This medal was awarded for a variety of operations over a fifty-year period. Due to this long period, there were five obverse issues of the medal, although the reverse design has remained constant. The obverse types are: GVR (1915-36); GVIR "Indo. Imp." (1936-49); GVIR "Fid. Def." (1949-52); EIIR "Br. Omn." (1952-53) EIIR "Dei Gratia" (1953-62). The medal is always found named in one of two styles; the GVR issue is in large impressed capitals, and includes the name of the recipients' ship; all other issues are in small, impressed capitals and omit the name of the ship, including only 'RN' or 'RM' in the naming. With the later issues, examples are found with only the initials and name of the recipient, and these are usually to civilians serving with the Royal Fleet Auxiliary. The fifteen clasps vary greatly in their rarity and the type of operations for which they were awarded. The first, for "Persian Gulf 1909-14" was issued to the crews of some 17 vessels (some of which are rarely seen on the market) for operations against pirates and gun-runners. Thirteen Army officers received this clasp. The clasp for "Iraq 1919-1920" is very rare, being awarded to only 128 officers and men for services on river gunboats July to November 1920. The rarest clasp of the series is "N.W. Persia 1920", which was awarded to only four officers and four ratings who formed the Naval Mission in the area. Of the post-1945 clasps, those for "Palestine 1945-48" and "S.E. Asia 1945-46" are scarce, whilst those for "Arabian Peninsula" and "Brunei" are very scarce. The "Yangtze 1949" clasp is much sought-after, especially to a confirmed recipient on HMS 'Amethyst'. Both clasps for the clearance of bombs and mines are very rare, particularly the latter, which was only awarded to a small diving team between 1953 and 1960. Medals with two clasps are scarce, those with three or more clasps being rare. The ribbon is of crimson with three white stripes.

There is a complete roll of recipients of this medal which is obtainable from The Naval & Military Press.

Persian Gulf 1909-14	£75
Iraq 1919-20	£800
N.W. Persia 1920	£1,500
Palestine 1936-39	£60
S.E. Asia 1945-46	£85
Minesweeping 1945-51	£100
Palestine 1945-48	£65
Malaya (GVIR)	£65
Malaya (EIIR)	£65
Yangtze 1949	£225
Yangtze (H.M.S. Amethyst)	£500
Bomb & Mine Clearance 1945-53	£450
Bomb & Mine Clearance Mediterranean	£1,000
Cyprus	£60
Near East	£60
Arabian Peninsular	£150
Brunei	£150

153. GENERAL SERVICE MEDAL 1918-62

This medal, which was instituted in 1923, was awarded for many years for services in campaigns outside Africa and India, for which separate medals were awarded. It was awarded to the Army and RAF, the Royal Navy receiving a separate medal until 1962, when all three services became entitled to one new medal. The 1918 issue covers a very wide range, being issued to many different units over a period of 44 years; 16 different clasps were issued for various campaigns. All issues of the medal have a common reverse, ribbon and suspension, although there are six obverse types; GVR coinage head (1918-32); GVR crowned head (1932-36); GVIR "Indo. Imp." (1936-49); GVIR "Fid. Def." (1949-52); EIIR 'Br. Omn.' (1952-53); EIIR "Dei Gratia" (1953-62). The rarest type is the GVR crowned head, as this was issued only with the rare clasp for "Northern Kurdistan". The first EIIR type is scarce. The first clasps - "S. Persia" "Kurdistan" "Iraq" "N.W. Persia" - were issued for fighting in the Middle East against various tribesmen in the wake of the First World War. The clasps for "Southern Desert: Iraq" and "Northern Kurdistan" were issued mainly to the RAF, the first being scarce and the second rare; the operations for which these clasps were issued were in the same area as for the first four clasps, but they provide a good example of how the RAF took over the role of peacekeeping from the Army in the 1920s, being thought to be cheaper and more efficient. Those who served in the Arab Revolt of 1936-39 received the clasp "Palestine", and after the Second World War further troubles in the area resulted in the award of the second clasp - that for "Palestine 1945-48". Also immediately after the end of the war, a clasp was awarded to those who took part in the reoccupation of the Dutch East Indies and French Indo-China and the civil wars that followed. Since 1945, other campaigns and operations in Malaya, Cyprus, Egypt, Aden and Brunei have been recognised by the award of a clasp. These are all fairly common with the exception of the last. The medal is usually named in small impressed capitals, although some RAF issues are engraved. The post-1945 clasps can be found to almost every regiment and corps in the Army, and can make an interesting collection. Recipients who were mentioned in dispatches were allowed to wear an oakleaf emblem on the ribbon. The ribbon is of purple, with a green central stripe.

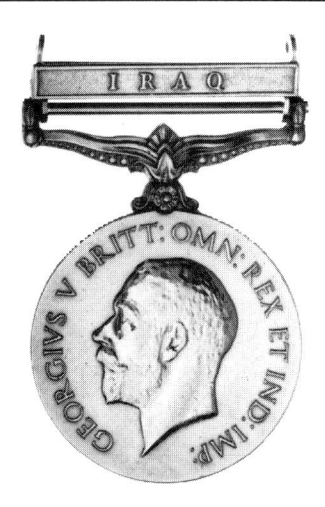

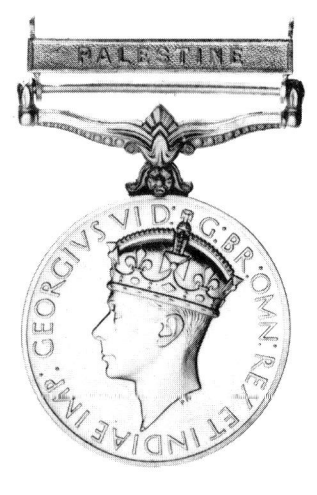

	British Army	R.A.F.	Indian and Local Units
S. Persia		£350	£30
Kurdistan	£40	£150	£20
Iraq	£35	£150	£18
N.W. Persia	£40	£300	£25
Southern Desert Iraq	*	£250	£120
Northern Kurdistan	*	£300	£120
Palestine	£30	£35	£20
S.E. Asia 1945-46	£45	£60	£20
Bomb & Mine Clearance 1945-46	£200	£260	*
Bomb & Mine Clearance 1945-56	£325	£325	*
Palestine 1945-56	£20	£20	£15
Malaya (George VI)	£25	£25	£20
Malaya (Elizabeth II)	£25	£25	£20
Cyprus	£25	£25	£20
Near East	£40	£50	*
Arabian Peninsular	£30	£30	£20
Brunei	£120	£120	£60

154. INDIA GENERAL SERVICE MEDAL 1936-39

This medal, the fourth and last award in the IGS series, was introduced in 1938 to replace the 1908-35 issue, the accession of George VI being a convenient time to change the entire medal rather than merely the obverse. There were two issues of this medal, the most noticeable difference being in the claw connecting the suspension to the medal; the Royal Mint issue has a rather decorative claw, whilst the Calcutta Mint version has a plain claw without shoulders. Two clasps were issued for services in Waziristan bearing the appropriate dates of the campaign in which the recipient fought. Although several British regiments were present, this medal is scarce to Europeans, and even those to Indian troops are not as common as the 1908-35 issue. Awards to the RAF, which had nine squadrons present, are scarce. Naming for all units is by impressed capitals, those to Indian troops being in larger and cruder letters. The ribbon is of a grey centre, with a red and green stripe at each side.

	British Units	R.A.F.	Indian Troops
North West Frontier 1936-37	£45	£65	£20
North West Frontier 1937-39	£50	£75	£25
Two Clasp medal	£65	£100	£30

155. 1939-45 STAR

This bronze star, which is identical to others in the series except for the obverse inscription, is the commonest star awarded for the Second World War. It was awarded for services between the declaration of war in September 1939 and the surrender of the Japanese in 1945. Naval recipients had to complete six months at sea in a theatre of war, but qualified in a shorter period if involved in a commando raid or with the Fleet Air Arm. The basic qualifying time of six months also applied to the Army, the exceptions being service at Dunkirk, in Norway or in certain airborne and commando operations. For RAF aircrew, the award was gained by two months' operational service, groundcrew qualifying under the same general conditions as the Army. The Merchant Navy received the award for six months' service afloat, which had to include at least one voyage in a theatre of war. In addition to these regulations, any service curtailed by death, injury or capture qualified for the award, as did the award of a decoration or mention in despatches. Only one bar was issued on this star, that inscribed "Battle of Britain" being issued to aircrew engaged in these operations in 1940. In addition to the British forces, many awards were issued to Commonwealth and Imperial forces for their services. The star is worn before all other campaign awards for the Second World War. The ribbon, which is of equal stripes of dark blue, red and light blue, is symbolic of the Royal Navy, Army and RAF respectively.

£5

156. ATLANTIC STAR 1939-45

The star was issued for services during operations in the Atlantic for the entire duration of the war. The star is of bronze, and is similar to other awards in the series except for the obverse inscription; it was issued unnamed. In most cases, this award could not be won until the recipient had qualified for the 1939-45 Star. Service on Russian convoys was counted, but the qualifying period for this award could not be used towards the France and Germany Star. For the Merchant Navy, six months had to be spent at sea, with at least one voyage in the prescribed area of operations. RAF recipients had to complete two months' service in the area after qualifying for the 1939-45 Star. If the recipient won this star first, and subsequently won the Air Crew Europe or France and Germany Stars, a bar was worn on the ribbon to show the second award, as no two of these three stars could be worn together. Those who received an award for gallantry, or whose service was cut short by death or injury, were automatically entitled to the award. The ribbon is of dark blue, white and green stripes and is watered.

£15

157. AIR CREW EUROPE STAR 1939-44

This award was issued to aircrew who flew from Britain over Europe from the beginning of the war up to D-Day in June 1944. The star is of bronze, and is similar to other stars in the series, except for the obverse inscription; it was issued unnamed. The award was superceded by the France and Germany Star on 6th June 1944. Recipients who were captured whilst on operations were entitled to the award provided they had previously qualified for the 1939-45 Star. Termination of service by death or injury, or the receiving of an award for gallantry, conferred automatic entitlement to the star. The basic qualification for the award was four months' aircrew duty, of which any two months could be a qualification for the star. A few Army personnel were entitled to the star, the necessary qualifications being much the same as those for the RAF. A recipient of this star could not receive the Atlantic or France and Germany Stars, but wore a bar on the ribbon to show entitlement to a further star — either "Atlantic" or "France and Germany". The ribbon is of light blue, black and yellow stripes, symbolic of the RAF operating night and day. This is the rarest star in the series, and commemorates some of the most important operations of the war. Care should be taken with this award, as copies are known.

£100

158. AFRICA STAR 1940-43

This bronze star, similar to other awards in the series except for the obverse inscription, was awarded for services in North Africa between June 1940 and May 1943. The Royal Navy and Merchant Navy qualified for the award by any service in the Mediterranean or off the Horn of Africa during the qualifying period; those naval personnel who served ashore qualified under the same rules as the Army. The qualification for the latter was any service in North Africa, Abyssinia, Sudan, Eritrea and Malta during the prescribed period, the same being true for RAF groundcrew; aircrew qualified by flying over enemy-occupied territory. Three different bars were awarded on this star, only one of which could be worn at a time; those for "8th Army" and "1st Army" are self-explanatory. The bar "North Africa 1942-3" was awarded to the Royal and Merchant Navies for inshore operations. The ribbon is of buff, with a central red stripe and thinner stripes of dark blue and light blue, representing the desert, Army, Royal Navy and RAF respectively.

£4

159. PACIFIC STAR 1941-45

This star was awarded to personnel of all three services for operations in the Pacific area from the action at Pearl Harbour until the final surrender of the Japanese in September 1945. The star, which is of bronze, is similar to others in the series, except for the obverse inscription. It was issued unnamed, although those to Australian troops are often impressed on the reverse with the number and name of the recipient. For the Royal Navy, the areas of operations were the Pacific, South China Sea, and the eastern sector of the Indian Ocean. The 1939-45 Star had to be earned first before the qualifying period for this star could commence, but after this only one operational sortie in the area was needed to qualify. The Army qualification was service in a territory subjected to enemy invasion; thus the main category of Army awards were those who fought in Malaya, Singapore and Hong Kong in 1941-42. Australian and New Zealand troops received the star for the difficult campaigns in New Guinea and the South Pacific. For the RAF, one operational sortie over the area qualified for the star. Though many were entitled to this and the Burma Star, the two stars could only be worn together, and only the first one for which the recipient qualified was issued, with a bar for the other award; therefore this star is found with the bar 'Burma' on the ribbon. The ribbon is of green, yellow, dark blue, red and light blue - 'these are symbolic of forests, beaches, the Navy, Army and RAF respectively. Those who were captured in 1941-42 and who remained as POWs received this star.

£25

160. BURMA STAR 1941-45

This bronze star was awarded for services in Burma from the invasion in December 1941 until the surrender of the Japanese in September 1945. It is similar to other awards in the series except for the obverse inscription and the ribbon. For the Navy, the main qualifications for the award were possession of the 1939-45 Star and service in the Bay of Bengal. For the Army, one days' service in the prescribed area during the period qualified for the award, with the following additions; service in Bengal or Assam between May 1942 and September 1945, and services in China or Malaya between February 1942 and September 1945. For RAF aircrew, one operational sortie over the area qualified for the award, the rules for other RAF personnel being similar to those for the Army. Those on tours of inspection had to serve for 30 days to receive the star. This award could not be worn in addition to the Pacific Star of 1941-45, and those entitled to both had the bar 'Pacific' on the ribbon. The ribbon is of dark blue, red and orange stripes.

£15

161. ITALY STAR 1943-45

This award was issued to personnel of all three services for operations in Sicily and Italy from June 1943 until May 1945. The star is similar to others in the series except for the obverse inscription; it is of bronze and was issued unnamed. For the Royal Navy and Merchant Navy, the star could only be awarded to those who were entitled to the 1939-45 Star, Service in the Aegean, the Dodecanese, and off the Greek and Yugoslav coasts during the relevant period also qualified for the star. For the Army, service in any of the prescribed areas for one day or more qualified for the award. RAF personnel who served on land qualified in the same way as the Army, and aircrew who flew in operations over the theatre were entitled. As this star was issued in addition to, and not instead of, other stars, no bars were worn on the ribbon,. The ribbon is of red, white and green stripes, the national colours of Italy.

£8

162. FRANCE AND GERMANY STAR 1944-45

This award was issued for services during the campaigns in North West Europe from D-Day until the final German surrender in May 1945. The star, which is of bronze, is similar in design to the other stars in the series, except for the obverse inscription. It was issued unnamed. For the Royal Navy, the basic qualification for the award was services afloat or on land in support of the invasion of Europe or subsequent operation. It should be noted that naval personnel involved in the invasion of Southern France received the Italy Star. Army personnel were entitled to the award for any services on land during the specified period, and the RAF were entitled to the award on the same lines as the Army for personnel serving on the ground, whilst one or more operational sorties over the theatre qualified air crew. This star could not be awarded in conjunction with either the Atlantic or Air Crew Europe Stars, and recipients of any two of these awards wore the appropriate bar on the ribbon. The ribbon is of red, white and blue stripes, symbolising Britain, France and the Netherlands.

£12

163. DEFENCE MEDAL 1939-45

This medal was issued for services during the Second World War, and is probably the commonest campaign award ever issued. Struck in cupro-nickel for all recipients except Canadians, whose award was in silver, the award is found both singly and in groups. The major qualifications for the award were; service in the forces and other allied organisations in a non-operational area threatened by air attack or invasion, the minimum period being three years; non operational service outside the country of residence for one year or more, the minimum time being six months if service was in an overseas territory threatened by invasion or air attack. The award was available to police, fire and ambulance services as well as other bodies such as the Civil Defence and Home Guard. Any services curtailed by death or injury, or which resulted in an award or commendation, automatically qualified the recipient for the award. The obverse shows the uncrowned head of George VI with an inscription, whilst the reverse depicts the Crown on the stump of an oak tree with two lions. In addition to this there are the dates '1939' and '1945', and the title of the medal in full in the exergue. The award was issued unnamed and was suspended from a straight, non-swivelling suspender. The ribbon is of a wide central orange stripe, with green edges, each containing thin black stripes.

British Issue	£12
Canadian Issue	£16

164. WAR MEDAL 1939-45

This medal was awarded to all personnel in any of the British or Commonwealth forces who served for a minimum of 28 days during hostilities. This service could be operational or non-operational. Recipients whose service was terminated by death, injury or capture were automatically entitled to the award. In addition, anyone qualifying for one of the campaign stars was awarded this medal. The medal is of cupro-nickel, except for the Canadian issue (700,000) which is of silver. No clasps were issued, and the medal was usually issued unnamed, although some recipients had their medals privately named. However, those issued to South African and Australian troops are usually impressed with the number and name of the recipient. Those who were mentioned in dispatches during the war affixed the oakleaf emblem to the ribbon of this medal. This award is one of the commonest that is encountered, and the large number issued and lack of naming make them one of the least expensive. The ribbon is of red, white and blue stripes.

| British Issue | £4 |
| Canadian Issue | £12 |

165. INDIA SERVICE MEDAL 1939-45

This medal, which was sanctioned in 1946, was awarded to officers and men of the Indian forces for services between September 1939 and September 1945. The medal is of cupro-nickel, and the obverse design is similar to that of the War Medal of 1939-45; the reverse depicts a map of India. The basic qualification for the award was three years' non-operational service in India or elsewhere. It was awarded in addition to the various campaign stars and the War Medal of 1939-45, but could not be issued to those who qualified for the Defence Medal of 1939-45. All ranks of the Indian forces were entitled, including Reserve, State and Womens' forces. In addition, personnel attached to the Indian Army were entitled. In all some 220,000 were awarded. The medal was issued unnamed, and the ribbon is of dark and light blue stripes.

£12

166. CANADIAN VOLUNTEER SERVICE MEDAL 1939-47

This medal, issued in silver only, was sanctioned in 1943. The basic qualification for the award was 18 months' voluntary service in the Canadian armed forces and other recognised organisations between September 1939 and March 1947. The late finishing date was allowed so that those who began their service towards the end of the war could qualify. Those who served for less than 18 months were entitled to the award if they received an honourable discharge. In addition, those who served overseas for six days or more were entitled to wear a bar on the ribbon; this was plain with a maple leaf in the centre. Prior service in the British or American forces counted towards the award, as did any service curtailed by death or injury. The obverse depicts seven marching figures representing the various services, together with maple leaves and an inscription. The reverse contains the Canadian coat of arms. The suspension, the design of which is unique, was by a loop attached to the medal and a hole in the suspender, the two being joined by a loose ring. The medal was issued unnamed. The ribbon is of stripes of green, scarlet and blue.

| Medal | £15 |
| Medal with clasp | £22 |

167. AFRICA SERVICE MEDAL 1939-45

This medal, sanctioned in 1943, was awarded to the South African forces for service during the Second World War. The obverse shows a map of Africa with an inscription, whilst the reverse depicts a leaping springbok. The basic qualification for the award was the signing of an oath to serve in the Union forces in Africa or overseas.

Full-time service of 30 days or more in South Africa qualified the recipient for the award. About 190,000 medals were struck, all in silver. They are usually named in small impressed capitals with the number and name of the recipient. The prefix of the number can give some indication of the service of the recipient, or whether he was a native ('N') or coloured ('C'). The ribbon is of a central orange stripe, with one green and one gold stripe on each side.

£8

168. AUSTRALIA SERVICE MEDAL 1939-45

This award was issued to members of the Australian forces for services between September 1939 and September 1945, and was sanctioned in December 1949. The medal, which was issued in nickel-silver only and without any clasps, was usually named in impressed capitals showing the recipients' number and name. The prefix of the number shows the state in which the recipient enlisted. The basic qualification for the award was eighteen months' service overseas or three years' service at home by members of the regular and reserve forces. Service terminated by death, injury or capture led to automatic qualification for the award. About 180,000 were issued. The ribbon is of stripes of dark blue, khaki, light blue and red, symbolic of the Navy, Army, Air Force and Mercantile Marine respectively.

£25

169. NEW ZEALAND WAR SERVICE MEDAL 1939-45

This medal was issued to all members of the New Zealand forces who served during the Second World War and completed either one month of full-time service or six months of part-time service. The qualifying period was between September 1939 and September 1945. Apart from awards to regular forces, many Reserve and Home Guard units were entitled to the medal. Termination of service caused by death, injury or capture resulted in the automatic award of the medal. It was issued in cupro-nickel, with no clasps and was unnamed. About 240,000 were issued in all. The ribbon is of black, with white edges.

£20

170. SOUTH AFRICA MEDAL FOR WAR SERVICE 1939-46

This award, sanctioned in 1946, was awarded to both men and women for services between September 1939 and February 1946. The main qualifications were two years service in an official voluntary organisation in South Africa or elsewhere. At least one year had to be continual service, and in addition the work had to be unpaid and voluntary. Any service which counted towards the award of the Africa Service Medal of 1939-45 could not count for this award, and thus it is very unusual to find the two awards in a group. The medal, which was issued in silver only, was issued unnamed and had a straight suspender. The obverse shows the South African coat of arms, whilst the reverse has a protea wreath and a bilingual inscription. Those mentioned in despatches or commended wore a bronze protea leaf on the ribbon, which is of three equal stripes of orange, white and blue. Some 17,000 of these medals were issued.

£30

171. SOUTHERN RHODESIA WAR SERVICE MEDAL 1939-45

This very scarce medal, issued in cupro-nickel, was awarded only to those who served in Southern Rhodesia at any time during hostilities; those who qualified for a campaign star or medal were not eligible for this award, and as so many Rhodesians served overseas, only about 1700 were issued. No clasps were awarded, and the medal was issued unnamed. The reverse design depicts the arms of Southern Rhodesia. The ribbon is of dark green, with black and red stripes at each edge.

£185

172. NEWFOUNDLAND VOLUNTEER WAR SERVICE MEDAL 1939-45

Instituted by the Province of Newfoundland as late as July, 1981, for award to any person in the Provence who volunteered to serve in the Imperial Forces during the 1939-45 War, but did not receive a volunteer service medal. Basically, this means that it was given to those who served in the British Army, Navy or Air Force, those serving with the Canadians being disqualified by reason of having received the Canadian Volunteer Service Medal.
The obverse shows the Royal Cypher of George VI with crown above on which stands a staff caribou. This is surrounded by the name of the medal and dates. The reverse shows a figure of Britannia being stalked by two lions on a scalloped background. The deep claret ribbon with red, white and blue edges hangs from a straight suspender.

£400

173. KOREA MEDAL 1950-53

This medal was awarded to members of the British and Commonwealth forces who took part in the operations in Korea between July 1950 and June 1953. All issues were in cupro-nickel except for the Canadian issue (27,500), which is in silver and has 'Canada' under the obverse bust. The reverse depicts Hercules fighting the Hydra. No clasps were issued to the medal, but there were two obverse types, differentiated by the inscription. The first issue is the most common, but the second issue (without "Britt. Omn.") is scarce. The British and Commonwealth force in Korea was small compared to the American and Korean armies, but the Commonwealth Division saw much heavy fighting. The most desirable medals in this series are those to the men of the Gloucestershire Regiment who took part in the epic battle at the Imjin River. A roll of these men has been published, and their medals are worth a considerable premium. The three services had differing conditions of service for the award. Naval recipients had to serve one day on land or 28 days in Korean waters; Army personnel had to serve one day on land; and the RAF requirement was one sortie over Korea or one day on land. Medals to British recipients are impressed in small capitals, whilst those to Canadian, Australian and New Zealand recipients are named in larger impressed capitals. Those who were mentioned in despatches during the war wore a bronze oakleaf on the ribbon. The ribbon is of yellow, with two blue stripes.

British Issue	£60
Canadian Issue	£60
Australia/New Zealand Issue	£65
Gloucester Regt. present at the battle of Imjin River	£325

174. UNITED NATIONS KOREA MEDAL 1950-53

This bronze medal was sanctioned in 1951 by the United Nations, and was awarded to all those who served with the UN forces during the Korean War of 1950-53. Various types were issued to different national contingents, the British issue being awarded to all Commonwealth forces. The basic qualification was one days' service in Korea, with a longer period for those on tours of inspection. Personnel who served in Japan were entitled to the award, and it was always awarded to those who held the British medal, although the converse not necessarily true. Those who served in Korea after the 1953 armistice were also entitled to the medal. The obverse depicts the UN emblem, and the reverse has an inscription. The suspension is by a fixed bar, the clasp "Korea" being standard. The award was issued unnamed, except for those issued to Canadians, which were named in small block capitals. The ribbon is of seventeen equal stripes - nine blue and eight white.

£25

175. SOUTH AFRICA KOREA MEDAL 1950-53

This rare medal was awarded to members of the South African forces who served with the UN contingent in Korea. The obverse shows maps of South Africa and Korea, whilst the reverse shows the South African coat of arms and the royal cipher. The medal was instituted by a Royal Warrant in 1953 and was issued in silver only. Some 800 were issued in all, and apart from 10 Army officers attached to the Commonwealth Division, all the recipients came from the 2nd (Cheetah) Squadron, South African Air Force. The suspension was by ring and clasp, and the naming was in impressed block capitals. The ribbon is of sky blue, dark blue and orange stripes.

£300

176. GENERAL SERVICE MEDAL 1962

This medal, issued to all three services, is the only campaign award still on issue to the British forces. It was instituted in 1964, and replaced the Army/RAF and Royal Navy issues to coincide with the new unified Ministry of Defence. To date, ten clasps have been issued. Those for "Borneo" and "Malay Peninsula" were awarded for services during the Indonesian Confrontation, and whilst the former is common to all three services, the latter is scarce to Army personnel. Medals with one or both of these clasps are sometimes found to personnel of the Australian and New Zealand forces who served alongside British troops; awards to native policemen and trackers are also encountered. The next two clasps, which can again be grouped together, were for "South Arabia" and "Radfan". The former clasp was awarded for services in Aden state, whilst the latter, scarcer, clasp was for services in the mountainous area to the north. The clasp for "South Vietnam" is the rarest of the series, only about 70 being issued to members of the Australian Army Training Team Vietnam for services between 1962 and 1964. The clasp was replaced by the Vietnam Medal of 1964. Probably the commonest clasp in terms of numbers issued is that for "Northern Ireland", which has been awarded since August 1969 and is still on issue. It is found to members of all three services, as well as to auxiliary units such as the UDR, MOD Police and AFS. About 120,000 of these clasps have been issued so far. The clasp "Dhofar", was awarded for services in Oman between 1969 and 1976 in support of the Sultan's Armed Forces in operations against Yemeni rebels. This clasp is very scarce, and is usually found to RAF personnel, although various specialist teams and members of the SAS also received the clasp Most of the subsequent clasps are not frequently seen on the market. "Lebanon" was issued to a small number of troops for operations in that country in 1983-84 and the clasps "Mine Clearance – Gulf of Suez" (1984) and "Gulf" (1986-89) are even scarcer. The clasp "Kuwait" was given for service between March and September 1991 in Kuwait or the Northern Gulf, and is unique in that those who failed to gain the Gulf Medal because of insufficient service may count that time towards the Kuwait clasp. The final clasp to date, "N. Iraq & S. Turkey" was given to personnel engaged in the protection of the Kurds in Northern Iraq during operation Haven between April and July, 1991. The maximum verified number of clasps seen on one medal is five, and the medal was not issued without a clasp. Recipients who have been mentioned in dispatches wear a bronze oakleaf on the ribbon. The naming is always in small, impressed capitals, and the ribbon is of purple with green edges.

Borneo	£30
Radfan	£50
South Arabia	£30
Malaya Peninsula	£30
South Vietnam	Rare
Northern Ireland	£25
Dhofar	£95
Lebanon	£400
Mine Clearance – Gulf of Suez	£40
Gulf	£250
Kuwait	£500
N. Iraq & S. Turkey	£450
Two Clasps	£35
Three Clasps	£95
Four Clasps	£150

177. VIETNAM MEDAL 1964

This award, sanctioned in 1965, was awarded to Australian and New Zealand troops for services in Vietnam after 28th May 1964. The period of service necessary to obtain the award was one day on land, twenty-eight days at sea, or thirty days on an official visit. The obverse shows the crowned bust of Elizabeth II, whilst the reverse depicts a figure separating two symbolic ideological spheres. The suspension is by a swivelling bar of the General Service Medal type. This medal was the first to be designed and produced in Australia, and was issued named in one of two styles: large impressed capitals for Australian forces, and small impressed capitals for New Zealand recipients. 18,000 of the former and 4,000 of the latter were awarded. The ribbon is of dark blue, light blue, red and yellow stripes, representing the three services and the national colours of South Vietnam.

Australian Recipient	£150
New Zealand Recipient	£150

178. SOUTH VIETNAM CAMPAIGN MEDAL 1964

This award was issued by the South Vietnamese government to Australian and New Zealand troops for those operations recognised by the Vietnam Medal of 1964. The basic qualification was six months' service in Vietnam, and therefore this award should be accompanied by the Australian medal, although the reverse is not necessarily true. The award is in the form of a six-pointed star, with gold rays between each of the points; the obverse is of white enamel, the centre showing a map of Vietnam and flames. The reverse is plain, except for an inscription in the centre. The original issue was unnamed and rather crude, after which the Australians took over the manufacture of the award and named them on the reverse with the number and name of the recipient. The ribbon is of white and green stripes and bears a metal bar with date 1960 -.

Named	£20
Unnamed	£10

179. THE RHODESIA MEDAL 1980

Made of rhodium plated cupro-nickel, this medal was awarded for 14 days service in Rhodesia during the period between 1 December, 1979 to 20 March, 1980 which led to Independence and the first elections. The medal should be accompanied by the Zimbabwe Independence Medal.
The obverse shows the crowned head of the Queen with usual titles and the reverse bears a Sable Antelope, the title of the Medal and the date 1980. The ribbon, which is sky blue with a narrow band of red, white and dark blue in the centre, hangs from a straight non-swivelling suspender. The medal seems to have been named in impressed capitals to army recipients, but issued unnamed to Royal Air Force and Police. Approximately 2,500 were issued.

Though frequently worn by recipients with other campaign medals in date order of award, this is, in fact, a commemorative or miscellaneous medal and its precedence is very low, being ranked just after the Civil Defence Long Service Medal.

£300

180. THE SOUTH ATLANTIC MEDAL 1982

Issued to commemorate the successful conclusion of the operations to re-take the Falkland Islands after their occupation by an Argentine invasion force. Qualifying service was a) one day in the Falkland Islands or their Dependencies or in the South Atlantic south of 35° south or b) 30 days in the South Atlantic south of 7° south. Those qualifying under a) wear a large rosette on the ribbon. The medal was widely awarded, not only to the military and naval forces engaged, but to all kinds of other organisations including the Civil Service and public relations personnel serving on Ascension Island. Some 30,000 were issued in total.

The obverse shows the crowned head of the Queen with usual titles and the reverse has the arms of the Falkland Islands with the title of the medal above. It is attached to the shaded and watered blue, white and green ribbon by a straight suspender. It was struck in cuprco-nickel and named in impressed capitals.

Medal to Royal Navy recipient	£150
Royal Marines	£175
Royal Fleet Auxiliary	£175
Army	£200
Royal Air Force	£220
Merchant Navy & Civilians	£120

181. THE GULF MEDAL 1990-91

Issued to commemorate the operations by the United Kingdom and its Allies against Iraq as a consequence of its invasion and occupation of Kuwait. The area of operations is very widely drawn and includes most of the Middle East and Cyprus. Service required is a) thirty days continuous service between 2 August, 1990 and 7 March, 1991 or b) seven days between 16 January, 1991 and 28 February, 1991 or c) service in the Kuwait Liaison Team on 2 August, 1990. Two clasps are authorised: for those qualifying under b) a clasp dated "16Jan-28 Feb 1991", and for those qualifying under c) a clasp dated "2 Aug 1990".

The medal is in cupro-nickel and bears on the obverse the Queen's crowned head and titles and, on the reverse, the title of the medal above and the date 1990-91 below a design of an eagle, anchor and automatic rifle symbolising the three services. The ribbon has a sand coloured centre bordered by stripes of light blue, red and dark blue and hangs from a straight suspender.

A rosette is worn on the ribbon in undress uniform to indicate the possession of a clasp. Naming is in impressed capitals.

According to official statistics, the United Kingdom committed over 45,000 troops to this operation but it is thought that the eventual issue of the medal will be even larger.

Clasp, 16 Jan-28 Feb 1991	£140
Clasp, 2 Aug 1990	£1,500
No Clasp	£100

182. UNITED NATIONS MEDALS

The first medal issued by the United Nations was that for Korea which has already been described. Since that time two different types of medal have been issued for a variety of purposes.

United Nations Emergency Force Medal
A bronze medal showing the U.N. emblem below the letters UNEF. The reverse is plain with the inscription "In the Service of Peace". Issued for the patrolling of the Israel-Egypt border from 1956 to 1967. The suspension was by a ball and ring and the ribbon sand with a central UN blue stripe and narrow dark blue and green stripes towards each edge.

The United Nations Medal
This medal is the same design as the Emergency Force Medal described above except that the letters above the emblem on the obverse are reduced to UN instead of UNEF. This design became the general purpose medal of the United Nations and was used for a number of operations, the only difference between these being the design of the ribbon.

UNTSO - United Nations Truce Supervision Organisation. Ribbon blue with two narrow white stripes towards each edge.

UNOGIL - United Nations Observation Group in Lebanon. Ribbon as for UNTSO.

ONUC - Organisations des Nations Unies an Congo. Ribbon at first the same as UNTSO then changed to green with white and blue edges.

UNTEA - United Nations Temporary Executive Authority. Ribbon blue

182. UNITED NATIONS MEDALS *continued*

with three central stripes of dark green, white and light green.
UNMOGIP - United Nations Military Observer Group in India and Pakistan. Dark green centre fading to light green with a white and blue edge.
UNIPOM - United Nations India/Pakistan Observation Mission. Ribbon as for UNMOGIP.
UNYOM - United Nations Yemen Observation Mission. Ribbon brown centre bordered by yellow and light blue edges.
UNFICYP - United Nations Force in Cyprus. Ribbon UN blue with a central white stripe bordered by a thin dark blue stripe. This medal was widely awarded to British forces.
UNEF 2--United Nations Emergency Force 2. Ribbon UN blue with a sand centre bearing two dark blue stripes.
UNDOF - United Nations Disengagement Observer Force. Ribbon red, white, black, UN blue.
UNIFIL - United Nations Interim Force in Lebanon. Ribbon UN Blue with a green centre bordered with white and red.
UNIIMOG - United Nations Iran-Iraq Military Observer Group. Ribbon UN blue with red, white and green edges.
UNAVEM - United Nations Angola Verification Mission. Ribbon pale blue with yellow edges separated by thin stripes of red, white and black.
ONUCA - Observadores de las Naciones Unidas en Centro America. (United Nations Observer Group in Central America.) Ribbon light blue with dark blue edges and nine thin central stripes of green and white.
UNTAG - United Nations Transitional Assistance Group. For service in Namibia in 1990. Ribbon sand with pale blue edges and thin central stripes of black, yellow, red, green and dark blue.
ONUSAL - Observadores de las Naciones Unidas en El Salvador. (United Nations Group of Observers in El Salvador.) Ribbon UN blue with a white centre bordered by dark blue stripes.
UNIKOM - United Nations Iraq/Kuwait Observation Mission. Ribbon sand with a narrow central UN blue stripe.
MINURSO - Mission des nations unies pour le referendum dans le Saraha Occidental. (United Nations Mission for the Referendum in Western Saraha). Ribbon has a wide central band of sandy brown, representing the Saraha Desert, with two narrow bands of UN blue at either end.
UNIMAC - United Nations Advanced Mission in Cambodia. Ribbon has a white central stripe flanked by dark blue, gold and red stripes representing the Cambodian flags. These are followed on either side by a band of UN blue.
UNTAC - United Nations Transitional Authority in Cambodia. Ribbon green with a central stripe of white flanked by red, UN blue and darker blue.
UNPROFOR - The United Nations Protection Force. Ribbon is UN blue with a central stripe of red, edged white. The blue edge nearest centre chest bears a stripe of green and the other blue edge a stripe of brown. Numerous British troops are currently qualifying for this medal.
UNMIBH - United Nations Mission in Bosnia Herzegovina. Blue ribbon with white central stripe, edged with one green and one red stripe.
UNPREDEP - United Nations Preventative Deployment in Yugoslavia. Blue ribbon with central re stripe bearing four yellow lines and flanked by white edging.
UNTAES - United Nations Transitional Authority in Eastern Slovenia. Pale blue ribbon with yellow, red edged with white, and green stripes.
UNOSOM - United Nations Operation in Somalia. Ribbon yellow buff with a central stripe of UN blue flanked by stripes of dark green.
UNOMIL - United Nations Observer Mission In Liberia. Pale blue ribbon flanked with white stripes with dark blue or red edges.
ONUMOZ - United Nations Operations in Mozambique. Ribbon shows a central wide band of UN blue flanked by two narrow bands of white and two bands of green.
UNOMUR - United Nations Observer Mission in Uganda/Rwanda. Pale blue central stripe edged by white and flanked by equal stripes of black, orange and red.
UNAMIR - United Nations Assistance Mission in Rwanda. Pale blue central stripe edged with white and flanked by equal stripes of black, green and red.
UNOMIG - United Nations Observer Mission in Georgia. Pale blue central stripe flanked by equal stripes of white, green and dark blue.
UNMOT - United Nations Peacekeeping Force in Tadjikistan. Blue ribbon with central green stripe flanked by white stripes.
UNMOP - United Nations Mission of Observers in Pravlaka. Dark blue ribbon with central yellow stripe edged with white and two pale blue stripes.
UNMOGUA - United Nations Military Observers in Guatemala. Purple with central blue stripe and two white stripes each with central green line.
UN Special Service - reward for special service. Blue ribbon with white edges.
General Service Medal for service at U.N. Headquarters, New York. Ribbon plain, UN blue.

Any medal regardless of ribbon	£10

Long Service and Good Conduct Medals and Meritorious Service Medals

At one time or another, almost every uniformed organisation from the armed services to the Women's Royal Voluntary Service has issued a medal to reward long and meritorious service and so this particular series forms a large and most interesting aspect of medal collecting. Medals for meritorious service have been included in this section as, apart from the period 1916-1928, they have almost always been used to reward senior N.C.Os. for exceptionally long service. The order in which medals have been grouped is Royal Navy, Army, Royal Air Force, Indian Army, Colonial, Police, Colonial Police and Miscellaneous. References to obverse types are as below:

GVR 1st/Admiral/Field Marshall. The bust of George V in robes or in the uniform of an Admiral of the Fleet or a Field Marshall.

GVR Coinage. The head only of George V as used on coins. This was introduced in 1931.

GVIR 1st type. Head of George VI including the words "Ind. Imp." in the inscription. In use 1937-48.

GVIR 2nd type. "Ind. Imp." omitted post 1948.

EIIR 1st type. Head of Elizabeth II with the long legend including the inscription "Brit. Omn." used 1953-4.

EIIR 2nd type. Inscription "Brit. Omn." omitted. This version is still current on most medals.

Those collectors with an interest in the series of Naval Long Service awards should not be without a copy of the standard work, *THE NAVAL LONG SERVICE MEDALS* by Capt. K.J. Douglas-Morris, published by the author in 1991. Those concerned more with military awards cannot do better than acquire the ongoing range by John Tamplin in the Spink Medal Booklet series. So far twelve long service medals and decorations have been exhaustively covered and others are in preparation.

183. ROYAL NAVY LONG SERVICE AND GOOD CONDUCT MEDAL

This medal was instituted in 1830, shortly before the institution of the Army LSGC; it is on current issue. Initially, the qualification for the award was 21 years in the ranks of the Royal Navy, but it was later reduced to 10 years in 1874 and extended to 15 years in 1885. Conduct throughout has to be very good. Due to the length of time this award has been on issue, there are eleven discernible types. The William IV issue, the 'anchor type' was smaller than later issues and was pierced for suspension. This issue is found with several different die flaws. The naming is in the centre of the reverse, where the rank, name, ship and number of years served is engraved. This type, of which about 750 were issued, ended in 1841, although a few were still being issued in the late 1840s, presumably to use up stocks. The next type was the QV first issue, which had the 'young head' obverse, and the reverse design which has remained, with a few small die variations, until the present day. This issue was made between 1841 and 1874, and is discernible from later issues by the wider suspender—1½" as against 1¼". About 100 of this type have the date "1848" under the reverse head, whilst some 4000 of the wide suspender type are without this date. These medals are engraved on the rim, usually in block capitals. In 1874 the narrow suspender (1¼") type was introduced. At first (1875-77) these were engraved, and some 4400 were issued. After 1877, the medals were impressed in tall, seriffed capitals. This type, which was issued until 1901, is fairly common, some 18,000 being issued. The EVIIR issue is standard; the GVR (1st) issue is also standard, although it is possible to differentiate between swivelling (early) and non-swivelling (later) types. The final issues are the GVIR first and second types, and the EIIR first and second types. The EIIR second type with fixed suspender is very scarce, being issued 1954-55. During the reign of George VI, clasps were sanctioned for further periods of 15 years' service. This medal is always issued named, and usually has the name of the ship on which the recipient was serving at the time of the award on the rim. The exception to this is the awards to the Royal Marines, which show only 'RMLI' or 'RM'. From the GVR issue onwards, this medal was awarded to Colonial Navies; these awards are exactly the same as the British issue, except for the naming, for example 'RAN' 'RCN' 'RNZN'. The Wm IV issue had a dark blue ribbon, and later issues added a white stripe at each edge. The current qualifying period for this medal is 15 years.

Wm IV (Anchor)	£400
QV (Wide suspender)	£175
QV (Wide suspender) '1848'	£1,000
QV (Narrow suspender - Engraved)	£50
QV (Narrow suspender - Impressed)	£40
EVIIR	£30
GVR (Admiral)	£25
GVR (Coinage)	£28
GVIR (1st)	£28
GVIR (2nd)	£28
EIIR (1st) (Fixed)	£35
EIIR (2nd) (Swivel S)	£25

ROYAL NAVY LONG SERVICE AND GOOD CONDUCT MEDAL *continued*

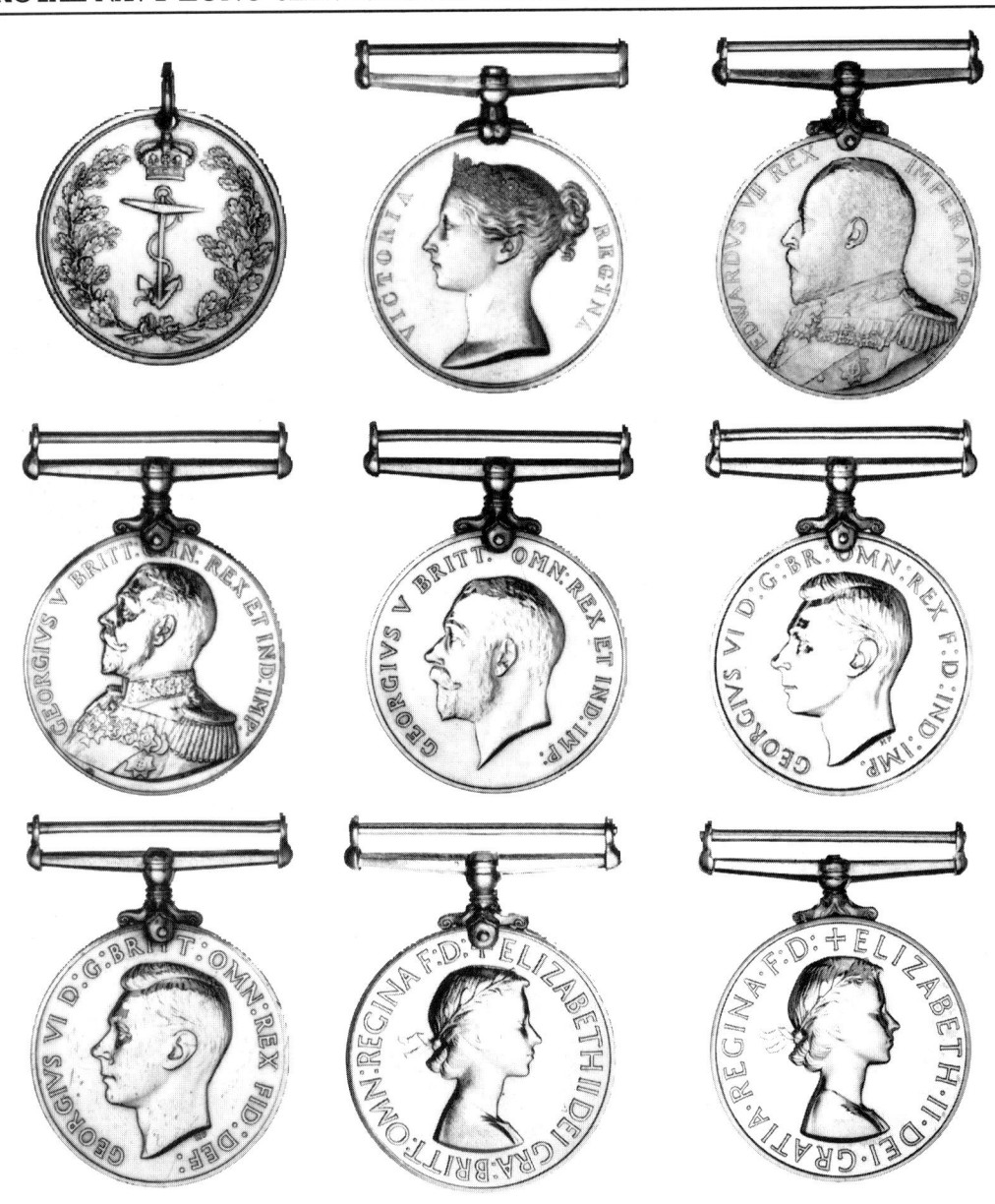

184. ROYAL NAVAL RESERVE DECORATION

This decoration was instituted in 1908, and is currently on issue. It was designed as a naval counterpart to the Volunteer and Territorial Decorations and, like these is awarded only to commissioned officers. The basic qualifying time is 15 years' commissioned service, with the exclusion of service in the rank of Midshipman. Recipients must have completed the required training, and their character and conduct must be consistently good. Wartime service counts double towards the award of the decoration. Bars were awarded for further periods of service; recipients are allowed to put the letters 'RD' after their name. In 1958 the RNVR was merged with the RNR, and the RNR Decoration became the award for all reserve Naval officers, with the exception of the Royal Marines Reserve and Dominion

184. ROYAL NAVAL RESERVE DECORATION *continued*

Navies. The ribbon was originally plain dark green, but in October 1941 a white stripe at each edge was added. The reverse is plain on all issues, although later issues have the date engraved at the foot of the reverse. There are five obverse types, distinguishable by the cipher: EVIIR, GVR, GVIR (1st-GRI), GVIR (2nd-GVIR), and EIIR. This award is similar to the RNVR Decoration.

EVIIR	£100
GVR	£85
GVIR (1st)	£85
GVIR (2nd)	£90
EIIR	£120

185. ROYAL NAVAL RESERVE LONG SERVICE AND GOOD CONDUCT MEDAL

This medal was instituted in 1908, and continues today with certain modifications. It was introduced to reward men of the Royal Naval Reserve who had served for 15 years, with good conduct and a high standard of training. Bars were sanctioned for a further period of 15 years' service after the award of the medal. War service counted double towards the award of the medal. The medal was issued to colonial Naval Reserves, although these are rarely found. The only discernible difference between British and Dominion issues is the naming—for example, 'RCNR' or 'RANR'. These medals are always named in impressed capitals, the earlier issues having large type and the later issues the smaller type. The ribbon was plain green until 1941, when three white stripes were added, one in the centre and one at each edge. With the introduction of a unified Reserve in 1958, a new ribbon of five equal stripes of blue, white, green, white blue was taken into use. There is one reverse type common to all issues, and there are seven obverse types; EVIIR, GVR (Admiral), GVR (Admiral), GVR (Coinage), GVIR (1st), GVIR (2nd), EIIR (1st), EIIR (2nd).

EVIIR	£20
GVR (Admiral)	£15
GVR (Coinage)	£20
GVIR (1st)	£16
GVIR (2nd)	£25
EIIR (1st)	£45
EIIR (2nd)	£40

186. ROYAL NAVAL VOLUNTEER RESERVE DECORATION

This decoration was instituted in 1908, and was issued until May 1966. On this latter date, the decoration was superseded by the RNR decoration, following the merger of the RNR and RNVR on 1st November 1958. Some awards were made after 1966 to officers of the Royal Marines Reserve and Dominion Navies. The basic qualifying period of service for the award was 20 years' commissioned service in the Royal Naval Volunteer Reserve. Service did not necessarily have to be continuous, but service below the age of 17 years was not allowed to count. Service in the ranks of the RNVR counted half, whilst war service was counted double. Service in the RNR or the auxiliary elements of the other service was allowed to count towards the award of the decoration. Recipients were allowed to put the letters 'VRD' after their name. If a recipient had served in the ranks and had received the RNVR Long Service Medal, he was allowed to possess and wear both awards. The decoration is issued unnamed, although they are sometimes found privately engraved by the recipient; EVIIR issues are hallmarked, and later issues often have the date of award engraved on the reverse. Before 1919, the ribbon was plain green, but since that date it has been navy blue with a green centre stripe flanked by two narrowed stripes. The plain reverse is common to all issues, although there are five obverse issues; EVIIR, GVR, GVIR (1st-GRI), GVIR (2nd-GVIR), and EIIR. This award is similar to the RNR Decoration.

EVIIR	£100
GVR	£85
GVIR (1st)	£85
GVIR (2nd)	£90
EIIR	£120

187. ROYAL NAVAL VOLUNTEER RESERVE LONG SERVICE AND GOOD CONDUCT MEDAL

This award was instituted in 1908, and was issued until 1958, when the RNVR merged with the RNR. It was awarded to ratings of the Royal Naval Volunteer Reserve who had completed 12 years' service, and who had completed the necessary training; conduct throughout had to be very good. War service was allowed to count double towards the award of the medal. The medal itself is very similar to the RNR LSGC, the main differences being in the naming and in the ribbon. The medals are named in impressed capitals, and often the Division of the RNVR in which the recipient served is given. Awards to Dominion Navies were issued from the GVIR type onwards, being recognisable by the naming, for example 'RCNVR' 'RANVR'. These Dominion issues are very scarce. Clasps were sanctioned for further periods of 12 years' service. The ribbon has a broad green central stripe, with a thin red stripe on each side. There is a blue stripe at each edge. There is one reverse type common to all issues. There are six obverse types; EVIIR, GVR (Admirals' Bust), GVR (Coinage), GVIR (1st), GVIR (2nd), and EIIR.

EVIIR	Rare
GVR (Admiral)	£50
GVR (Coinage)	£60
GVIR (1st)	£50
GVIR (2nd)	£60
EIIR (2nd)	£75

188. ROYAL FLEET RESERVE LONG SERVICE AND GOOD CONDUCT MEDAL

This medal was instituted during the reign of George V and has been on issue to the reign of Elizabeth II. Recipients of this award had to serve for 15 years in the Royal Fleet Reserve, and their conduct, character and standard of training and attendance has to be very good. Service in the Royal Navy counted towards the award of the medal, but those already in possession of the RN LSGC were not eligible for this medal. Bars were sanctioned for a further period of 15 years' service. The medal is generally similar to the RNR LSGC, but is immediately discernible from it by the ring suspension, and on closer examination by the naming. Whilst the earlier issues of this medal are common, latter issues are scarce; awards to the members of the Royal Marines Reserve are also scarce. The medals are always issued named in impressed capitals, and the lettering often appears to be widely-spaced. The ribbon is of a wide blue centre stripe, flanked by narrow red stripes, and with white stripes at the edge. There is one reverse design common to all types. There are, however, six obverse types: GVR (Admiral), GVR (Coinage), GVIR (1st), GVIR (2nd), EIIR (1st), and EIIR (2nd).

GVR (Admiral)	£20
GVR (Coinage)	£20
GVIR (1st)	£25
GVIR (2nd)	£30
EIIR (1st)	£60
EIIR (2nd)	£40

189. ROYAL NAVAL AUXILIARY SICK BERTH RESERVE LONG SERVICE AND GOOD CONDUCT MEDAL

This medal was instituted in 1919, and was issued until the disbandment of the RNASBR in 1949. There were three issues—GVR, GVR (Coinage) and GVIR. The award is similar to the Royal Naval Reserve LSGC in every respect, except for differences in the naming. These differences are, firstly, the rank (for example 'SBA' or 'LSBA'), and secondly the letters 'RNASBR' instead of 'RNR'. The Sick Berth Reserve originated in 1901, when the Medical Director of the Navy asked the Commissioner of the St John Ambulance Brigade to form a reserve of Sick Berth personnel which could be mobilised in the event of war to provide ancillary medical services for the Fleet. The Commissioner agreed, and the RNASBR dates from 1903. As most RNASBR personnel were from the St. John organisation, this medal is often found with awards of the Order of St. John. The medal was awarded by the Navy (and not by the Order of St. John as has been stated), although the presentations were made by the St. John Commissioner. The first issues were made in 1919. Approximately 1500 of these medals were awarded, about 780 being awarded before 1939, and about 715 between 1939 and 1949. The medals are usually named in a similar style to the RNR LSGC, that is, impressed in small capitals. Until 1941, the ribbon was plain green, but after that date a central white stripe and white edges were added. The reverse of the medal is common throughout. The three obverse types are: GVR (Admiral), GVR (Coinage), GVIR.

GVR (Admiral)	£90
GVR (Coinage)	£100
GVIR	£90

190. ROYAL NAVAL WIRELESS AUXILIARY RESERVE LONG SERVICE AND GOOD CONDUCT MEDAL

This medal, instituted in 1939, was issued until 1957, when the RNWAR was disbanded. It is similar in most respects to the RNR, RNVR and RFR long service awards mentioned elsewhere, the only difference being in the naming, with 'RNWAR' on the rim. The award was made to members of the RNWAR for 12 years service, with good conduct and high standards of training. Bars could be awarded for further periods of 12 years. Service in the RNVR was allowed to count towards the award of the medal. The medal is very scarce on the market, only about 200 being issued up to 1949. The ribbon is of a wide green stripe in the centre, with a narrow red stripe on each side, and blue edges. The reverse of this medal is constant throughout.

GVIR (1st)	£250
EIIR	£250

191. ROYAL NAVAL AUXILIARY SERVICE LONG SERVICE MEDAL

Instituted in 1965 for award to members of the Royal Naval Auxiliary Service (RNXS), formerly the Royal Naval Minewatching Service, for 12 years satisfactory service, whether full or part-time. A clasp is available for an additional 12 years service. Broken service, if spent with the armed services, is permitted and service with the old Minewatching Service from 1952 was allowed to count.

Issued in cupro-nickel, the obverse has the crowned head of the Queen and the reverse shows a slightly tilted fouled anchor with crown above surrounded by a wreath. Around all is the inscription 'Royal Naval Auxiliary Service Long Service'. The suspender is straight and the ribbon is the same as the Naval Long Service, but with a thin green stripe through each colour. Naming is in impressed capitals showing initials and name only. Women, however, have the prefix Miss or Mrs.

EIIR	£100

192. THE BOARD OF TRADE ROCKET APPARATUS VOLUNTEER LONG SERVICE MEDAL
THE COAST LIFE SAVING CORPS LONG SERVICE MEDAL
THE COAST GUARD AUXILIARY SERVICE LONG SERVICE MEDAL

These three titles cover what is basically one medal, but reflects the changes in the name of the organisation throughout the years and a slight widening of eligibility. Instituted in 1911 and still being awarded, the basic requirement for qualification is 20 years service with the Rocket Apparatus, now the Coastguard Auxiliary, during which conduct had to be continuously good. The recipient must have been prompt at all times when called out for duty and have attended all drills and training.

The obverse of the medals bears the head of the reigning monarch with the words 'Instituted 1911' below the bust; the reverse bears one of four different inscriptions, but all have space for the name to be engraved in the centre. The ribbon is watered azure with broad scarlet edges. There may be five obverse types, of which only those priced below have been noted: George V coinage, George VI 1st and 2nd and Elizabeth II 1st and 2nd. There are four reverse types. From 1911 to 1942 the inscription was 'Presented by the Board of Trade to ……… For Long Service with the Rocket Life Saving Apparatus' and from 1942 to 1954 it read 'Rocket Apparatus Volunteer Medal Presented to ……… For Long Service'. Between 1954 and 1966 the title was changed to 'The Coast Life Saving Corps' and the current version from 1966 reads 'The Coastguard Auxiliary Service'.

GVR	£45
GVIR 1st type, BoT Reverse	£80
GVIR 1st type, Rocket App. Reverse	£80
GVIR 2nd type, Rocket App. Reverse	Rare
EIIR 1st type, Coast Life Saving	Not known
EIIR 2nd type, Coast Life Saving	£90
EIIR 2nd type, Coastguard Auxiliary	£90

193. ROYAL NAVAL DOCKYARD POLICE (HONG KONG) LONG SERVICE MEDAL

Instituted in 1921 for award to the Dockyard Police, subject to a character rating of 'Very Good' on completion of 15 years service. The award of the medal carried additional monetary allowances. The Dockyard was closed in 1961, but those men who transferred to work elsewhere under their previous conditions of service continued to be awarded the medal, the last qualifying in 1973. There is a partial roll of recipients in Douglas-Morris. Approximately 280 medals were issued.

The obverse of this bronze medal shows the head of the reigning monarch, and it is believed that the obverse die of the Board of Trade Sea Gallantry Medal was used for the purpose. The reverse has the inscription 'Royal Naval Dockyard Police Hong Kong'. Suspension is by a ring and the ribbon is golden yellow with two centrally placed stripes of royal blue. The recipient's details are engraved on the edge.

There are believed to be four obverse types of this medal: GVR Coinage, GVIR 1st and 2nd and EIIR. As the last batch of these medals was minted in 1955, it is thought that the EIIR version is the 1st type.

GVR Coinage	£250
GVIR 1st type	£200
GVIR 2nd type	£250
EIIR	£250

194. MERITORIOUS SERVICE MEDAL (ROYAL NAVY)

This medal was instituted in 1919, and was effective until 1928, when it was replaced by the British Empire Medal for Gallantry or Meritorious Service. It was awarded to non-commissioned officers and men of the Royal Navy or Royal Marines for arduous or specially meritorious service, or for an act of gallantry performed whilst not in the presence of the enemy. There was only one issue of this medal—the GVR 'Admiral of the Fleet' type obverse. It can be recognised by the large epaulettes on the King's uniform. The naming is by large capitals with serifs, the style being dissimilar to that on Army MSMs. All awards are listed in the London Gazette, and awards are found therein from 1919 to 1923. A list of recipients is given in the Navy List 1919-20, but the practice was discontinued thereafter. Just over 1000 of these medals were issued including 175 to Royal Marine recipients. The ribbon is similar to the Army MSM—red, with three white stripes. The Royal Navy MSM was reintroduced on 1st September 1977. The qualifications for the award of this new medal are 27 years service, with special emphasis on a very high standard of character and service. To maintain high standards, only a limited number of awards can be made each year. Recipients must be of the rate of Petty Officer or above. The medal and ribbon are similar to the current Army MSM, and the only discernible difference is in the naming. Due to the limited numbers awarded so far, this medal is very rare on the market, and will continue to be most scarce. There is a complete list of recipients in *The Meritorious Service Medal to Naval Forces* by Ian McInnes.

GVR (Admiral)	£200
EIIR (2nd)	£300

195. ARMY LONG SERVICE AND GOOD CONDUCT MEDAL

This medal was authorised by Army Circular 685 of 1830 and was issued until replaced with the Military Long Service and Good Conduct Medal in 1930. It was the first officially issued medal to recognise long service, the basic requirement being 21 years service in the ranks, from 1870 reduced to 18 years, with a high standard of conduct. Due to the length of time the medal has been on issue, there are seven different issues. The first type of William IV, issued only during 1830-31, showed the Hanoverian arms on the obverse and the words 'For Long Service and Good Conduct' on the reverse in large letters with a small ring and steel clip suspender. From 1831-37 this was altered to a large ring or rectangular suspender. Queen Victoria's first issue (1837-55) was similar but the arms no longer showed the centre shield bearing the white horse of Hanover. Her second type, issued from 1855 to 1874 introduced the well-known scroll suspender and the lettering on the reverse was smaller. The last type (1874-1901) was similar. The issues of Edward VII and George V show the head of the King on the obverse while retaining the same reverse and suspension.

The William IV medals were impressed with the same machine used to name the Waterloo Medals and they are dated on the rim, as are some very early Victorian issues. The 1855 issue is named in the same style as the Military General Service Medal and some Crimea medals. The 1874-1901 series generally has impressed naming a particularly scarce type being those engraved in running script to Europeans serving in the Indian Army. Since 1901, the vast majority of medals are named in small impressed capitals of various types. The first ribbon was plain maroon but, in 1916, narrow edges of white were added.

William IV 1830-31	£400
William IV 1831-37	£380
Victoria 1837-55	£100
Victoria 1855-74	£85
Victoria 1874-1901	£50
Edward VII	£30
George V	£25

195a. LONG SERVICE AND GOOD CONDUCT MEDAL (Military)

The Long Service and Good Conduct Medal (Military) was introduced in 1930 to replace the old Army medal and standardise the award for use by all the regular forces of the Empire. Thus, it also replaced the Permanent Forces of the Empire Beyond the Seas LSGC at the same time. Though the traditional wording was retained on the reverse and the monarch's head on the obverse, the suspender was redesigned to incorporate a rectangular bar upon which appeared the title of the force or area. British issues have the words "Regular Army" on this bar but many others are met with including Australia, Canada and India. The time qualification remained at 18 years until 1977 when all three armed forces were brought into line at 15 years. Rectangular sew-on bars bearing the Royal Crest are available for award to those completing a further period of 18 or 15 years. During the 1939-45 War, due to a large number of men being commissioned from the ranks, the award of the medal was extended to officers, provided that they had served a minimum of 12 years in the ranks. There is only one reverse type of this medal but five obverse types: GVR, GVI 1st type, GVIR second type and EIIR 1st and 2nd types. The ribbon remained as established with the earlier medal, maroon with white edges. In the table below, the value given for a Commonwealth bar is that of the commoner issues.

195a. LONG SERVICE AND GOOD CONDUCT MEDAL (Military) *continued*

GVR Regular Army	£25
GVR Commonwealth Bar	£85
GVIR 1st type Regular Army	£20
GVIR 1st type Commonwealth Bar	£85
GVIR 2nd type Regular Army	£25
GVIR 2nd type Commonwealth Bar	£85
EIIR 1st type Regular Army	£35
EIIR 1st type Commonwealth Bar	£100
EIIR 2nd type Regular Army	£20
EIIR 2nd type Commonwealth Bar	£90

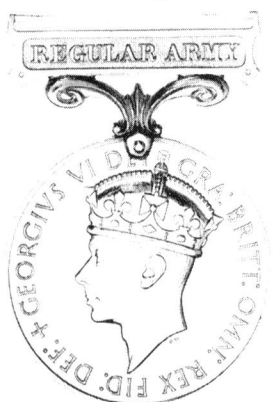

196. THE MEDAL FOR LONG SERVICE AND GOOD CONDUCT (ULSTER DEFENCE REGIMENT)

Instituted in 1982 as a separate medal, this is really a variation of the standard Military Long Service and Good Conduct Medal with top bar "U.D.R.". It is awarded upon the recommendation of a senior officer to soldiers of the Permanent Cadre of the Ulster Defence regiment for 15 years service after 1 April 1970, provided that character and conduct have been irreproachable. A clasp is available for a further period of 15 years service. It is also awarded to officers of the permanent cadre, provided that at least 12 years of their 15 years service has been in the ranks.

Of silver, the medal bears on the obverse the crowned head of the Queen with usual legend and the obverse is the same as the standard medal. The ribbon is also the standard Military Long Service and Good Conduct, but with an added stripe of green in the centre.

In view of recent announcements, it is possible that changes will have to be made to this medal.

Other Ranks	£100

197. VOLUNTEER OFFICERS DECORATION

This decoration was instituted by Royal Warrant on 25th July 1892. It was issued until 1908, when it was superseded by the Territorial Decoration in the United Kingdom. The revolutionary design of the VD was due to the desire of the War Office to make it immediately discernible from a campaign award. The ribbon, of plain green, set a precedent which has remained up to date, that of green being the predominant colour in most volunteer medal ribbons. recipients of the VD could not wear the Volunteer LSGC Medal as well, although they were permitted to possess both. The qualifications for this award were that the recipient should have served in the Volunteer Force as a commissioned officer for 20 years, and that this service had been 'efficient and capable'. Awards were listed in the London Gazette, and could be forfeited by detrimental conduct. Service in the ranks was counted half towards the award. In 1894, Volunteer Officers in India and the Colonies were allowed to receive the award under the same conditions as in the United Kingdom, except that the qualifying period was 18 years in India. Those awards to UK recipients have the cipher 'V.R.', whilst overseas awards have the cipher 'V.R.I.'. The VD is incomplete without the top suspension bar which was issued with the piece. recipients were allowed to put the letters 'VD' after their name. Although the VD was issued unnamed, many recipients had their names, and sometimes other details, engraved on the reverse. There is almost always a hallmark on the reverse, as the VD was often made by contractors, and not by the Royal Mint. There are three issues of this award: the two VR types mentioned above, and the EVIIR Type. For a comprehensive account of this award, see '*The Volunteer Officers Decoration*' by J.M.A. Tamplin.

VR (U.K.)	£55
VRI (Overseas)	£225
EVIIR	£75

198. VOLUNTEER FORCE LONG SERVICE AND GOOD CONDUCT MEDAL

This medal was instituted in 1894, and was issued until 1908, when it was replaced by the Territorial Force Efficiency Medal in the United Kingdom. Only the Indian Auxiliary Forces continued to use the medal, and this stopped in 1930. Thus almost all GVR issues of this medal are to Indian Volunteers. The basic qualification for the award of this medal was 20 years' service in the Volunteer Forces of Britain, India and the Colonies. The character and conduct of the recipient had to be uniformly good. Although usually found named to other ranks, this medal is sometimes found named to officers who had spent a portion of their service in the ranks. No bars were issued to the medal for further service. The QV issues are sometimes found named, but most are not named. The EVIIR issues are almost always named, usually in impressed capitals, although some, particularly those to officers, are found with engraved naming. The QV issue has two obverse types: the 'Victoria Regina' legend was issued to troops in the United Kingdom, whilst the 'Victoria Regina et Imperatrix' type was issued to troops in India and the Colonies. The EVIIR issue has two types also: the 'Rex Imperator' legend is found on medals issued to British troops, whilst the 'Kaisar-I-Hind' type was issued to volunteers in India. The GVR issue is found in only one type, and is almost always named to Indian volunteers, although a few awards were made to the 7th (Isle of Man) Battalion of the Liverpool Regiment, which remained in the Volunteer Force after 1908. The ribbon for all issues is plain green, although the Honourable Artillery Company was allowed to wear a ribbon similar to the racing colours of Edward VII—half scarlet, half dark blue, with bright yellow edges. The reverse type is common throughout, and there are five obverse issues: QV 'Regina'; QV 'et Imperatrix'; EVIIR 'Kaisar-I-Hind'; EVIIR 'Imperator'; GVR.

There is a detailed study of this medal in *The Volunteer Long Service Medal* by J.M.A. Tamplin.

QV (GB)	£35
QV (India & Colonies)	£50
EVIIR	£50
EVIIR (India)	£40
EVIIR (Colonies)	£70
GVR (India)	£30

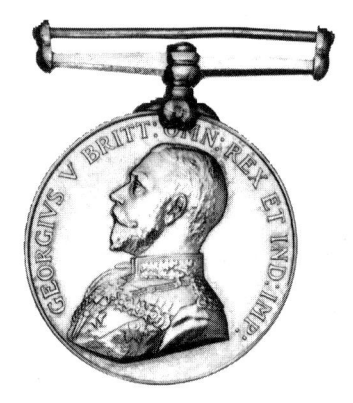

199. TERRITORIAL DECORATION

This award was instituted by a Royal Warrant on 29th September 1908, and replaced the Volunteer Officers Decoration in the United Kingdom, the Volunteer Force being replaced by the Territorial Force in 1908. It was issued until 1930, when it was replaced by the Efficiency Decoration with bar-brooch 'Territorial'. The basic qualification for the award of the decoration was 20 years' service in the Territorial Force as a commissioned officer. Service by officers in the Yeomanry was allowed to count towards the award. Recipients had to be recommended by their commanding officer as being efficient, capable and worthy of the award. Service in the ranks could only count half towards the award. Awards were notified in the London Gazette. Those awarded the decoration were allowed to put the letters 'TD' after their name. These awards are often found unnamed, but sometimes the recipient has had his details of service engraved on the reverse. There is almost always a hallmark on the reverse. The ribbon was green with a central yellow stripe. The reverse is common to all issues, but there are two obverse types: EVIIR, and GVR. There is a detailed study of this decoration in *The Territorial Decoration 1908-1930* by J.M.A. Tamplin.

EVIIR	£85
GVR	£50

200. TERRITORIAL FORCE EFFICIENCY MEDAL

This medal was instituted in 1908, on the setting up of the Territorial Force. It replaced the Volunteer LS Medal in the UK. The basic qualifications for award were that the recipient had to serve for 12 years, with consistent good conduct, and had to attend the required camps and trainings. The medal was replaced in 1930 by the Efficiency Medal with suspender 'Territorial'. The medal was named in impressed lettering only. In 1920, there were two major changes to the medal due to the change of title from Territorial Force to Territorial Army. Firstly, the reverse inscription was changed, and secondly the ribbon was altered. Until 1920 the ribbon was green with a central yellow stripe; after 1920 the ribbon was green with yellow stripes at each edge. Until 1920, the reverse inscription read 'Territorial Force Efficiency Medal'; whilst after 1920 it read 'Territorial Efficiency Medal'. There were two reverse types, as mentioned above; and two obverse types; EVIIR and GVR. There is a detailed study of this medal in *The Territorial Force Efficiency Medal 1908-1921* and *The Territorial Efficiency Medal 1922-1930* by J.M.A. Tamplin in the Spink Medal Booklet Series.

EVIIR	£65
GVR ('TFEM')	£40
GVR ('TEM')	£30

201. EFFICIENCY DECORATION

This decoration was awarded from 1930 onwards, it being instituted on 17th October 1930, when a Royal Warrant appeared in the London Gazette. The basic qualification for receiving the decoration was 20 years' continuous commissioned service by officers of the territorial and auxiliary forces of Britain and the Commonwealth reduced to 12 years after 1949. Recipients had to have consistently high standards of conduct and training. Service in the ranks was allowed to count towards the award, although it counted half. In addition, and of great relevance to this award bearing in mind that the Great War was in the period covered, war service counted double. The decoration was instituted to standardise the method of rewarding reserve officers, and replaced the Territorial Decoration in the United Kingdom, the Colonial Auxiliary Forces Decoration in the Colonies, and the Volunteer Decoration in India. Although the decoration itself was standard, there was still a differentiation between the awards to British, Colonial and Indian officers by means of various 'bar-brooches', that is a bar from which the

201. EFFICIENCY DECORATION *continued*

ribbon and decoration hung. This was inscribed with the name of the Dominion or Colony in which the recipient served, for example, 'Canada', 'Australia', 'India'. Those awarded to officers in the UK had the bar-brooch 'Territorial'. Service by officers which had counted towards the decorations replaced in 1930 was not allowed to count towards the Efficiency Decoration. Recipients were allowed to put 'TD' after their name in the UK, whilst those in the Dominions put 'ED' after their name. The decoration was issued unnamed in the UK though it is often found with the recipient's details engraved on the reverse. Later issues have the date of award engraved on the reverse. Clasps were issued for further periods of 6 years' service, and here again clasps issued from the 1940s onwards have the date of issue engraved on the reverse. The recipient had to be nominated by his commanding officer for the award, and lists of awards appear in the London Gazettes. The ribbon, common to all issues, is green with a central yellow stripe. The reverse is common to all issues, and is plain. On the setting up of the Territorial and Army Volunteer Reserve, the Efficiency Decoration has had the bar-brooch. 'T&AVR'; this has a ribbon half dark-blue and half green, with a central yellow stripe. Since 1982 the bar-brooch has reverted to 'Territorial' but the ribbon remains unchanged. There is a detailed study of this decoration in *The Efficiency Decoration, instituted 1930*, by J.M.A. Tamplin.

GVR 'Territorial'	£60
GVIR (1st) 'Territorial'	£50
GVIR (2nd) 'Territorial'	£55
EIIR 'Territorial'	£55
EIIR 'T&AVR'	£120
GVR 'India'	£85
GVIR (1st) 'India'	£75
With Colonial/Dominion Bar	from £150

201a. ARMY EMERGENCY RESERVE DECORATION

Instituted by Royal Warrant on 17th November 1952, the first issues of this new award were made in November 1953. It is really a variation of the Efficiency Decoration and was awarded to officers of the Emergency Reserve on the same terms, 12 years efficient commissioned service. Bars, of similar pattern to those of the Efficiency Decoration are available for further periods of six years service. Active service counts double and non-commissioned service counts half. Recipients may use the post-nominal letters ERD. The piece itself is identical to the Efficiency Decoration but it has a top suspender bar bearing the title "Army Emergency Reserve" and is worn from a ribbon of blue with a central yellow stripe. There is only one obverse to this ward, the EIIR. The Army Emergency reserve was abolished in 1967.

There is a detailed study of this decoration in *The Army Emergency Reserve Decoration and the Efficiency Medal (Army Emergency Reserve)* by J.M.A. Tamplin.

EIIR	£120

202. EFFICIENCY MEDAL

This medal was instituted by Royal Warrant on 17th October 1930. It was introduced to standardise awards to territorial and auxiliary forces throughout Britain, the Dominions and the Colonies. It superseded the Volunteer LSGC in India, the Colonial Auxiliary Forces LSGC in the Colonies, and in Britain replaced three medals – The Territorial Efficiency Medal, the Militia LSGC and the Special Reserve LSGC. This medal, which was in the oval form of previous awards, had a suspension bar on which was inscribed the country in which the recipient served, for example 'India', 'Canada', 'Australia'. Over 30 of these 'Colonial' inscriptions are known. In Britain, the usual bar was 'Territorial', although some were issued with the inscription 'Militia'. Naming was almost always in block capitals, and, particularly in some GVIR and EIIR issues, appears uneven and crude. The basic qualification for the award of this medal was that the recipient should be either in the Territorial Army, Militia, or the Colonial Auxiliary Military Forces; he, (or after the formation of the Auxiliary Territorial Service, she), had to serve 12 years with continual good conduct, and had to be recommended as deserving by the appropriate commanding officer. War service, and service in West Africa, counted double towards the award of the medal. In all but exceptional cases, service had to be continuous. Service in the Royal Navy and Royal Air Force was allowed to count. These medals are found named to officers, particularly GVIR issues due to the number of other ranks granted commissions in the Second World War; these men had started the service required in the ranks, but were commissioned before receiving the medal. Most issues of this medal are fairly common, for example some 11000 were issued with a 'Canada' suspension bar. The EIIR varieties are scarce, and some of the colonial issues are very rare indeed. The ribbon is green with yellow edges. The reverse design is common throughout, but there are five obverse types. GVR (Robes), GVIR first and second types, and EIIR first and second types. These medals are often found with clasps, which were awarded for a further period of six years' service. On the setting up of the Territorial and Army Volunteer reserve in the late 1960s, the 'Territorial' bar has been replaced by the bar 'T&AVR', and the ribbon for the T&AVR variant is half-blue, half-green, with a yellow stripe at each edge. In 1982, the suspension bar titled reverted to 'Territorial' but the new colours were retained for the ribbon.

There is a detailed study of this award in *The Efficiency Medal, Instituted 1930* by J.M.A. Tamplin.

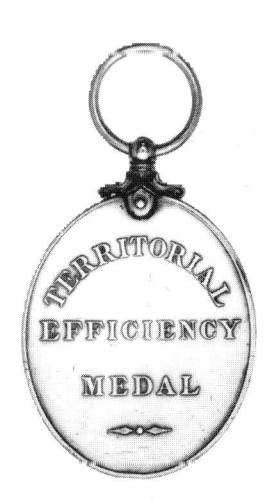

GVR (Robes) 'Territorial'	£20
GVIR (1st) 'Territorial'	£15
GVIR (2nd) 'Territorial'	£20
EIIR (1st) 'Territorial'	£35
EIIR (2nd) 'Territorial'	£28
GVR (Robes) 'Militia'	£40
GVIR (1st) 'Militia'	£40
GVIR (2nd) 'Militia'	£40
EIIR (2nd) 'T&AVR'	£75
GVR (Robes) 'India'	£35
GVIR (1st) 'India'	£80
With Colonial/Dominion Bar	from £150

202. EFFICIENCY MEDAL *continued*

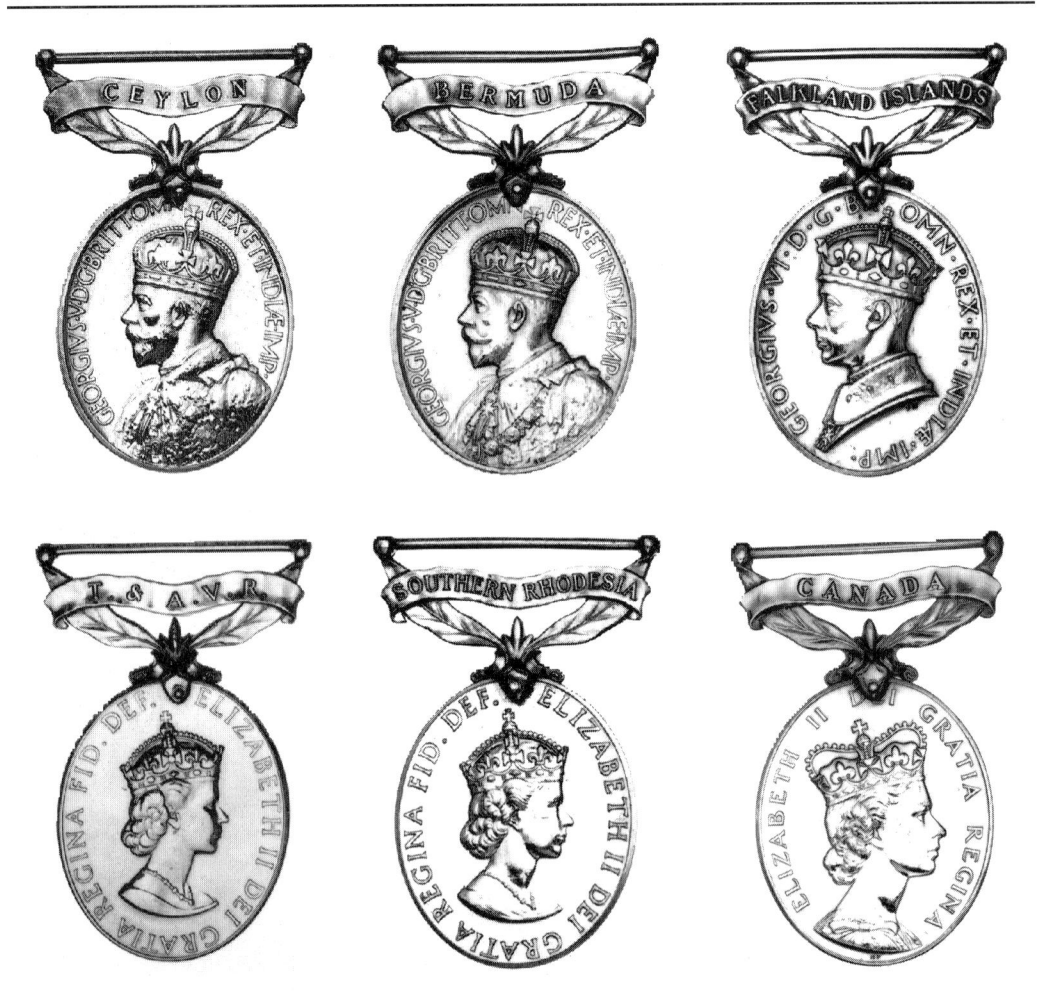

202a. THE EFFICIENCY MEDAL (ARMY EMERGENCY RESERVE)

Instituted by Royal Warrant dated 1st September 1953, the first awards of this decoration were not made until October 1955. It is really a variation of the Efficiency Medal and was awarded to non-commissioned officers and men of the Emergency Reserve on the same basis, 12 years efficient service. Bars of similar pattern to those of the Efficiency Medal are available for further periods of 6 years service. War service counted double. The award is identical to the Efficiency Medal but with the suspension bar title 'Army Emergency Reserve' worn from a ribbon of blue with three central stripes of yellow. There is only one obverse to this award, the EIIR second type. The Army Emergency reserve was abolished in 1967.

There is a detailed study of this medal in the *Army Emergency Reserve Decoration and the Efficiency Medal (Army Emergency Reserve)* by J.M.A. Tamplin.

EIIR 2nd Type	£150

Long Service and Good Conduct Medals

203. THE ULSTER DEFENCE REGIMENT MEDAL

Introduced, like its full-time counterpart, in 1982, this medal is the Ulster equivalent of the Efficiency Medal. It is awarded to all part time officers and soldiers of the Ulster Defence Regiment upon completion of 12 years continuous efficient service after 1st April 1970. A clasp is available for further periods of service of 6 years. Officers awarded this medal may use the post-nominal letters U.D.

Of silver and, unlike the Efficiency Medal, circular in appearance, the obverse bears the crowned effigy of the Queen with usual legend and the reverse shows the badge of the U.D.R. with surrounding legend 'Ulster Defence Regiment'. The suspender is the same type as used on the Efficiency Medal and the scroll bears the initial U.D.R.

The ribbon is green with a central gold stripe edged on either side by a narrow red stripe.

Officers	£100
Other Ranks	£75

204. IMPERIAL YEOMANRY LONG SERVICE AND GOOD CONDUCT MEDAL

This medal was instituted in Army Order No 211 of December 1904. It was the first long service award to be awarded exclusively to the Yeomanry, and indeed was the only such. Those qualifying for this medal were NCOs and men of the Imperial Yeomanry who had completed 10 years' service and ten 'trainings', or annual camps; their conduct had to be exemplary. The award was terminated in 1908, when the Yeomanry became part of the Territorial Force, the Yeomanry receiving the Territorial Force Efficiency Medal from this date. There was therefore only one issue of this medal – that with the bust of Edward VII. The medal is always named, almost always in sans-serif capitals, giving details of the number, rank, initials, surname and regiment of the recipient. Previous service in the Regular Army was not allowed to count towards the qualifying period, but service in other territorial or auxiliary forces could be counted, provided that the five years immediately preceding the award of the medal were served in the Yeomanry. Recommendations for the medal came via Commanding Officers, and lists of medals awarded were published in Army Orders. Some 1674 awards were made to over 50 different Yeomanry regiments. A complete account of the medal and a complete roll of recipients appears in *The Imperial Yeomanry LSGC Medal* by J.M.A. Tamplin (Spink, 1978). The ribbon is plain yellow.

EVIIR	£175

205. MILITIA LONG SERVICE AND GOOD CONDUCT MEDAL

This medal was instituted in Army Order 211 of December 1904, and was issued until 1930, when it was replaced by the Efficiency Medal with bar 'Militia'. It was awarded to NCOs and men of the Militia who had served for 18 years, not necessarily without a break, and who had attended at least 15 annual trainings. The recipient's character and conduct had to be very good. There were two obverse types of the medal - EVIIR and GVR - but only one common reverse. Naming was in impressed sans-serif capitals with the number, rank, initials, surname and regiment of the recipient. Service with the Regular Army was not allowed to count towards the award of the medal, but service with other territorial and auxiliary forces could count, provided that the last five years of the qualifying period were spent in the Militia. Breaks of service of less than twelve months were allowed. Recipients had to be recommended by their commanding officers, and lists of those recommended were forwarded to the War Office every three months. Lists of awards were then published in Army Orders. This medal was awarded between 1904 and 1930, and a total of 1587 were awarded. The vast majority were of the EVIIR issue, only about 140 being issued with the GVR obverse. There are some 200 different units shown on the roll. A full list of recipients appears in *The Militia LSGC Medal* by J.M.A. Tamplin.

EVIIR	£100
GVR	£200

206. SPECIAL RESERVE LONG SERVICE AND GOOD CONDUCT MEDAL

This award was instituted in Army Order 126 of June 1908; it was awarded to NCOs and men of the Special Reserve who completed 15 years' service and attended 15 or more trainings. Recipients had to have continual good conduct. There were two issues of the medal - EVIIR and GVR obverse, although there was a common reverse. Naming was by impressed sans-serif capitals with number, rank, initials, surname and regiment. Service with the Regular Army was not allowed to count towards the award of the medal, but service with any territorial and auxiliary forces could count, provided that the last five years of the qualifying period were spent in the Special Reserve. This medal was also awarded to the Irish Yeomanry (North and South Irish Horse) who had completed 10 years' service and 10 trainings. No recipient was allowed to have this medal and the Territorial Force Efficiency Medal. Recommendations were to come from commanding officers, and were forwarded to the War Office every three months. All recipients were listed in Army Orders. Awards were made between 1908 and 1936, with one late award each in 1947 and 1953. In all, some 1078 medals were awarded to over 100 different units. A full list of recipients appears in '*The Special Reserve LSGC*' by J.M.A. Tamplin. The ribbon is of dark blue, with a central light blue stripe.

EVIIR	£125
GVR	£140

Long Service and Good Conduct Medals

207. MERITORIOUS SERVICE MEDAL

This medal was instituted in 1845, and is still on current issue. It is a most unusual and complicated award, with different types and reasons for award. It is necessary first to explain the setting up of the award. By a Royal Warrant of 19th December 1845, a sum of £2000 was provided each year to be given to NCOs of the rank of Sergeant and above in the form of annuities, to be paid for life. Recipients of these annuities were either serving or retired NCOs. In addition, the annuitants were to receive the Meritorious Service Medal, which was instituted at the same time as the annuity fund. The annuity and medal were to be rewards for 'distinguished or meritorious service'. Because the annuities were paid for life and the sum of money available was limited, it follows that the number of MSMs has always been very limited, especially in the earlier part of its issue. Awards were evenly distributed amongst all regiments and corps, and so early MSMs to any particular regiment are very rare on the market. The sum of money available for annuities has been increased on several occasions since the institution of the award, but the yearly figure for issued MSMs has remained low. As the overriding aspect of this award was financial, awards were listed in Army Estimates from 1847 to 1926, and from 1885 to 1972 lists of recipients were published in Army Orders. The MSM has always been issued as a form of reward for long service to senior NCOs, although there are two exceptions to this statement, one minor and one major. The minor exception is a few early awards which were stated to be for gallantry, whilst the major exception is during the period 1916-28. During this period, MSMs were awarded for services in the field which fell short of the award of the MM or DCM. A very small number were awarded for gallantry not in the face of the enemy. This usage of the MSM ended in 1928 with the introduction of the BEM for Meritorious Service. Thus between 1916 and 1928, two types of MSM were awarded; firstly, the limited regular issue to annuitants for long service, and secondly, the large number of awards for services during the war. These two types can be told apart by the fact that the 'long service' issues have no mention of the recipient's number on the rim, whilst immediate awards for services in the war have the recipient's number. The vast majority of MSMs have been awarded to British Army personnel, but there are some rare Colonial issues known as Canada, Cape of Good Hope, Natal, and the various Australian states. These are similar to the British MSM, except for the name of the Colony or Dominion on the reverse above the normal inscription. Other very rare issues include the QV obverse type with '1848' under the bust, and the MSM issued to the Royal Marines with a similar obverse. The following figures for MSMs issued are approximate: there may be some overlap between consecutive issues. QV (dated 1847 on rim) - 110; QV (1848 in exergue) - 10; QV - 990; EVIIR - 725; GVR (swivel suspender) - 1050; GVR (fixed suspender) - 400; GVR (coinage head) - 550; GVIR (1st) 1090; GVIR (2nd) - 5600; GVIR (crowned head) - 55; EIIR (1st) - 125; EIIR (2nd) - 2750. Between 1916 and 1928 some 25,500 immediate MSMs were awarded, differentiated from the rarer MSMs by having the regimental number included in the naming. The Royal Marine variant is rare, approximate numbers issued being QV (1848 in exergue) - 40; QV - 110; EVIIR - 50; GVR (Field Marshall's bust) - 50; GVR (Admiral's bust) - 75; GVR (coinage head) - 17; GVIR (1st) - 60; GVIR (2nd) - 270. The ribbon was, before 1916, plain purple but after that date had three white stripes, one at each edge and one in the centre. The medal is always named; the QV issue has a variety of styles, although from the EVIIR issue on, most seen are impressed in capitals similar to various contemporary campaign medals. There is one type of reverse common to all issues from 1847 to date, except for the Colonial issues of various types. There are 12 types known:

QV (1847 on rim)	£320
QV (1848 under bust)	£1,500
QV	£150
EVIIR	£120
GVR (Immediate)	£50
GVR (Non-immediate)	£60
GVR (Coinage head)	£125
GVIR (1st)	£60
GVIR (Crowned head)	£800
GVIR (2nd)	£50
EIIR (1st)	£160
EIIR (2nd)	£120

207. MERITORIOUS SERVICE MEDAL *continued*

208. ROYAL AIR FORCE LONG SERVICE AND GOOD CONDUCT MEDAL

This award was instituted by Royal Warrant on 1st July 1919. There are five different obverse types - GVR (coinage head), GVIR first and second types, and EIIR first and second types. The last is on issue currently. The award is made to NCOs and men of the Royal Air Force who have served 18 years or, from 1977 onwards, 15 years and whose conduct has been exemplary. Naming is either impressed or engraved, almost always in block capitals. In 1944 a bar was sanctioned for those who served for a further 18 years or, from 1977, 15 years. Although there are five obverse types, all have a common reverse. The GVR and second EIIR issues have swivelling suspenders, whilst most GVIR and the first EIIR awards have fixed suspenders. Service in the army and navy was generally allowed to count towards the award of the medal, as most early RAF personnel came from one of these services. Provision was also made in 1919 for the award of the medal to personnel who, although not reaching the required standard of conduct, had shown 'exemplary conduct' in action or elsewhere, although this rule was dropped after the Second World War. In 1957 the first medal was issued to the Women's Royal Air Force. These medals are sometimes awarded to officers; to qualify, an officer must have served 18 years (or, from 1977, 15 years), of which 12 years are spent in the ranks; however, officers cannot receive clasps for further service. Air Ministry Orders 1919-41 and 1950-64 contain lists of recipients, though this has not been the practice outside these periods. Although fairly common overall, there are some scarce issues of this medal; there are only 3300 of the GVR types, and between 1950 and 1964 only about 330 clasps were issued. A gratuity of £5 was decreed in 1919 for recipients of this medal, a figure which has remained fixed until recently. The ribbon, unchanged since 1919, is of dark blue and maroon with white edges, and is worn with the blue farthest from the left shoulder.

GVR	£60
GVIR (1st type)	£30
GVIR (2nd type)	£35
EIIR (1st type)	£35
EIIR (2nd type)	£30

209. AIR EFFICIENCY AWARD

This decoration was instituted in September 1942 to reward service in the Auxiliary and Volunteer Air Forces of Britain, India and the Dominions. The basic qualification was 10 years service, provided that enlistment had been before September 1939 or after May 1945. Service commencing during the war did not qualify. Conduct had to be good and all required training satisfactorily completed. The award is common to both officers and other ranks but the former are now allowed to use the post-nominal letters *AE*. Names of recipients were published in Air Ministry Orders and the medal is named, usually rather crudely. The ribbon is green with two centrally placed stripes of light blue. There is one reverse type but four obverse types; GVIR 1st type, GVIR 2nd type and the two EIIR types.

209. AIR EFFICIENCY AWARD *continued*

GVIR (1st)	£75
GVIR (2nd)	£100
EIIR (1st)	£120
EIIR (2nd)	£85

210. ROYAL AIR FORCE LEVIES IRAQ LONG SERVICE AND GOOD CONDUCT MEDAL

This rare award was instituted in 1949, and was terminated in 1955. The basic qualification for the award was 18 years service with the RAF Levies in Iraq, the last 12 years of which service had to be assessed as 'exemplary'. There was a provision for a bar to be awarded for a further 18 years service. After the First World War the RAF took over responsibility for defending much of British territory in the Middle East, as a few aircraft were considered to be as efficient in remote areas as static army garrisons. In Iraq, local levies were raised to assist the RAF, and were for most purposes considered to be a part of the RAF, although they were commanded by army officers in the main. During the Second World War, the Iraq Levies remained loyal during the Rashid Ali Revolt (1941) and by 1944 they numbered over 10,000. After the war their strength was much reduced, and when the British withdrew from Iraq they were disbanded. In 1948 the Levies became eligible for the RAF LSGC Medal, which was subsequently awarded to them; the medal is in most aspects similar to the normal RAF LSGC, but with a clasp fixed to the medal, in a manner similar to campaign medals, bearing the inscription 'Royal Air Force Levies, Iraq'. A total of about 300 medals were issued, about 40% of which were awarded to locally-commissioned officers. The ribbon is similar to the RAF LSGC. For a full account of this medal see the article by Squadron Leader J. Routledge in the OMRS Journal, Summer 1978.

GVIR	£1,250
EIIR	£1,800

211. MERITORIOUS SERVICE MEDAL (ROYAL AIR FORCE)

In June 1918 the first awards of the Meritorious Service Medal were made to the Royal Air Force. The initial intention was to award medals similar to those which were being issued to the Army, but as the RAF had become a separate service in April 1918, it was decided to design and issue a new medal. This had the GVR 'coinage head' as the obverse design - similar to the Army MSM of 1930-36. The reverse design was similar to that of Army MSMs of all periods. The RAF MSM was issued from 1919 to 1924, after which no awards were made. In 1928 it was replaced by the British Empire Medal for Meritorious Service. The RAF MSM was instituted by Royal Warrant on 26th June 1918, and was to be awarded to other ranks of the RAF for 'valuable services rendered in the Field', although these services were to be 'distinct from actual flying service'. All awards of this medal were published in the London Gazette, and a total of 854 awards were made. Most were awarded for operations during the First World War, but some were for small post-war campaigns such as North and South Russia, Afghanistan, Somaliland, Kurdistan, etc. The ribbon is identical to that of the RAF LSGC, except for a thin white stripe down the centre. The naming is in two main types; the bulk of the awards, made between 1918 and 1920, are named in large serifed capitals similar to the naming on the DSM and Naval LSGC; later awards are named in thin capitals similar to early GVR General Service Medal issues. Apart from the naming, this medal can be told apart from the 1930-36 Army MSM as it has a swivelling suspender, which the Army issue does not. Unlike Army and Navy MSMs, the RAF MSM is worn before the appropriate LSGC. There is one reverse type and one obverse type. The RAF MSM was reintroduced on 1st December 1977. The qualification for the award of this new medal are 27 years service, with special emphasis on a very high standard of character and conduct. Recipients must be of the rank of Sgt. or above. To maintain the high standards of the award, only 70 awards per year can be made. The medal and ribbon are similar to the current MSM, and the only discernible difference is in the naming. Due to the small numbers awarded so far and the fact that some recipients are still serving, this medal is very rare on the market. A complete roll of all issues from 1918-1924 can be found in *The Meritorious Service Medal to Aerial Forces* by Ian McInnes.

GVR (RAF)	£275
EIIR (2nd)	£220

212. INDIAN ARMY LONG SERVICE AND GOOD CONDUCT MEDAL

Introduced by the Government of India in 1848 for award to Europeans only, this medal existed only until 1873, after which Europeans received the standard British issue Long Service Medal. It was awarded on discharge after completion of 21 years meritorious service. The obverse of the medal shows a trophy of arms with the shield of the Honourable East India Company in the centre. The reverse is engraved with the name of the recipient and date of award. The ribbon was the usual crimson.

The second type of this medal, issued from about 1860, has the young head of Victoria on the obverse and the words 'For Long Service and Good Conduct' surrounded by two oak sprays on the reverse. For some unknown reason, there is an anchor between the two sprays.

In 1888 a further Indian Long Service and Good Conduct Medal was introduced, but for Indian other ranks only after 20 years meritorious service. In silver, the obverse showed the head of the reigning monarch and the reverse the word 'India' in the centre of a wreath of lotus leaves surrounding the words 'For Long Service and Good Conduct'. This medal ceased to be issued with Indian Independence in 1947.

H.E.I.C.S. Shield issue	£400
Victoria anchor issue	£450
Victoria Lotus Wreath	£100
EVIIR	£100
GVR Kaisar-i-Hind	£30
GVR Ind. Imp.	£35
GVIR	£30

212. INDIAN ARMY LONG SERVICE AND GOOD CONDUCT MEDAL *continued*

213. INDIAN ARMY MERITORIOUS SERVICE MEDAL

The HEICS issue, which is rare, has the obverse Wyon head of Queen Victoria and the HEICS arms on the reverse. Those GVR (K-I-H) issues awarded for the First World War are listed in the Indian Army List and the theatre in which they were won is shown.

QV (HEICS)	£285
QV	£120
EVIIR	£100
GVR (K-I-H)	£50
GVR (Ind Imp)	£60
GVIR (1st)	£40

214. INDIAN ARMY VOLUNTEER OFFICERS' DECORATION

The Indian Volunteer Officers' Decoration was instituted by Royal Warrant on 18th May 1899 at the same time as the Colonial Auxiliary Forces Decoration, thus dividing the Volunteer Decoration into three groups: UK, Colonial and Indian. The Indian version is immediately recognisable by the words 'Indian Volunteer Forces' in the obverse design. The reverse was issued plain, but these awards are usually found with the recipient's details engraved here. The main qualification was 18 years commissioned service in the Volunteers, service in the ranks counting half. Although there was a great variety of units these awards are by no means common. It should be noted that a few naval formations such as Port Defence Corps were also entitled to the decoration. The award was replaced in 1930 by the Efficiency Decoration with the bar-brooch 'India'. Throughout its life the ribbon was green. There were two obverse types: the EVIIR issue and the GVR issue, the plain reverse was common to both. There is a detailed study of this decoration in *The Colonial Auxiliary Forces Officers' Decoration: The Indian Volunteer Forces Officers' Decoration* by J.M.A. Tamplin.

EVIIR	£120
GVR	£110

215. COLONIAL AUXILIARY FORCES OFFICERS' DECORATION

In May 1894 a Royal Warrant extended the award of the Volunteer decoration to officers outside the United Kingdom; this award was in force until 1899, when two new awards were created: the Indian VD, for officers in India, and the Colonial Auxiliary Forces Officers Decoration for all officers in Dominions and Colonies other than India. The latter was awarded until 1930, when it was replaced by the Efficiency Decoration with the appropriate bar-brooch. The basic qualification for the CAF Decoration was 20 years commissioned service in the reserve forces of the Colonies, with consistent standards of conduct and training. No figures are known as to the numbers issued, but a rough guide is that approximately 2700 were awarded in Canada, probably the largest issue to one colony. Awards to the forces of the smaller colonies are rare. There was one type of reverse - plain, except for a hallmark. Often the recipient had his name and other details engraved on the reverse. There were three obverse types: QV, EVIIR and GVR. The obverse is immediately recognisable from similar awards by the inscription. The ribbon was plain green. There is a detailed study of this decoration in *The Colonial Auxiliary Forces Officers' Decoration* by J.M.A. Tamplin in the Spink Medal Booklet Series.

QV	£180
EVIIR	£160
GVR	£130

216. COLONIAL AUXILIARY FORCES LONG SERVICE AND GOOD CONDUCT MEDAL

This award was instituted in 1899 as a concurrent award with the Colonial Auxiliary Forces Decoration. It was issued until 1930, when it was replaced by the Efficiency Medal with the appropriate bar. The basic qualification for the award was 20 years service in the ranks of the reserve forces of the Empire, excepting India. Good conduct and efficient service were also necessary for the award. There are no figures for the number issued, but as a rough guide, the numbers for Canada are: QV - 1350; EVIIR - 750; GVR - 4300. It is doubtful if any other dominion or colony had more awards than Canada, although it will be noted that the EVIIR issues is, in Canada at least, very scarce. The medals are always named, although the style and method of naming varies - both impressed and engraved types have been seen. The ribbon throughout was plain green. There was only one reverse type common to all issues, but there were three obverse types: QV; EVIIR; GVR. Prices below are for larger Dominions/Colonies; those to smaller territories can be valued higher. There is a detailed study of this medal in *The Colonial Auxiliary Forces Long Service Medal* by J.M.A. Tamplin in the Spink Medal Booklet Series.

QV	£125
EVIIR	£95
GVR	£75

217. PERMANENT FORCES OF THE EMPIRE BEYOND THE SEAS LONG SERVICE AND GOOD CONDUCT MEDAL

This medal was instituted in 1909 and replaced the issue authorised in 1895, which was the Army LSGC with the name of the Dominion or Colony on the reverse. It was replaced in 1930 by the LSGC Medal (Military) with the appropriate suspender bar. The medal was awarded to other ranks of the Permanent Forces of the Empire, as opposed to Auxiliary Forces and Militia. Due to the small size of the Regular Forces of most Colonies, there were few of these medals issued. Recipients had to serve 18 years, with a high standard of conduct and character. A few medals were made bearing the head of Edward VII, but these are very rare. Those medals which were issued have the GVR obverse. The naming is in various styles, varying from Dominion to Dominion. The naming is the only factor available in determining which army the recipient served in. No overall figure is known for the numbers issued, but as a rough guide some 900 were issued to Canadian troops, probably the largest issue to any Dominion. The ribbon is maroon, with a wide central white stripe. In the very centre is a thin black stripe.

EVIIR	£250
GVR	£85

218. CANADIAN FORCES DECORATION

This award was instituted by an Order-in-Council dated 15th December 1949. It was to be awarded to all ranks in any of the Canadian services who had completed 12 years long and meritorious service. The reverse design is symbolic of the Canadian Army, Navy and Air Force. This medal is unique in that it is the only decagonal award in the British and Dominion series. The two different issues - GVIR and EIIR - are different in many ways. The GVIR issue is made of silver and is finished in silver-gilt; it has a 'Canada' bar, on the reverse of which is machine-engraved the rank and name of the recipient. Some 13,500 of this type were issued. The EIIR issue is made of 'tombac'; it does not have the 'Canada' bar, and the name and rank of the recipient is stamped on the edge. Approximately 105,000 of this type have been issued. The ribbon is reddish-brown and is divided into quarters by three narrow white stripes. Clasps are awarded for periods of 10 years service after the award of the medal, and medals with a s many as three bars are known. Approximate numbers of bars issued are: 1st bar - 24,000; 2nd bar - 7,000; 3rd bar - 1,200. The obverses and reverses on the two issues are dissimilar.

GVIR	£55
EIIR	£35
EIIR (1 Bar)	£50
EIIR (2 Bars)	£80

219. THE NEW ZEALAND ARMED FORCES AWARD

'The New Zealand Armed Forces Award' is issued to officers serving on or after 1st December 1977 who have completed 15 years service, provided their service has not already been recognised by another long service award. A clasp will be awarded for each additional 15 years service.

The Award is a silver medal, struck by the Royal Mint, UK and bearing on the obverse the Crowned Effigy of the Queen and on the reverse emblems representing the three services.

The ribbon of dark blue, crimson and light blue with a central black stripe are the three service colours. The reverse of the award was designed by Mr. Maurice Conly, MBE, of Waikanae, and the ribbon by Mr. Philip O'Shea, New Zealand Herald of Arms Extraordinary.

£65

220. POLICE LONG SERVICE AND GOOD CONDUCT MEDAL

This medal was instituted in June 1951, and is on current issue. It was introduced to replace various unofficial medals issued by local authorities for many years; these unofficial awards could not be worn with the new medal. The basic qualification for award is 22 years; service in any United Kingdom police force, including Dockyard, Transport and Ministry police. This award was also issued to members of the Australian federal and state police forces under terms similar to the British issue. The only way of differentiating the Australian awards is by noting in the naming a rank not applicable in the British service. Recipients had to be of good character. The medal, which is of cupro-nickel, is always issued named in small impressed capitals. Where no rank is shown, it can be assumed that the recipient is a Constable. The recipient's full Christian name is usually given. The ribbon is of dark blue, with two stripes at each edge. there is one reverse design common to all issues. There are three obverse types: GVIR (2nd); EIIR (1st); EIIR (2nd). This medal was also awarded in Australia from 1951-1975.

GVIR (2nd)	£25
EIIR (1st)	£30
EIIR (2nd)	£25

221. ROYAL ULSTER CONSTABULARY SERVICE MEDAL

Established in 1982 for award to members of the Royal Ulster Constabulary and the Royal Ulster Constabulary Reserve for continuous service of 18 months from 1st January 1971. The grant of an Honour for gallantry or a Queen's Commendation received before the end of the qualifying period will be an immediate qualification.

The medal is of cupro-nickel and has the crowned head of the Queen on the obverse. The reverse shows the badge of the R.U.C. with the legend 'For Service'. The ribbon is apple green with three narrow stripes of dark red, black and dark green in the centre. The medal is named.

EIIR	£120

222. SPECIAL CONSTABULARY LONG SERVICE MEDAL

This medal was instituted in August 1919 to reward long service by members of the Special Constabulary, and is in current issue. For the purposes of convenience, the award of this medal can be divided into two - in peace and war. In peacetime, the normal qualifying period is 9 years, with 50 or more duties per year. During the two World Wars, the qualifying period was 3 years without pay, with 50 or more duties per year. This medal, which is always found in bronze, can be awarded to policemen of any rank in the Special Constabulary. Naming is by small impressed capitals. The first Christian name of the recipient is almost always given in full. The first issue of this medal, to those who had served in the First World War, had a bar sewn on the ribbon bearing the inscription 'The Great War 1914-18'. All other bars were awarded for 10 years service after the award of the medal, and these bore the date of award (for example, 'Long Service 1929'). As can be seen from the above qualifying periods, wartime service counted treble. Although earlier issues are very common, the small size of the Special

222. SPECIAL CONSTABULARY LONG SERVICE MEDAL *continued*

Constabulary in recent years has made some later issues quite scarce. The ribbon is of a wide red stripe in the centre, with one black and two white stripes on each side. There are six obverse types to this medal: GVR (Robes), GVR (Coinage), GVIR 1st Type, GVIR 2nd Type, EIIR 1st Type and EIIR 2nd Type. There are three reverse types. The standard issue reads 'For Faithful Service in the Special Constabulary' and there are two variants in use in Northern Ireland: 'For faithful Service in the Ulster Special Constabulary' and 'For Faithful Service in the Royal Ulster Constabulary Reserve'. These last two are scarce.

GVR Robes	£10
GVR Coinage	£10
GVIR 1st Type	£8
GVIR 2nd Type	£40
EIIR 1st Type	£25
EIIR 2nd Type	£25
EIIR Ulster reverse	£150
EIIR RUC Reserve reverse	£150

223. COLONIAL POLICE LONG SERVICE MEDAL

This medal was instituted by a Royal Warrant dated 23rd March 1934. It was awarded to members of the Colonial Police. The basic qualification for the award was eighteen years' service in a full-time force; generally, only junior officers and other ranks were entitled. The conduct of recipients had to be good, and they had to be recommended by a senior officer. The award was named on the edge, with details of the name, rank and force of the recipient. Both impressed and engraved styles of naming are known. The ribbon is of a broad green central stripe, with dark blue edges and two thin silver stripes. There is one reverse type common to all issues, and five obverse types: GVR; GVIR (1st); GVIR (2nd); EIIR (1st); and EIIR (2nd).

GVR	£95
GVIR (1st)	£65
GVIR (2nd)	£65
EIIR (1st)	£75
EIIR (2nd)	£75

225. COLONIAL SPECIAL CONSTABULARY LONG SERVICE MEDAL

This medal was instituted by Royal Warrant dated 1st April 1957. It was awarded in the Colonies and Territories which came under the Colonial Office to members of the Special and Reserve Constabularies. Recipients had to serve for a minium of nine years, and had to be recommended by a senior officer; those special policemen given any pay or allowances had to serve a minimum of fifteen years, and had also to be recommended by a senior officer. Service in regular police forces, or services towards the Colonial Police LSGC Medal, was not allowed to count towards this award. Those who served satisfactorily for a further ten years and were again recommended were allowed to wear a bar on the ribbon. On the introduction of this award, all unofficial local awards that had been worn were superseded, and could not be worn with the new medal. The medal is named on the rim with details of the recipient's rank, name and the force to which he belonged. The ribbon is of dark green with dark blue edges, with two thin silver stripes superimposed on the green.

EIIR (2nd)	£175

226. COLONIAL POLICE MERITORIOUS SERVICE MEDAL

This medal was instituted in May 1938 by a Royal Warrant. It was awarded to members of the police and fire brigades in the Colonies and Territories of the Empire. There were two types, differentiated by the reverse inscription: 'Gallantry' and 'Meritorious Service' Only the latter will be dealt with here. It was awarded for conspicuous and meritorious service over a period of time, rather than a specific act of gallantry. Lists of recipients were published from time to time in the London gazette, and a register was to be kept by the Secretary of State for the Colonies. A second award of the medal was possible, recognised by the award of a clasp. The ribbon is of dark blue with green edges and a thin silver stripe at each side separating the two. The medal was named on the rim with the rank, name and force of the recipient. Approximate figures issued: GVIR (1st) - 460; GVIR (2nd) - 435; EIIR - 2,200. There is one reverse type common to all issues.

GVIR (1st)	£150
GVIR (2nd)	£150
EIIR (1st)	£170
EIIR (2nd)	£110

227. COLONIAL PRISON SERVICE LONG SERVICE MEDAL

This rare medal was instituted by a Royal Warrant dated 28th October 1955. It was awarded to those below the rank of Assistant Superintendent who had served eighteen or more years in the Colonial Prisons Service. Conduct had to be exemplary, and the recommendation for the award had to come from the officer in charge of the prisons in the relevant colony. Unofficial, local medals for long service were ended with the introduction of this award, and could not be worn with the new medal. Further clasps could be issued - the first for 25 years service, the second for 30 years service. The medal was named with the rank, name and service of the recipient. The ribbon is of green with dark blue edges and a thin silver stripe in the centre. Only one obverse (EIIR 2nd) type and one reverse type have been issued.

EIIR (2nd)	£300

228. AFRICAN POLICE MEDAL FOR MERITORIOUS SERVICE

This very rare medal was instituted in 1915 by a Royal warrant, and was superseded in 1938 by the Colonial Police Medal (Meritorious Service). It was awarded to non-European members of various police forces in both East and West Africa. Only native NCOs and men were eligible for the award. It was awarded to those who were marked out by distinguished and meritorious service, the main qualification being at least fifteen years service with exceptional conduct and ability. The recipient had to be recommended by a senior officer, and lists of recipients were published in the government gazettes of the relevant colony. The medal was named with the rank, name and force of the recipient. The ribbon is of yellow with two red stripes.

GVR	£400
GVIR (1st)	Rare

229. ROYAL CANADIAN MOUNTED POLICE LONG SERVICE MEDAL

This medal was instituted by an Order-in-Council on 14th January 1933, and is a current issue. It was to be awarded to regular and retired members of the Royal Canadian Mounted Police who had served 20 years in the force with good and satisfactory conduct. The medal is engraved on the rim with the recipient's rank and name. Bars were issued for further service after the award of the medal; these were plain with bronze, silver and gold stars for 25, 30 and 35 years respectively. Approximate numbers issued are: GVR - 390; GVIR (1st) - 385; GVIR (2nd) - 330; EIIR - 6000+. The ribbon is blue with two yellow stripes. this medal, particularly the earlier issues, is much sought after by Canadian collectors. There are four variations of the obverse: GVR(Robes); GVIR 1st Type, GVIR 2nd Type, and EIIR. There are three variations of the reverse. The first, with King's Crown was used for the GVR, both GVIR and early EIIR issues. later, a Queen's Crown was introduced as was a French language version.

GVR Robes	£575
GVIR 1st Type	£575
GVIR 2nd Type	£525
EIIR (KC)	£525
EIIR (QC)	£300
EIIR French	£300

230. CEYLON POLICE LONG SERVICE MEDAL

Instituted in 1925 for 15 years active service in the Ceylon Police Force. The obverse showed the head of the reigning monarch and the reverse an elephant with crown above surrounded by an inscription. The suspender was by a ring and the ribbon was white with a central stripe of red and thin side stripes of blue. In 1934 this medal was replaced by the Colonial Police Long Service medal.

GVR (Coinage)	£350

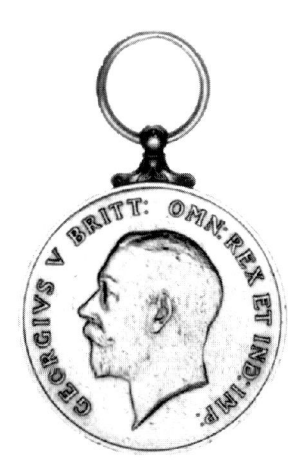

230a. CEYLON POLICE LONG SERVICE MEDAL (2nd TYPE)

This medal was re-instituted in 1950 for 18 years service in the Ceylon Police Force. Now in cupro-nickel instead of silver, the design was similar to the earlier version but, on the reverse, the inscription was re-arranged and the Crown omitted. The suspender was changed to the straight type and the ribbon was altered to become dark blue with light blue, white and gold edges. This medal became obsolete upon Independence in 1972.

GVIR	£250
EIIR	£250

231. MALTA POLICE LONG SERVICE AND GOOD CONDUCT MEDAL

This medal was instituted in 1921, and was issued until 1934, when it was superseded by the Colonial Police and Fire Brigade LSGC. There were two issues: GVR coinage head and GVR robed bust. The basic qualification for the award was 18 years service in Malta, with very high standards of character and conduct. Only service in the Malta Police was allowed to count towards the award. Officers of the rank of Sub-Inspector and above were eligible, provided they had completed 18 years in the ranks before being promoted. The medals are named on the rim with details of the recipient's number, rank, initials and surname. The few examples seen have been engraved in a variety of styles. There are no exact figures known for the numbers issued, but 99 names have been traced in the Malta Gazette; some names are listed in the Police Commissioners' Annual reports which are not in the Gazette. A roll of the 99 gazetted recipients appears in an article by J.M.A. Tamplin (OMRS Journal, Autumn 1973). The ribbon is of light blue, with a thin central white stripe.

GVR (Robes)	£350
GVR (Coinage)	£450

232. CYPRUS MILITARY POLICE LONG SERVICE AND GOOD CONDUCT MEDAL

This medal was instituted in 1929 and was issued for only 5 years, being replaced in 1934 by the Colonial Police and Fire Brigade LSGC Medal. There was only one type issued, the obverse having the bust of George V. The regulations and conditions of award were published in the Cyprus Gazette in 1929. The medal was to be awarded to other ranks in the Cyprus Military Police who had three good conduct badges and had served for 6 years after the third badge was awarded. Conduct throughout had to be very good, and those with more than four entries in the defaulters' book were not eligible. The overall qualifying period was therefore 15 years, and service had to be active - that is, service in offices and courts was not allowed to count towards the award of the medal. Officers who had risen from the ranks were eligible, provided that they had served the 15 years in the ranks and met the other requirements. Only one list of recipients has been found - in the Cyprus Gazette of 18th October 1929 - but there may be other awards. A list of the 7 officers and 54 other ranks traced as being entitled to the medal appears in an article by J.M.A. Tamplin (OMRS Journal, 1973). This rare medal is thought to have been named on the rim.

GVR	£500

233. NEW ZEALAND POLICE LONG AND EFFICIENT SERVICE MEDAL

This medal was instituted in 1886 and was issued until 1976, when it was replaced by a new award bearing the head of EIIR. The date of institution makes this one of the earliest colonial police awards. The medal was set up after questions in the New Zealand Parliament, although Queen Victoria's approval was not sought. The basic qualification was 14 years service in the New Zealand Police, the last 3 years of which had to be served without an entry in the defaulters' sheet. There have been seven issues of this medal, although the basic design has been constant; unlike most awards, the issues changed according to the manufacturer. The first type (1886-1900) was made by Kohn & Co., and was of a heavy gauge. The maker's name was in

233. NEW ZEALAND POLICE LONG AND EFFICIENT SERVICE MEDAL *continued*

the obverse exergue. The reverse was identical to the Regular Army LSGC of the period. This type had a ring suspender. The second type (1900-27) was made by White of Auckland. Early types of this issue had ring suspenders, replaced in 1906 by bar suspenders. The obverse die was better engraved, and the reverse lettering was smaller. The third issue, by Mayer & Kean, had a gauge that was further reduced, and is found with both fixed and swivelling suspenders. The fourth type, limited in number, was made in 1931-35 by Bock of Wellington; this had the manufacturer's name in the obverse exergue, and some were hallmarked on the reverse. The fifth type of Gaunt of Birmingham was issued 1954-60; features of this type were better engraving, wider gauge and a British War Medal-type suspension. The sixth type (1960-73) was by Dick & Watt, the main features being thick claws and suspension. The seventh type, by Goodwill Agencies, was of a thinner gauge, and had a hallmarked inscription 'silver' on the suspender. All medals were named on the rim, usually with details of number, rank, initials and surname; some also had the year of issue added. Early issues are well engraved, but from the 1940s on, the engraving was poor. Those issued 1971-76 are impressed. Bars were authorised in 1959 for further periods of 7 years service after award of the medal. The total length of service is inscribed on the bar, for example '28 Years'. The ribbon was originally crimson, but after about 1919 it became similar to the Permanent Forces Overseas LSGC.

£100

234. SHANGHAI MUNICAPL POLICE LONG SERVICE AND GOOD CONDUCT MEDAL

This semi-official award was instituted in 1929 by the Shanghai authorities to members of the Special Police for 12 years' active and efficient service. Full-time and paid policemen were not eligible, and service in any other organisation was not allowed to count towards the qualifying period. Awards were only made on the recommendation of a senior police officer. There are probably two types of this medal; the first, by far the commonest, has the reverse inscription 'For Long Service', but it is thought that a very small number, perhaps only one, exist with the reverse inscription 'For Distinguished and Valuable Services'. The medal is in silver, with the details of the recipient engraved on the rim - rank, number, initials and surname. Most awards were notified in the Shanghai Municipal Gazette, together with the details which the recipient could engrave on the medal. Bars were awarded for a further period of 5 years service. Some 52 medals and 8 bars have been traced in the Shanghai Gazette, although the actual figures issued might be slightly higher. The medal was not awarded after 1941. The ribbon is of dark brown, with three white stripes, each of which contain within them a yellow stripe.

£250

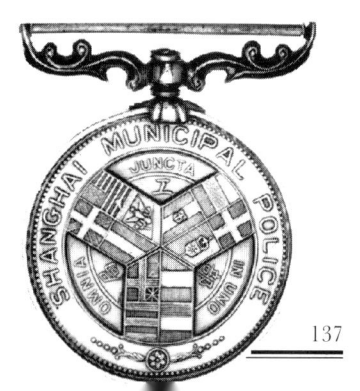

235. SOUTH AFRICAN POLICE GOOD SERVICE MEDAL

This medal was issued 1923-63 and in all 11,600 were issued. The first type was issued 1923-32, the second type 1932-51, and the third type 1951-63. The basic qualification for the award was 18 years service with exemplary conduct. A few awards were issued for gallantry and distinguished conduct, these having a clasp inscribed 'Merit - Verdienste'.

1st type - obverse 'Politie Dienst'	£30
2nd type - 'Poliesie Diens'	£25
3rd type - obverse 'Polisiediens'	£25

236. SOUTH AFRICAN POLICE MERITORIOUS SERVICE MEDAL

There is one reverse type common throughout. There are two obverse types: GVR (Coinage); GVIR (1st).

GVR (Coinage)	£85
GVIR (1st)	£75

237. SOUTH AFRICAN PRISON SERVICES LONG SERVICE MEDAL

£40

238. FIRE BRIGADE LONG SERVICE & GOOD CONDUCT MEDAL

Established by Royal Warrant of 1st June 1954, this medal is awarded to all full or part time members of Fire Brigades, other than the Auxiliary Fire Service, maintained by Local Authorities and Government Departments in the United Kingdom, regardless of rank. It is given for twenty years whole or part time service or an aggregate of both. Service in the Auxiliary Fire Service between 3rd September 1939 and 18th August 1941 and in the National Fire Service was allowed to count as was secondment in the Armed Forces during the 1939-45 War or in a British territory overseas. Candidates must be nominated by the Chief of their Brigade who certifies that their character and conduct have been very good. The medal is struck in cupro-nickel and is named on the rim. The ribbon is red with on either side a yellow stripe on which is superimposed a narrow stripe of red. It is a condition of the award of this medal that the grant of any unofficial or local long service and good conduct medals shall be discontinued and that any such already awarded shall not be worn by the recipients.

EIIR (1st)	£30

239. COLONIAL FIRE BRIGADE LONG SERVICE MEDAL

This rare medal was instituted in a Circular Despatch from the Secretary of State of the Colonies dated 11th June 1934. It was awarded to members of Colonial Fire Brigades. The basic qualification for the award was 18 years service in a full-time brigade; generally, only junior officers and other ranks were entitled. The conduct of the recipient had to be very good, and the recommendation for the award had to come from a senior officer. The award was named on the edge with details of the rank, name and brigade of the recipient. Both impressed and engraved styles of engraving are known. The ribbon is of a broad green central stripe, with dark blue borders and three thin silver stripes. There are five obverse types: GVR; GVIR (1st); GVIR (2nd); EIIR (1st); EIIR (2nd). All issues are very rare, and a minimum price for any issue of this award would be:

GVR	£300
GVIR (1st)	£250
GVIR (2nd)	£250
EIIR (1st)	£250
EIIR (2nd)	£250

240. CADET FORCES MEDAL

This medal was instituted in February 1950 and was to be awarded to commissioned officers and adult NCO Instructors for 12 years service with the Cadet Forces. Those forces involved were the cadets of the Army, Navy and Royal Air Force in the United Kingdom and the Dominions. Although the reverse design remains constant there are three obverse types - GVIR second type and EIIR first and second types. The medal is a current issue. Bars are awarded for further periods of 8 years service, and medals are known with up to four bars. The medal, which is of cupro-nickel, is always issued named in either impressed capitals, for Army and Navy recipients, or in the modern engraved style, to RAF recipients, the latter being found on long service and campaign medals to the RAF. Awards to officers are notified. Only service with cadets was allowed to count towards the award, and service in other arms which went towards other long service awards was not admissible. The 12 years had to be of continuous service. These medals are sometimes found with only the surname and initials of the recipient on the rim; these are usually WOs and senior NCOs of the cadets, medals to

240. CADET FORCES MEDAL *continued*

officers being shown by the addition of the rank to the naming. These awards are most commonly found named to the ACF (Army Cadet Force) and CCF (Combined Cadet Force). The main difference between these two designations is that the ACF is administered directly by the Army, and is open to all, whilst CCFs are based on schools, and are officered by teachers, with training support from touring Army instructors. The ribbon has a green central stripe with stripes of red, blue or grey and yellow towards the edge. The ribbon is worn with the grey stripe on the recipient's left.

GVIR (2nd)	£55
EIIR (1st)	£85
EIIR (2nd)	£55

241. CIVIL DEFENCE LONG SERVICE MEDAL

This medal was instituted by Royal Warrant in March 1961. It was awarded to members of several organisations, namely - Civil Defence, Auxiliary Fire Service, Warning and Monitoring Organisation, and the National Hospital Service Reserve. The qualifying period was 15 years' efficient service in any of these organisations. A bar was sanctioned for a further period of 12 years' service. Awards were made by the Home Office, to whom recommendations were to be made, and by whom a list of recipients was kept. There were the usual articles providing for the return of the award should the person later prove unsuitable. Some 35 organisations, large and small, were eligible for the medal, including the four major ones above. In 1963 the award was extended to CD personnel in Malta, Gibraltar and Hong Kong. In 1968, with the disbandment of the CD organisation, the medal ceased to be generally awarded. Since 1968 the only organisation to be awarded the medal has been the Warning and Monitoring Organisation. To September 1980, 14,164 of these medals have been awarded, with only 57 clasps. The ribbon is of dark blue, with three narrow stripes of yellow, green and red, the yellow stripe being worn farthest from the left shoulder. There is one obverse type, but three reverse designs; the usual design was issued to all recipients, except for those in Northern Ireland who received a medal with the Ulster reverse, distinguished by the use of the initials AFRS and HSR. A third reverse showing a wreath with crossed palms between the words 'Civil Defence' and 'Long Service' was instituted when the award was extended to Malta, Gibraltar and Hong Kong. Only the last area appears to have awarded this variation.

EIIR (General issue)	£15
EIIR (Ulster issue)	£120
EIIR (Hong Kong)	£300

242. ROYAL OBSERVER CORPS MEDAL

This award was instituted in January 1950 and is on current issue. The basic qualification for award was 12 years satisfactory service by part-time and 24 years service by full-time members of the Royal Observer Corps. Both Officers and Observers were eligible. The ROC was part of the Warning and Monitoring Organisation, but the rest of the latter received the Civil Defence Long Service Medal (q.v.). The medal is almost always engraved in the distinctive style found on modern RAF issues. Bars were sanctioned for further periods of 12 years' service after the award of the medal. This award, which was of cupro-nickel, had a reverse common to all issues; in addition, there were two obverse types; EIIR (1st) and EIIR (2nd). The ribbon is of light blue, with a central stripe of silver-grey bordered on each side by narrow dark blue stripes.

EIIR (1st)	£100
EIIR (2nd)	£80

243. WOMEN'S VOLUNTARY SERVICES MEDAL

This medal was instituted in 1961 and is a current issue. It is of cupro-nickel, and is issued unnamed. The basic qualification for the award is 15 years' service in the WVS. Bars are issued with the inscription 'Long Service' for each additional period of 12 years' service. The WVS was raised in 1938 as a voluntary, trained body of women to aid the civil population in the event of war. During the Second World War, the WVS had a strength of over a quarter of a million, and performed many important ancillary tasks. In 1961, the Queen approved the award of this medal to WVS members who had served 15 years, and had completed their basic training and 60 hours duty. Service in the Civil Defence counted towards the award of the medal. The WVS itself administered the award of the medal, though the cost was borne by the Home Office. WVS Headquarters in London holds rolls of recipients, as do regional Headquarters. The names of recipients were published in the WVS Magazines whilst this was in print.

£15

244. SERVICE MEDAL OF THE ORDER OF ST. JOHN OF JERUSALEM

Instituted in 1898 by Chapter-General, the medal is awarded for valuable services to the Order but, in the St. John Ambulance Brigade, it is usually given for voluntary service of 15 years. Bars are awarded for each further period of service of 5 years. At first these bars bore the words 'Five Years Service', but since about 1924 they bear a spray of St. John's Wort with a Maltese Cross in the centre. In 1990 the term of service was reduced to 12 years, but the period for the bar remained unchanged.

The medal bears the head of Queen Victoria on the obverse, the only currently issued medal to do so, and on the reverse a design incorporating the Royal Arms and the Arms of the Order. It originally had a ring suspender but, since about 1914, the ribbon of three black and two white equal stripes has hung from a straight suspender.

Until 1947, the medal was of silver; later issues were of silver-plated cupro-nickel and, currently, of rhodium plated cupro-nickel. Until recently, medals were named with the rank, name, unit and year of issue.

Silver Medal ring suspension	£15
Silver Medal straight suspension	£10
Base metal issues	£5

245. VOLUNTARY MEDICAL SERVICE MEDAL

Established in 1932 for award to members of the British Red Cross Society and the St. Andrew's Ambulance Brigade for voluntary service of 15 years. For further periods of 5 years a plain bar is provided bearing, for the former organisation a Geneva Cross and, for the latter, a St. Andrew's Cross.

The obverse shows a female bust symbolic of Florence Nightingale, and the reverse the Geneva and St. Andrew's Crosses with the legend 'For Long Efficient Service'. Originally the medal was issued in silver but, for the last twenty years or so, all issues have been in cupro-nickel. The medal hangs from a straight suspender and the ribbon is of red with yellow and white stripes, the name of the recipient is impressed on the rim of the medal, with the first name in full. Occasionally a rank such as Sister will be found.

Silver issue	£15
Cupro-nickel issue	£10

245a. THE ACCUMULATED CAMPAIGN SERVICE MEDAL

A Royal Warrant concerning this new British commemorative medal was published as Command Paper No. 2447 on 27th January 1994. Its purpose is to reward long campaign service rendered by members of the Armed Forces since the 14th August 1969, in those operations for which the award of the General Service Medal 1962 is deemed to be appropriate.

Entitled the Accumulated Campaign Service Medal, the medal is circular in form and of silver. It will bear on the obverse the crowned effigy of the Sovereign and, on the reverse, the inscription "FOR ACCUMULATED CAMPAIGN SERVICE" set within a four part ribbon surrounded by a branch of oak leaves with laurel and olive leaves woven through the motto ribbon. It is worn immediately after the Medal for Meritorious Service and hangs from a ribbon of purple and green having a central stripe of gold to denote excellence.

The Medal is awarded to holders of the General Service Medal, 1962, whether military or civilian, serving or retired, on completion of thirty six months accumulated campaign service since 14th August 1969, as defined in the regulations. It may be awarded posthumously to the next of kin of deceased personnel whose service prior to their deaths met the criteria.

Any holder of the Accumulated Campaign Service Medal will be awarded a clasp for each further period of 36 months accumulated campaign service as defined in the regulations. A rose emblem is worn on the ribbon to denote possession of a clasp when ribbons alone are worn. Silver emblems are worn for the first three clasps awarded, a silver gilt emblem for the fourth clasp and two silver gilt emblems for any further clasps. Part-time members of the Royal Irish Regiment are eligible on completion of one thousand days qualifying service as defined in the regulations and a clasp for each further period of one thousand days.

The Regulations referred to above were issued on 11th March 1994, as Defence Council Instruction GEN 65/94. As intimated in the Command Paper, service within the following areas may be aggregated in calculating entitlement to the Accumulated Campaign Service Medal.

Northern Ireland	14th August 1969 to a date to be decided
Dhofar	1st October 1969 to 30th September 1976
Lebanon	7th February 1983 to 9th March 1984
Mine Clearance Gulf of Suez	15th August 1984 to 15th October 1984
Gulf	17th November 1986 to 28th February 1989
Kuwait	8th March 1991 to 30th September 1991
Northern Ireland and Southern Turkey	6th April 1991 to 17th July 1991

Service in respect of any future clasps to the General Service Medal 1962 will count towards the Accumulated Campaign Service Medal. If and when the Medal is superseded, the regulations governing its successor will make clear whether the same arrangements will apply.

The purpose of the Accumulated Campaign Service Medal is to recognise 36 months service in areas which have qualified for clasps on the General Service Medal 1962. Service counting towards medals which were specific to certain theatres of operations, e.g. Rhodesia, South Atlantic, Gulf, will NOT count towards the Accumulated Campaign Service Medal.

246. ROYAL HOUSEHOLD FAITHFUL SERVICE MEDAL

Instituted by Queen Victoria in 1872 to reward Royal Servants for long and faithful service. Like the Royal Victorian medal, it is normally given to those who are not of the 'officer' class, i.e. footmen, chambermaids, grooms, etc. In silver, it is given for 20 years service and bars are available for each further period of 10 years, bearing the title 'Thirty Years' etc. on them. The obverse of the medal shows the head of the reigning monarch and the reverse has the inscription 'For Long and Faithful Service'. The suspender of the Victorian issue is very ornate but this was standardised by George V to become a crowned royal cypher. Dates of service are usually found engraved on the obverse suspender. The ribbon changes with the monarch. The Victorian was a version of the Royal Stuart tartan; George V's was red with blue stripes from top right of the wearer towards bottom left; George VI's the reverse of this; and the current ribbon is blue with three thin red vertical stripes.

QV	£600
GVR	£250
EVIIR	Rare
GVIR	£300
EIIR	£325

Coronation and Jubilee Medals

Although medallions had been issued for hundreds of years to commemorate Royal events, coronations, jubilees and visits, the first official commemorative medal which was designed to be worn, albeit in limited circumstances, was the Empress of India Medal of 1877. From this time onwards, medals were issued regularly for such royal events.

While most awards were issued unnamed, it is still quite possible to build up an interesting collection of commemorative issues. Some of the earlier ones, particularly those given to the Police, were named and the Coronation Medal of 1911, for instance, gives ample scope for building up a display of many different Forces including City, County and Borough units. In addition, commemorative medals are often found privately named to proud civilian recipients who, although only receiving one or two of these medals, nevertheless had very interesting and varied careers which are not difficult to research. Collectors are advised always to make a double check on any commemorative medal offered: check any naming for scarce or senior ranks and check the reverse of the medal for type. Remember that the 1911 Coronation had ten different reverse types and that you could strike lucky with a rare one. Clearly, the field of commemorative medals cannot offer the same interest, excitement and research potential as campaign or gallantry awards, but it should not be neglected. There is a varied selection and, apart from the rarest, they are not expensive.

The specialist standard work on this series is **Coronation and Commemorative Medals** by Lt. Col. H.N. Cole. This book gives far more detail than most. Those interested in the Police series should obtain a copy of the Orders and Medals Research Society's **Miscellany of Honours No. 7** where there is a very detailed article by John Farmery.

247. EMPRESS OF INDIA MEDAL 1877

This large (2.3" diameter) medal was struck in gold and silver. It commemorated the proclamation of Queen Victoria as Empress of India on 1st January 1877. Most recipients were high-ranking civil and military officers, and the medal was also awarded to Indian princes, who received the gold issue. In addition, the medal was awarded in silver to a selected soldier from each regiment - both British and Indian - serving in India at the time. The medal was to be worn round the neck rather than on the chest, but could not be worn by military personnel when they were in uniform. Due to its size, this medal is unique among commemorative awards. The ribbon is of maroon, with a thin yellow stripe at each edge. The medals were issued unnamed, although some are found privately named by the recipients.

Gold	£1,800
Silver	£250

248. JUBILEE MEDAL 1887

This medal, which was issued in gold, silver and bronze, was awarded to a wide range of civil and military recipients. It was given to those who were present on the day of the Jubilee Procession in an official capacity, or to those who assisted in any of the celebrations at which the Queen was present. The gold issue was awarded to members of the Royal Family, whilst the silver was given to middle-ranking civilians and officers of the two services. The bronze issue was awarded to other ranks present at the Jubilee Procession or at the Spithead review of the Navy. The medal was issued unnamed, but is sometimes found privately engraved by the recipient. The ribbon is of a central wide blue stripe, with wide white stripes at each edge. Recipients of this medal who were also awarded the Jubilee Medal 1897 could not have both medals, and were instead awarded a bar, bearing the date '1897' which was affixed to the ribbon. The first price below is for the medal only, the second price being for the medal and '1897' bar.

		With bar
Gold	£750	£900
Silver	£100	£125
Bronze	£75	£95

249. JUBILEE MEDAL 1887—POLICE ISSUE

This award was made to all ranks of the Metropolitan and City of London Police Forces who were serving on the day of the Jubilee procession through London, 21st June 1887. originally, the intention was to award the medal to the Metropolitan Police, but a claim by the City Police could not really be denied. The bronze medal has on the obverse the head of Queen Victoria and, on the reverse, the words 'Jubilee of Her Majesty Queen Victoria' within a circular wreath with the date below. Around the top rim appears the name of the Force. The medal has a straight swivelling suspender. For some reason, the original colour of the ribbon, which was plain dark royal blue, seems to have become darker as each new batch has been woven and the ribbon on offer at present is so dark as to be almost black. This is incorrect. Those men who later qualified for the Police Jubilee Medal issued to commemorate the 1897 Jubilee were not permitted to receive that in addition, but had to send their medal back to have a simple rectangular bar bearing the later date fitted. The medal is therefore found with and without clasp. Approximately half of each Force later received this clasp.

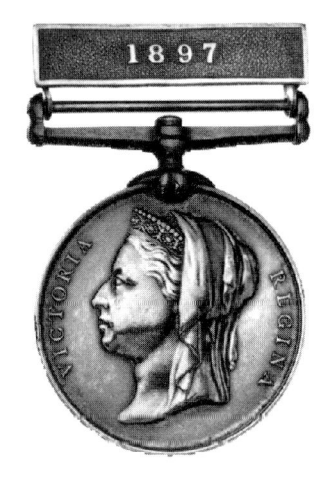

		With bar
Metropolitan Police (5,300)	£20	(8,700) £20
City of London Police (400)	£55	(484) £50

250. JUBILEE MEDAL 1897

This medal, issued to commemorate the Diamond Jubilee of the reign of Queen Victoria, is very similar in appearance to the Jubilee medal of 1887, except for the different date on the reverse inscription. The medal was struck in gold, silver and bronze, and was issued to the same categories of recipient as the 1887 award. Approximately 1,000 medals or '1897' clasps were issued to Army officers. The ribbon is of a wide central stripe of blue, and white stripes at each edge.

Gold	£850
Silver	£60
Bronze	£50

251. JUBILEE MEDAL 1897—MAYORS' AND PROVOSTS' ISSUE

This unique, diamond-shaped award was truck in gold (for Lord Mayors and Lord Provosts) and in silver (for Mayors and Provosts). The central circular designs on the obverse and reverse are similar to the official commemorative medallion issued at the time. Only 14 gold and 512 silver awards were made, the medals being issued unnamed. The ribbon is of a central white stripe, with a blue stripe at each side, and a thin white stripe at each edge.

Gold	£1,000
Silver	£225

252. JUBILEE MEDAL 1897—POLICE ISSUE

Once again, after the Jubilee procession through London on 25th June 1897, it was decided to issue a Jubilee medal to all ranks of the Metropolitan Police Force who were serving on that day. This time, however, other organisations were ready and successful applications for the same medal were made not only by the City of London Police but by the Police Ambulance Service, the St. John Ambulance Brigade and the London County Council Metropolitan Fire Brigade. Approximate numbers issued appear in the table below. The medal was issued in bronze only and is identical to the 1887 medal apart from the date at the bottom of the reverse. Around the top reverse rim appears the name of the Force.

Those men who had qualified for the Police Jubilee medal issued in 1887 did not receive this medal but had to send their earlier medal back to have a simple rectangular bar bearing the later date fitted.

Metropolitan Police	(7500)	£15
City of London Police	(535)	£55
Police Ambulance	(210)	£200
St. John Ambulance Brigade	(910)	£65
London County Council Metropolitan Fire Brigade	(950)	£60

253. VISIT TO IRELAND MEDAL 1900

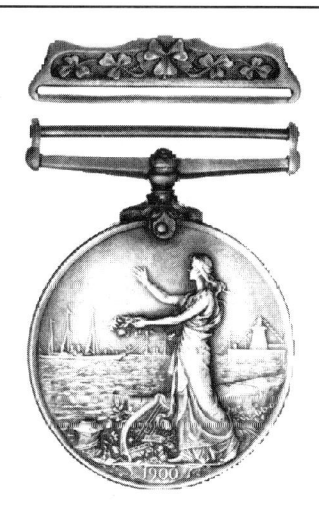

This medal was issued mainly to members of the Dublin Metropolitan Police and the Royal Irish Constabulary, of any rank, who were on duty in connection with the visit of Queen Victoria to Ireland in April 1900. It was issued in bronze only. The obverse bust of Queen Victoria is similar to that used on the Queen's Sudan medal of 1896-98. The reverse scene is of the figure of Hibernia looking out over Kingstown Harbour, in which the Royal Yacht is anchored. This medal is incomplete without the ornate top suspension bar. Some 2300 medals were issued, and are almost always named on the edge in engraved capitals with the rank, name and police force of the recipient. The ribbon is of plain dark blue.

Bronze issue	£65

254. CORONATION MEDAL 1902

This medal, which was issued to commemorate the coronation of Edward VII, was awarded in both silver and bronze. The categories of recipient were spread rather more widely than previous awards, although the bulk of awards still went to the Army and Navy - silver for officers, bronze for other ranks. The medal was issued unnamed. The ribbon is of a central red stripe, with a wider dark blue stripe at each side, and a thin white stripe at each edge.

Silver issue	£60
Bronze issue	£40

255. CORONATION MEDAL 1902—MAYORS' AND PROVOSTS' ISSUE

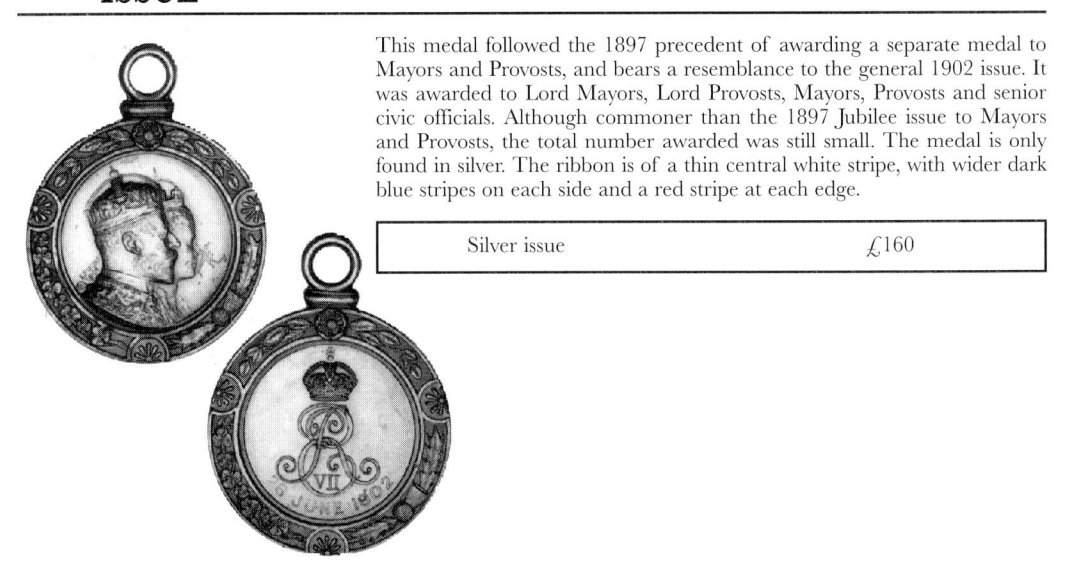

This medal followed the 1897 precedent of awarding a separate medal to Mayors and Provosts, and bears a resemblance to the general 1902 issue. It was awarded to Lord Mayors, Lord Provosts, Mayors, Provosts and senior civic officials. Although commoner than the 1897 Jubilee issue to Mayors and Provosts, the total number awarded was still small. The medal is only found in silver. The ribbon is of a thin central white stripe, with wider dark blue stripes on each side and a red stripe at each edge.

Silver issue	£160

256. CORONATION MEDAL 1902—POLICE ISSUE

In line with the practice already established for the late Queen's Jubilees, this medal was instituted to reward the Police Forces and allied organisations which had been on duty during the Coronation celebrations. In the Metropolitan Police it was awarded to all those who were serving in the Metropolitan Police Area on the actual day. The obverse of the medal shows the crowned head of the King with the legend 'Edwardus VII Rex Imperator' and the reverse shows a wreath of oak and laurel at the base with a crown above and the name of the organisation around the upper rim. It has a straight swivelling suspender and hangs from a ribbon of pillar box red with a central royal blue stripe.

The same five organisations which qualified for the 1897 Jubilee also qualified for this medal but the title of the London Fire Brigade is this time shown only by its initials. A very few silver medals were awarded to senior officers. Numbers of both silver and bronze medals issued are given below.

	Bronze		Silver	
Metropolitan Police	(16,709)	£12	(51)	£300
City of London Police	(1060)	£30	(5)	£500
Police Ambulance Srvice	(204)	£150	(1)	*
St. Johns Ambulance Service	(912)	£45		*
L.C.C.M.F.B.	(1000)	£40	(9)	£400

257. VISIT TO IRELAND MEDAL 1903

This medal was awarded to commemorate the visit of Edward VII to Ireland in July 1903. It was awarded to members of the Dublin Metropolitan Police and the Royal Irish Constabulary who were on duty during the visit. About 7700 were awarded in all, and were made in bronze only. Particularly rare are those medals named to the Belfast Harbour Police and the Irish Coastguard. The medal is incomplete without the suspender brooch with which it was issued. Most examples are found named with details of the rank, name and force to which the recipient belonged. The ribbon is of plain turquoise.

Bronze issue	£65

258. VISIT TO SCOTLAND MEDAL 1903

This medal, which followed the precedent set by the Visit to Ireland Medal of 1900, was awarded to commemorate the visit of Edward VII to Scotland in May 1903. It was mainly awarded to members of the Scottish Police who were on duty during the King's visits to Edinburgh and Glasgow. The medal is very similar to the Coronation Medal 1902 (Police Issue), except for the reverse design and the ribbon. It is incomplete without the top suspension brooch, which was issued with it. 2950 medals were issued, and were usually named with details of the rank and name of the recipient. Particularly scarce are medals named to the St. Andrew's Ambulance Association. The medal was only issued in bronze, and had a plain red ribbon.

Bronze issue	£65

259. DELHI DURBAR MEDAL 1903

This medal, which commemorated the Durbar of 1st january 1903, was issued in gold and silver. It is somewhat larger than most commemorative issues, and is unusual in that the bust of Edward VII faces to the right. 140 medals were issued in gold to the rulers of various Indian states, and 2500 silver medals were issued to a wide range of recipients, including the Indian Civil Service and prominent civilians in Indias. In the case of the Army (for which issue a roll exists), the medals were evenly distributed to each regiment. Only 4 or 5 being issued to each unit. The medal was issued unnamed, but many are found privately engraved by the recipient. The ribbon is of light blue, with three thin dark blue stripes, one in the centre and one at each edge.

| Gold | £950 |
| Silver | £100 |

260. CORONATION MEDAL 1911

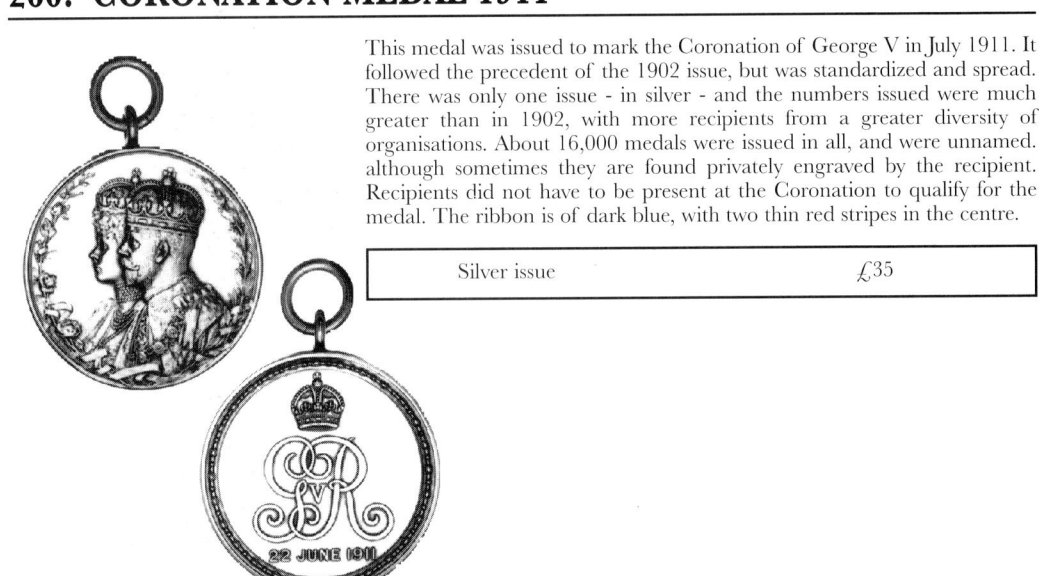

This medal was issued to mark the Coronation of George V in July 1911. It followed the precedent of the 1902 issue, but was standardized and spread. There was only one issue - in silver - and the numbers issued were much greater than in 1902, with more recipients from a greater diversity of organisations. About 16,000 medals were issued in all, and were unnamed. although sometimes they are found privately engraved by the recipient. Recipients did not have to be present at the Coronation to qualify for the medal. The ribbon is of dark blue, with two thin red stripes in the centre.

| Silver issue | £35 |

261. CORONATION MEDAL 1911 – POLICE ISSUE

This medal is, without doubt, the most interesting and diverse of the entire commemorative series. New organisations joined those qualifying and, for the first time Police Forces outside London were able to participate. The medal was issued in silver to all ranks and has, on the obverse, the crowned head of George V with titles 'Georgius V Rex et Ind: Imp'. The reverse design is very simple, showing a central crown with an encircling ornate band: in the outer circle between this and the rim appears the title of the organisation and at the foot the words 'Coronation 1911'. Suspension is by a ring and the ribbon is red with three narrow royal blue stripes. These medals are found named and unnamed, those to the provincial police often falling into the latter category. As will be seen from the figures given below, some of the issues are quite scarce.

261. CORONATION MEDAL 1911 – POLICE ISSUE *continued*

Metropolitan Police (19,783)	£15	
City of London Police (1,400)	£40	
County and Borough Police (2,565)	£40	
Scotiish Police (280)	£100	
Royal Irish Constabulary (585)	£75	
Royal Parks (119)	£300	
London Fire Brigade (1,374)	£40	
Police Ambulance Service	} (2,623)	£300
St. John Ambulance Brigade		£40
St. Andrew's Ambulance Corps		£150

262. VISIT TO IRELAND MEDAL 1911

Following the precedents set in 1900 and 1903, George V visited Ireland in July 1911, and a commemorative medal was issued. This was mainly issued to members of the Dublin Metropolitan Police and the Royal Irish Constabulary, although some were also awarded to senior civic figures. Recipients had to be on duty during the King's visit to Dublin to qualify for the award. The medal was very similar to the Coronation Medal of 1911 (Police Issue), except for the reverse inscription and the ribbon. Some 2,500 of these medals were awarded, and were issued unnamed. The ribbon is of dark green, with a thin red stripe towards each edge. The medal was only issued in silver.

Silver issue	£65

263. DELHI DURBAR MEDAL 1911

The award of this medal followed the precedent set in 1903. The medal was issued in gold and silver, the former to only 200 Indian princes and rulers and a few very senior officials. Some 30,000 were issued in silver to a wide variety of civil and military recipients. Recipients did not have to be present at the Durbar to receive the medal. About 10,000 silver medals were awarded to military personnel in both the British and Indian armies. Those who had received the Coronation Medal of 1911 were not issued with this medal, but received a clasp bearing the word 'Delhi' for attachment to the ribbon; 130 Indian Army officers and other ranks were entitled to this clasp. The medal was issued unnamed, but is often found privately named by the recipient. The ribbon is of dark blue, with two thin red stripes in the centre.

Gold issue	£800
Silver issue	£30

264. JUBILEE MEDAL 1935

This medal was issued to commemorate the 25th year of the reign of George V. Some 85,000 medals were struck, all in silver. As can be seen from the number struck, medals were awarded to the widest possible range of civil and military personnel, and organisations which had not previously been entitled to medals were included in the 1935 issue. Many were issued throughout the Empire. The medal is found named by the recipient, but most are found unnamed as issued. This is the first commemorative medal which adopts one standard design for all recipients. The ribbon is of red, with three narrow stripes at each edge, two dark blue and one white.

Silver issue	£18

265. CORONATION MEDAL 1937

This medal, of which 90,000 were issued, was struck to commemorate the Coronation of George VI. As with the Jubilee Medal of 1935, only one design was used for all recipients, and a very wide cross-section of recipients received the medal. The medal was issued unnamed, but is sometimes found privately engraved by the recipient. The ribbon is of blue, with three narrow stripes at each edge, two white and one red.

Silver issue	£18

266. CORONATION MEDAL 1953

This medal was issued to commemorate the Coronation of Elizabeth II in June 1953. There was only one design of the medal, and all were issued in silver. A total of 129,000 were issued to a very wide range of recipients, and the high number issued makes this the commonest commemorative medal issued, although not necessarily the commonest on the market. The medal is worn after gallantry and campaign awards, but before long service awards. Generally issued unnamed, the medal is occasionally found privately named by the recipient; a very small number were issued impressed to members of the Mount Everest expedition of 1953. The ribbon is of dark red, with two thin dark blue stripes in the centre, and a thin white stripe at each edge.

Silver	£35

267. JUBILEE MEDAL 1977

This award was issued to commemorate the Jubilee of Elizabeth II. Some 30,000 were issued, including 9,000 to service recipients. It is worn after gallantry and campaign awards, but before long service awards. As with previous awards, a wide cross-section of recipients received the medal. There is a Canadian version of this medal, which is basically similar to the British issue, except for the reverse design. The ribbon os of white, with thin red stripes at each edge, with a wide blue stripe in the centre and a thin red stripe superimposed on this.

Silver issue	£120
Canadian issue	£65

Miscellaneous Medals

268. ARMY BEST SHOT MEDAL

Instituted by a Royal Warrant of 30th April 1869 as an annual award to the best shots in the British Army, it was also known as 'The Queen's Medal'. It was first issued in bronze, changed to silver in 1872. The obverse depicts the diademed and veiled bust of Queen Victoria with the legend VICTORIA REGINA. The reverse shows the figure of Fame standing on a dais and placing laurel wreath on a warrior, who holds on his knee a target with three arrows through the centre and in his right hand a bow and quiver. The medal is 1.42 ins in diameter with a watered ribbon which has a wide crimson centre flanked by black, white and black stripes. Naming is in block letters giving rank, name and the regiment and then the year of the award. The competition ended in 1882 but it was revived in 1923 when the medal, logically, became known as 'The King's Medal' until 1952. The same reverse was used and provision was made for subsequent success by a bar noting the year and a silver rose emblem to be worn on the ribbon. The rules were revised in 1962, dividing the forces eligible for the award into three categories:
- The Military Forces at Home
- The Army Emergency Reserve
- The Military Forces of Canada, Australia, New Zealand, Ceylon and Rhodesia, the British South Africa Police, and the Ghana Armed Forces.

Victoria Bronze	Rare
Victoria Silver	£850
George V	£700
George VI	£700
Elizabeth II	£700

269. NAVAL GOOD SHOOTING MEDAL

Introduced by King Edward VII in August 1902 to encourage good gunnery performances at the annual Fleet Competitions, the medal was awarded for every type of gun used in the Royal Navy between 1903 and 1914, as it was awarded to seamen who scored well with their own particular weapon. The medal was discontinued in 1914 and it is now rare. The obverse shows the bust of either Edward VII or George V, both in naval uniform and with the legends EDWARDUS VII REX IMPERATOR or GEORGEIUS V BRITT OMN REX ET IND IMP. The reverse has the nude figure of Neptune facing right, grasping five thunderbolts in each hand, in the background the bows of a trireme and three horses' heads; around the edge is the lettering AMAT VICTORIA CURAM. The ribbon is dark blue with a red centre flanked by white stripes. The recipient's ship, number, rank and name, year of award and calibre of the gun involved are impressed in block letters on the rim. Subsequent success was recognised by a bar impressed with the ship, year and calibre of the gun. A total of 974 medals and 62 bars were awarded.
The Naval Good Shooting Medal 1903-1914 by R.J. Scarlett, published in 1990 contains a complete roll of recipients and detailed study.
A medal of the same reverse design but with the head of the present Queen on the obverse is now used as a Champion Shot Medal for the Naval and Marine Forces. It is only awarded, however, for land based shooting with small arms in the same way as the Army Best Shot and the RAF Queen's Medal. All awards have a clasp bearing the year of the award and the original ribbon is still in use.

EVIIR	£200
GVR	£225
EIIR	£700

270. QUEEN'S MEDAL FOR CHAMPION SHOTS OF THE AIR FORCE

The medal was introduced on 12th June 1953 and it is competed for annually at the RAF Small Arms Meeting at Bisley. It is 1.42 ins in diameter, in silver, and is worn on a 1.25 ins wide ribbon of dark crimson with dark blue, light blue and dark blue stripes at each edge. A straight fixed suspender was used for the first issue and a straight swivelling one for the second.

The obverse shows the crowned effigy of the sovereign. The first issue has the legend ELIZABETH II D.G. BR. OMN. REGINA F.D., and the second, ELIZABETH II DEI GRATIA REGINA F.D. The reverse depicts the kneeling figure of Hermes throwing a javelin while mounted on a hawk in flight. The recipient's name is engraved on the rim. Each award has a bar giving the year and any subsequent awards are indicated by an additional bar and a silver rosette on the ribbon.

EIIR	£800

271. EDWARD VII MEDAL FOR SCIENCE, ART AND MUSIC

£800

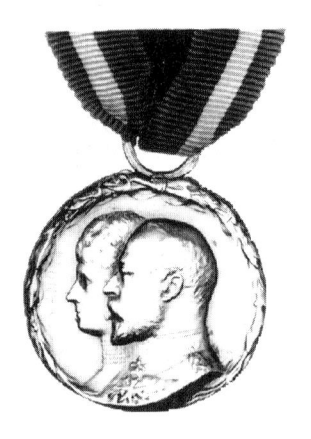

272. ARCTIC MEDAL 1818-55 & 1875-76

A retrospective medal for polar expeditions was sanctioned on 30th January 1857. Together with the subsequent special issue of 1876 it was styled the Arctic Medal as the services recognised took place in the northern polar regions only. Civilian volunteers (e.g. scientists) were eligible and awards were also made to the French Navy and to members of expeditions recognised by the United States government or of any other expeditions financed by the state, by the Hudson's Bay Company, or by private enterprise. The first issue is fairly common, the second rare.

1818-1855
The medal is silver, octagonal in shape and 1.3 ins in diameter. The obverse shows the head of Queen Victoria wearing a tiara, between the words VICTORIA REGINA and has a beaded edge. The reverse depicts a three-masted sailing ship with icebergs in the background and a sledge party in the foreground; around the top is the lettering FOR ARCTIC DISCOVERIES and the dates '1818-1855' appear in the exergue. The suspension is particularly interesting - a small claw fixed to the top of the medal and above it a star of five points with five small points between them, representing the Pole Star. The ribbon is plain white. The medal was issued unnamed and there were no bars. A total of 1,486 were awarded, 1,106 to the Royal Navy and the remainder to civilians and foreigners.

1875-1876
Sanctioned on 28th November 1876 for exploration by HMS **Alert** and **Discovery** between 17th July 1875 and 2nd November 1876, authority was also given for its extension to the crew of the private yacht **Pandora** which voyaged in the Arctic regions June-October 1875 and June-November 1876. The medal is silver, circular, 1.3 ins in diameter, with a raised milled edge and a plain white ribbon. The obverse has the crowned and veiled bust of Queen Victoria and the legend VICTORIA REGINA 1876. The reverse shows an ice-bound ship against a sky full of clouds. The medal was issued with name and rank given in small block lettering and there were no bars. A total of 170 awards were made.

A convenient check-list of officers who served in the Arctic up to 1873 can be found in the 1992 reprint of *The Arctic Navy List* by C.R. Markham.

QV (unnamed) 1818-55	£280
QV (named) 1875-76	£750

273. POLAR MEDAL

The current medal for Arctic and Antarctic exploration, it was introduced by Edward VII in 1904 and since then has appeared with the heads of all the sovereigns except Edward VIII. It is issued in silver and formerly in bronze, each being regarded as separate awards. With the exception of the 1902-04 bronze award, each medal has a bar, with further bars for subsequent voyages. The medal is octagonal, 1.315 ins in diameter, with an ornamental swivelling suspender and a plain white ribbon. The obverse shows the sovereign's effigy: the Edward VII and early George V issues in Admiral's uniform; later George V issues have a crowned head and robed bust and subsequently a coinage head; and all the George VI and Elizabeth II issues have a coinage head. The reverse depicts the ship **Discovery** with a sledge party of six in the foreground, together with a heavily laden sledge bearing a square sail.

The medal is issued named, Edward VII, George V and George VI issues in engraved capitals, and Elizabeth II in small impressed lettering. There are 91 bars and the later ones are engraved. Notable bars include: **Antarctic 1902-04** awarded for Captain Scott's first expedition - 38 silver medals and bars to the landing party and 60 bronze medals to the supply ships' crews; **Antarctic 1907-09** for Shackleton's expedition; and **Antarctic 1910-13** for Captain Scott's last expedition.

A total of 641 silver medals/bars and 275 bronze was awarded for the Antarctic up to 1971, and 71 silver for the Arctic 1930-54. The awards are gazetted, although often several years after the event. Conditions for the award have changed over the years and it is now made for notable achievements only rather than given automatically to all members of an expedition. In October 1933 George V ordered that in future silver medals only should be struck, but bronze issues persisted up to **Antarctic 1936-39**. The standard reference work for this medal is *The White Ribbon* by Lt. Col. N.W. Poulsom published by Seaby in 1968. In spite of its age, it is still a valuable reference tool.

	Silver	Bronze
EVII	from £1,000	from £750
GVR (Admiral)	from £900	from £650
GVR (Robes)	*	from £650
GVR (Coinage)	from £900	*
GVIR	from £950	from £650
EIIR	from £950	—

274. NAVAL ENGINEERS' MEDAL

Introduced in 1842, the medal was abolished four years later. Its purpose was to reward First Class Engineers of the Royal Navy whose conduct and ability deserved special recognition. Recommendations were made by the ship's captain and final approval was given by the Admiralty. The medal was designed by the great Wyon. Its obverse depicts a two-masted paddle steamer with a trident in the exergue. The reverse has an inner circle containing an anchor surmounted by a crown, and surrounding it are the words FOR ABILITY & GOOD CONDUCT. The name of the recipient, with his rank, ship and year, is engraved at the bottom, between the inner circle and the edge. The medal is 1.38 ins in diameter and was customarily worn with the Naval Long Service and Good Conduct ribbon - 1.5 ins wide with white edges - suspended by a small ring. Grounds for the award ranged from inventing a tide motor to participation in the reopening of the Parana River to trade. However, only eight awards were made, so that this is an extremely rare medal indeed!

Named medal	£3,000

Life Saving Medals

275. ROYAL NATIONAL LIFEBOAT INSTITUTION MEDALS

The institution was founded in 1824 and its first medals bearing the head of King George IV were awarded in 1825. This type was used until about 1864 when the head of Queen Victoria was substituted for that of King George IV. The reverse showing three men in a boat rescuing a fourth man from the sea, remained the same for both types. The distinctive dolphin suspender was not introduced until about 1852. Prior to this a ring fitted through the medal or to its edge was used. In 1903 a new medal was produced with the head of King Edward VII on the obverse and a new reverse depicting 'Hope' adjusting the life jacket of a lifeboatman. When George V became monarch his head was used on the obverse and the original reverse reverted. Up to this time the medals had only been awarded in gold and silver but in 1917 the bronze medal was introduced. When King George VI came to the throne it was not possible to use his head on the obverse as it had been decided that only medals awarded by the King could bear his effigy. The Institution chose to honour its founder Sir William Hillary by using his effigy on the obverse of its medals. The reverse remained unchanged. The ribbon used is blue in colour. The name of the recipient together with the date of the Committee meeting at which the award was voted is engraved on the edge of the medal. Further acts of gallantry were originally denoted by the award of a small gold or silver rowing boat. These were superseded during 1840-50 by bars inscribed 'Second Service' having the date of award on their reverse. The medals are awarded for individual acts of gallantry in saving life from the sea. They are not only awarded to the Institution's lifeboatmen; ordinary people who risk their lives to save others are also eligible. it should be noted that some of the awards made during the early part of the last century were either honourary or for improvements in life saving equipment.

George IV	Gold	£1,200
	Silver	£250
Victoria	Gold	£1,200
	Silver	£300
Edward VII	Gold	£1,400
	Silver	£800
George V	Gold	£1,400
	Silver	£400
	Bronze	£350
Sir William Hillary	Gold	£1,000
	Silver	£275
	Bronze	£225

276. LIVERPOOL SHIPWRECK AND HUMANE SOCIETY MEDALS

This Society which was founded in 1839 is unique in that it awards separate medals for three specific types of lifesaving, i.e. the 'Marine' medal for saving life from drowning, the 'Fire' medal for saving life from fire, and the 'General' medal for an act of saving life that does not meet the conditions of the other two categories. The earliest awards to be made by the Society were the Marine Medals in 1840. These were medallions 56mm in diameter and not intended for wearing. The obverse shows a man on a spar helping to lift a child from its mother who is just visible in the sea and the legend 'Lord Save Us: We Perish'. The reverse shows the name of the Society together with a wreath with the date 1839 at its base and in the centre the 'Liver' bird. This medallion was replaced in about 1867 by an oval shaped medal which has a similar obverse but including the name of the Society whilst the reverse has only a wreath in the centre of which is engraved the name of the recipient. The dark blue ribbon was attached to the medal by a 'Liver' bird suspender. The third type of Marine Medal was introduced in about 1874 and was a copy of the earlier medallion type but only 38mm in diameter. This was fitted with a scroll suspender and dark blue ribbon. Medals were awarded in gold, silver and bronze depending on the risk involved in the rescue. Plain bars with the date of the award engraved on them were awarded for subsequent rescues.

Special types of Marine Medal are also awarded. These are the Camp and Villaverde Medal which was first issued in 1847 and is similar to the third type Marine Medal but the reverse has the legend 'Camp and Villaverde Medal for Saving Life at Sea' and the date 1847 instead of the normal one. Also the Bramley-Moore Medal which is the same as the third type Marine Medal but has the legend 'Bramley-Moore Medal for Saving Life at Sea' and the date 1872 on the reverse. This was first awarded in 1874. An 'In Memoriam' Medallion was also awarded to the relatives of those who were unsuccessful in their rescue attempts. The medallion is identical to the first type Marine Medallion.

The Fire Medal was first awarded in 1883 and has the same reverse as the third type Marine Medal. The obverse shows a fireman descending the stairs of a burning house carrying three children, one of whom he is giving to the mother. In the exergue is the legend 'For Bravery in Saving Life'. the ribbon is bright scarlet and hangs from a scroll suspender. Plain bars engraved with the date of award were given for subsequent acts of bravery.

The General Medal was introduced in 1894 for acts of bravery in saving life on land. The reverse is the same as the third type Marine Medal but the obverse has the legend 'For Bravery in Saving Life' together with the date 1894 and shows an Imperial Crown encircled by a wreath superimposed on a cross pate. The ribbon has five equal stripes of red and white. Plain bars engraved with the date of award were given for subsequent acts of bravery.

Marine Medallion	Gold	£1,800
	Silver	£400
Marine Medal (oval type)	Silver	£475
Marine Medal (round type)	Gold	£900
	Silver	£55
	Bronze	£40
Fire Medal	Gold	£1,800
	Silver	£180
	Bronze	£150
General Medal	Gold	£1,800
	Silver	£75
	Bronze	£50
Camp & Villaverde Medal	Silver	£450
	Bronze	£400
Bramley-Moore Medal	Gold	£1,600
	Silver	£450
	Bronze	£400
'In Memoriam" Medallion	Silver	£400

277. SHIPWRECKED FISHERMEN & MARINERS ROYAL BENEVOLENT SOCIETY MEDALS

The Society was formed in 1839 to provide benevolent aid to shipwrecked mariners and their families. It awarded its first medals in 1851 and since that time about 650 medals have been presented. The ribbon is navy blue. Details of the recipient together with the date of the award are engraved on the edge of the medal. The medal has a variety of suspenders: the first is plain but the second to fifth have a pair of dolphins variously affixed to the suspender. The sixth type has the suspender as shown in the illustration with the dolphins loose but fixed to the ribbon.

| Gold | £900 |
| Silver | £175 |

278. ROYAL HUMANE SOCIETY MEDALS

The Society was founded in 1774 and issued its first medals in the same year. These were struck in silver, 51mm in diameter, the obverse showing a naked boy blowing on an extinguished torch with the legend 'Lateat Scintillula Forsan' above and 'Soc. Lond. in Resuscitat, Intermortuorum Inst. MDCCLXXIV' below. The reverse shows a wreath encircled by the legend 'Hoc Pertium Cive Servato Tulit', the area in the centre of the wreath being engraved with the details of the award. The medal was issued without any form of suspension for wearing. Later medals of similar design were struck in silver and bronze, and some were unofficially fitted with a ring so that the medal could be worn. Where a rescue attempt was unsuccessful the legend on the reverse was omitted. In 1869 the size of the medal was reduced to 38mm in diameter and it was fitted with a scroll suspender to accept a navy blue ribbon. The design remained basically the same as the earlier issues, only small changes being made. Details of the award were engraved on the edge of the medal. Bars were issued for subsequent acts of bravery and consisted of an oval plaque, inscribed with the initials of the Society, mounted on a scroll sweeping up under the plaque at each side. The ribbon for the silver medal was changed at the end of the First World War to include a central thin yellow stripe and similar white stripes on each side. Once a year the Society awards the Stanhope Gold Medal to the recipient of the silver medal whose act of gallantry was considered the bravest. The medal is struck in gold and is of the same design as the silver and bronze medals, but has an additional suspension bar inscribed 'Stanhope Medal'. (Early examples also have the year of award on the bar.)

Large Medal	(successful)	Silver	£160
		Bronze	£85
	(unsuccessful)	Silver	£350
		Bronze	£150
Small Medal	(successful)	Silver	£140
		Bronze	£50
	(unsuccessful)	Silver	£150
		Bronze	£50
Stanhope Gold Medal			£1,400

279. SOCIETY FOR THE PROTECTION OF LIFE FROM FIRE MEDALS

The first two types of medal issued by this Society (founded in 1836) had a large eye within a garter on their obverse with the dates 1836 and 1844 respectively. The reverse had a wreath of oak leaves with the details of the award engraved in the centre. The medals were fitted with ring suspenders. By 1852 a new medal had been introduced which had a new obverse showing a man carrying a woman on his shoulder from a fire and, again, the engraved details on the reverse. This medal was replaced by a fourth type whose obverse showed a man rescuing a woman and two children from a fire. The reverse now contained the legend 'Duty and Honor' with the recipients name inscribed on the rim. The ribbon for all the medals was scarlet. The current issue of the medal is bronze with 'Duty and Honor' on the obverse and the recipients name inscribed on the reverse field; it has no suspender.

Engraved type	Silver	£380
'Eye' type	Silver	£380
Third type	Silver	£175
Fourth type	Silver	£150
	Bronze	£120

280. DRUMMOND CASTLE MEDAL

This medal was awarded by Queen Victoria to those inhabitants of Brest, Ushant and Molene who displayed generosity, humanity and kindness when the Castle Liner S.S. 'Drummond Castle' struck a reef off Ushant on 16th June 1896 and became a total loss. There were only three survivors from the 247 passengers and crew. About 252 medals were awarded none of which were named but there is a full list of the recipients in the London Gazette dated 28th may 1896. the ribbon was crimson in colour.

Silver	£200

281. CQD MEDAL

On 23rd January 1909 off the coast of America the liner 'Republic' collided with the Italian steamship 'Florida' which was carrying 800 emigrants. In response to a C.Q.D. (Come Quick - Danger) wireless message the liner 'Baltic' arrived and assisted in the rescue of the crew and passengers of the 'Republic', which subsequently sunk. This rescue is notable as being one of the first occasions on which wireless telegraphy was used to send out a distress call. The medal was given to the crew of all three ships by the saloon passengers of the 'Baltic' and 'Republic'. The ribbon is dark blue.

Silver	£150

282. ORDER OF ST. JOHN OF JERUSALEM LIFE SAVING MEDAL

Instituted in 1874 for gallantry in saving life, the first type was awarded in silver and bronze up to 1888, when the second type was introduced and also gold were awarded. The second type has on its obverse the Badge of the Order encircled by the legend 'For Service in the Cause of Humanity' and the reverse a sprig of St. John's Wort with scrolls bearing the words 'Jerusalem' and 'England' encircled by the legend 'Awarded by the Grand Priory of the Order of the Hospital of St. John of Jerusalem in England'. The ribbon of the first medal was black with the Badge of the Order embroidered on it. The second type had a plain black ribbon which was altered in 1954 to include scarlet and white stripes at each side. All the medals are named on the edge. Bars could be issued for subsequent acts of gallantry.

First type	Silver	£500
	Bronze	£325
Second type	Gold	£1,000
	Silver	£400
	Bronze	£300

283. LLOYD'S WAR MEDAL FOR BRAVERY AT SEA

This medal was awarded to officers and men of the Merchant Navy and Fishing Fleets fore exceptional bravery at sea in time of war. It was instituted in December 1940 with the last awards being made in December 1947 and altogether 523 medals were awarded. The ribbon is white with blue side stripes. the medals are named on the edge with the recipient's name, date of the incident and the name of the vessel.

Silver	£600

284. LLOYD'S MEDAL FOR SAVING LIFE AT SEA

First instituted in 1836 the medal was 73 mm in diameters and was not intended for wearing. In 1896 the size was reduced to 36mm and fitted with a ring suspender. The ribbon was bright blue with two broad white stripes. The date of the award and the recipient's name are engraved on the edge of the medal. The design of the large and small medals is identical. From 1974 the words 'at Sea' were dropped from the side of the medal.

Large type	Silver	£400
	Bronze	£200
Small type	Gold	£185
	Silver	£150

285. LLOYD'S MEDAL FOR MERITORIOUS SERVICES

The first type instituted in 1893 was a nine pointed star struck in bronze with the Lloyd's shield of arms on the obverse and on the reverse the inscription 'Presented by Lloyd's for Meritorious Services'. The ribbon was red with blue stripes at each side. The second type was an oval silver medal introduced in 1900 with a blue ribbon having silver stripes at each side. In 1913 the design was changed again to the third type which is circular (37mm in diameter) and has the Lloyd's shield of arms encircled by the legend 'Presented by Lloyd's' on its obverse. The reverse shows a wreath with the legend 'For Meritorious Services'. The ribbon was the same as for the oval type.

Star type	Bronze	£85
Oval type	Silver	£400
Round type	Silver	£300
	Bronze	£285

286. TAYLEUR FUND MEDAL

Instituted in 1854 as a result of surplus funds raised for the benefit of survivors from the wreck of the emigrant ship 'John Tayleur' in Bantry Bay. The medal has a plain reverse on which are engraved the details of the award. The ribbon is dark blue. A total of six different rescues have been recorded resulting in the award of two gold and 38 silver medals. In 1913 the Fund was wound up and surplus funds transferred to the R.N.L.I. and no further awards were made.

Silver	£985

287. R.M.S. CARPATHIA AND S.S. TITANIC MEDAL

When the S.S. 'Titanic' sunk in the Atlantic on 15th April 1912, one of the ships which helped in the rescue was the R.M.S. 'Carpathia'. As a token of their gratitude the survivors of the 'Titanic' had this medal struck and presented to each of the officers and crew of the 'Carpathia'. It was given in gold, silver or bronze depending on the rank of the recipient. The total number of medals was approximately 300 of which 14 were gold. The ribbon was dark blue.

Gold	£1,200
Silver	£350
Bronze	£200

288. BINNEY MEMORIAL MEDAL

This medal is awarded annually to the British citizen who displays the most bravery in support of law and order within the areas administered by the Metropolitan and City of London Police Forces. That person must not be a member of any Police or other force maintaining law and order. Established as a memorial to Captain R.D. Binney, C.B.E., R.N. who was killed on 8th December 1944 in the City of London whilst attempting, single handed, to apprehend two thieves. The medal was first awarded in 1947. The reverse of the medal has the legend 'For Courage in Support of Law and Order Awarded to' and the recipient's name and date of award engraved on a tablet below the legend. The medal is 48mm in diameter.

Bronze	£450

289. HUNDRED OF SALFORD SOCIETY MEDAL

This Society was founded in 1789 and after a period of dormancy was revived in 1824. Two types of medal were issued. The first class was circular and struck in silver and bronze. The second type medal was issued around 1884 and was in the form of a hollow cross struck with gold or silver. Both types had the recipient's name and a date engraved on the reverse. The ribbon for both types was dark blue. The last issue of the medal is thought to have been in 1922.

1st type Silver	£120
Bronze	£100
2nd type Silver	£80

Life Saving Medals

290. CARNEGIE HERO FUND MEDAL

The Carnegie Hero Fund was established by Andrew Carnegie in the United States in 1904. In 1908, a Hero Fund Trust was established by Carnegie in Britain and their first bronze medallion (Case No. 1) was awarded on 26th November 1909. To date, 171 awards of the medallion have been made - in recent decades it has been awarded very sparingly. There are ten Carnegie Foundations throughout the world, most of whom issue a medal or medallion. The illustrations show the obverse and reverse of the British medallion (88mm diameter).

Bronze	£220

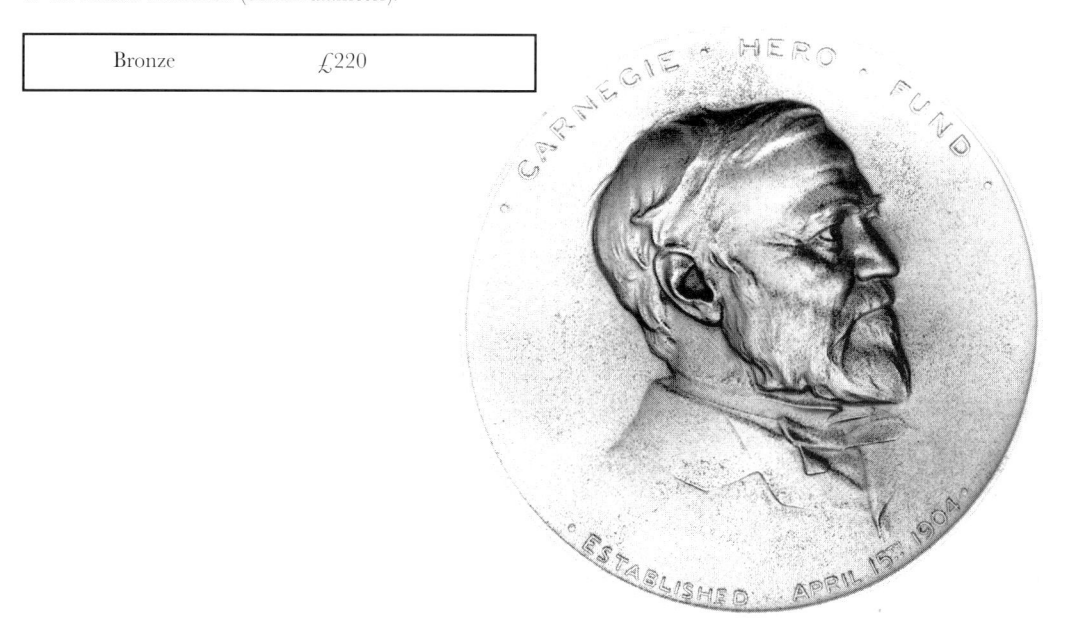

291. CORPORATION OF GLASGOW BRAVERY MEDAL

The Corporation of Glasgow instituted this medal in 1924 and over 600 awards had been made before it was superseded by the Strathclyde regional Council Medal for Bravery in 1974. Two medal types have been issued. The first (see illustration) has a characteristic 'Gallantry' brooch bar, the second has 'For Bravery' within a laurel wreath on the obverse and the Glasgow coat of arms and the recipient's name on the reverse. Both medals were struck in gold, silver and bronze with a green ribbon with narrow red edges.

Gold	£120
Silver	£75
Bronze	£65

292. R.S.P.C.A. LIFE-SAVING MEDAL

This medal is awarded in two classes of silver and bronze in recognition for gallantry in saving the lives of animals where there is great risk to the rescuer. The medal was first awarded in 1909. The class of medal awarded depends on the amount of risk involved in carrying out the act of gallantry. each medal has its own ribbon. The Silver medal has a blue ribbon with three white stripes, the centre one being narrower than the other two. The ribbon for the Bronze medal is blue with a central white stripe flanked on either side by narrow red and white stripes. Both medals are suspended from a brooch bar inscribed 'For Humanity'. The name of the recipient is usually inscribed on the rim of the medal.

Silver	£95
Bronze	£65

293. BOY SCOUTS ASSOCIATION GALLANTRY CROSS

Awarded in classes of Bronze, Silver and Gilt depending on the degree of risk of heroism involved. Somewhat unusually the Bronze Cross is the highest award. The Bronze Cross was first awarded in 1909 and the Silver Cross in 1913. Each Cross has its own ribbon; the Bronze has a red ribbon, the Silver a blue ribbon, and the Gilt a red and blue in two equal stripes. Bars could be awarded for subsequent acts of gallantry. These are plain and have the name of the recipient and date of award engraved on the reverse.

Bronze	£175
Silver	£250
Gilt	£350

The Medals Year Book
1999 Edition

Index of Medals

Index of Medals

Medal	Number
Abyssinia Medal 1867-68	103
Accumulated Campaign Service Medal	245a
Afghanistan Medal 1878-80	107
Africa General Service Medal 1902	140
African Police Medal for Meritorious Service	228
Africa Service Medal 193945	167
Africa Star 194043	158
Air Crew Europe Star 1939-44	157
Air Efficiency Award	209
Air Force Cross	27
Air force Medal	43
Albert Medal	31
Allied Subjects Medal The	50
Arctic Medal 1818-55 & 1875-76	272
Army Best Shot Medal	268
Army Emergency Reserve Decoration	201a
Army Gold Medal 1806-14	75
Army Gold Cross 1806-14	74
Army Long Service & Good Conduct Medal	195
Army of India Medal 1799-1826	82
Ashantee Medal 1873-74	105
Ashanti Medal 1900	139
Ashanti Star 1896	123
Atlantic Star 1939-45	156
Australia Service Medal 1939-45	168
Bagur and Palamos Medal 1810	67
Baltic Medal 1854-55	97
Baronet's Badge, The	14
Bath, The Most Honourable Order of the	4
Binney Memorial Medal	288
Board of Trade Rocket Apparatus Volunteer Long Service Medal	192
Boulton's Trafalgar Medal 1805	64
Boy Scouts Association Gallantry Cross	293
British India, The Order of	28
British North Borneo Company's Medal 1897-1937	127
British South Africa Company Medal 1890-97	116
British War Medal 1914-20	147
Bronze Memorial Plaque	151
Brunswick Medal for Waterloo, The	78
Burma Gallantry- Medal	39

Medal	Number
Burma Medal 1824-26	70
Burma, Order of	29
Burma Police Medal	46
Burma Star 1941-45	160
Cadet Forces Long Service & Good Conduct Medal	240
Canada General Service Medal 1866 70	104
Canadian Volunteer Service Medal 1939-47	166
Canadian Forces Decoration	218
Candahar-Ghuznee-Cabul Medal 1841-42	85
Cape Copper Company's Medal, The	136
Cape of Good Hope General Service Medal 1880-97	109
Capture of Louisbourg 1758, Medal for the	54
Capture of Rodrigues, Isle of Bourbon and Isle of France	66
Carnegie Hero Fund Medal	290
Central Africa Medal 1891-98	119
Ceylon Medal 1795-96	58
Ceylon Police Long Service Medal	230
Ceylon Police Long Service Medal (2nd Type)	230a
China 1842 - Original Design	89
China Medal 1840-42	88
China Medal 1900	137
Civil Defence Long Service Medal	241
Coast Life Saving Corps Long Service Medal	192
Coast Guard Auxiliary Service Long Service Medal	192
Colonial Auxiliary Forces Long Service & Good Conduct Medal	216
Colonial Auxiliary Forces Decoration	215
Colonial Fire Brigade Long Service Medal	239
Colonial Police Long Service Medal	223
Colonial Police Medal for Gallantry (Police)	47
Colonial Police Medal for Gallantry (Fire Brigade)	48
Colonial Police Meritorious Service Medal	226
Colonial Prison Service Long Service Medal	227
Colonial Special Constabulary Long Service Medal	225
Companions of Honour, The Order of the	13
Conspicuous Gallantry Medal (Royal Navy and Royal Air Force)	34

Medal	Number
Constabulary Medal (Ireland)	44
Coorg Medal 1837	71
Coronation Medal 1902	254
Coronation Medal 1902-Mayors' & Provosts' Issue	255
Coronation Medal 1902-Police Issue	256
Coronation Medal 1911	260
Coronation Medal 1911-Police Issue	261
Coronation Medal 1937	265
Coronation Medal 1953	266
Corporation of Glasgow Bravery Medal	291
CQD Medal	281
Crimea Medal 1854-56	98
Crown of India, The Imperial Order of the	9
Cyprus Military Police Long Service & Good Conduct Medal	232
Davison's Nile Medal 1798	59
Davison's Trafalgar Medal 1805	65
Deccan Medal 1778-84	56
Defence Medal 1939-45	163
Defence of Gibraltar Medals 1779-83	55
Defence of Kelat-I-Ghilzie Medal 1842	87
Delhi Durbar Medal 1903	259
Delhi Durbar Medal 1911	263
Distinguished Conduct Medal	32
Distinguished Conduct Medal (Colonial and Dominion)	33
Distinguished Flying Cross	26
Distinguished Flying Medal	42
Distinguished Service Cross	24
Distinguished Service Medal, The	40
Distinguished Service Order	20
Drummond Castle Medal	280
Earl St. Vincent's Medal 1800	61
East & West Africa Medal 1887-1900	117
East & Central Africa 1897-99	126
Edward Medal (Mines)	37
Edward VII Medal for Science Art, & Music	271
Edward Medal (Industry)	37a
Efficiency Decoration	201
Efficiency Medal	202
Efficiency Medal (Army Emergency Reserve)	202a
Egypt Medal 1801, Hon. East India Company's	62
Egypt Medal 1882-89	110
Empress of India Medal 1873	247
Fire Brigade Long Service & Good	

Medal	Number
Conduct Medal	238
France & Germany Star 1941-45	162
Garter, The Most Noble Order of the	1
General Gordon's Star for the Siege of Khartoum	112
General Service Medal 1918-62	153
General Service Medal 1962	176
George Cross	19
George Medal	35
Ghuznee Medal 1839	83
Guelphic Order, The Royal	5
Gulf Medal 1990-91, The	181
Gwalior Star 1843	91
Hanoverian Medal for Waterloo, The	79
Hong Kong Plague Medal 1894	120
Hunza Nagar Badge 1891	118
Imperial British East Africa Company's Medal, The	115
Imperial Service Order and Medal	21
Imperial Yeomanry Long Service & Good Conduct Medal	204
India General Service Medal 1854-95	96
India General Service Medal 1908-35	143
India General Service Medal 1936 39	154
India General Service Medal 1895-1902	121
India Service Medal 1939-45	165
Indian Army Meritorious Service Medal	213
Indian Army Long Service & Good Conduct Medal	212
Indian Distinguished Service Medal	38
Indian Empire, The Most Eminent Order of the	8
Indian Mutiny Medal 1857-59	100
Indian Order of Merit, The	22
Indian Police Medal	45
Indian Volunteer Decoration	214
Italy Star 1943-45	161
Java Medal 1811	68
Jellalabad Medals 1842	86
Jubilee Medal 1887	248
Jubilee Medal 1887-Police Issue	249
Jubilee Medal 1897	250
Jubilee Medal 1897-Mayors' & Provosts' Issue	251
Jubilee Medal 1897-Police Issue	252
Jubilee Medal 1935	264
Jubilee Medal 1977	267
Jummoo & Kashmir Medal 1895	122

Medal	Number
Kabul to Kandahar Star 1880	108
Kaisar-I-Hind, The	30
Khedive's Star 1882-91	111
Khedive's Sudan Medal 1910	144
Khedive's Sudan Medal 1896-1908	125
Kimberley Medal, The	134
Kimberley Star, The	133
King's Medal for Courage in the Cause of Freedom	51
King's Medal for Service in the Cause of Freedom	52
King's South Africa Medal, The	131
King's or Queen's Police and Fire Service Medal, The	36
Knight Bachelor's Badge, The	15
Korea Medal 1950-53	173
Liverpool Shipwreck & Humane Society Medals	276
Lloyd's Medal for Meritorious Services	285
Lloyd's Medal for Saving Life at Sea	284
Lloyd's Star Medal for Bravery at Sea	283
Long Service & Good Conduct Medal (Military)	195a
Long Service & Good Conduct (Ulster Defence Regiment)	196
Malta Police Long Service & Good Conduct Medal	231
Mediterranean Medal 1899-1902	130
Mercantile Marine Medal 1914 18	149
Meritorious Service Medal	207
Meritorious Service Medal (Royal Air Force)	211
Meritorious Service Medal (Royal Navy)	194
Military Cross	25
Military General Service Medal 1793-1814	76
Military Medal	41
Militia Long Service & Good Conduct Medal	205
Mysore Medal 1790-92	57
Nassau Medal for Waterloo, The	80
Natal Medal 1906	142
Naval Engineers' Medal	274
Naval General Service Medal 17931840	73
Naval General Service Medal 1915-62	152
Naval Gold Medal 1795-1815	72
Naval Good Shooting Medal	268
Nepaul Medal 1814-16	69
New Zealand Armed Forces Award	219
New Zealand Cross	18

Medal	Number
New Zealand Medal 1845-47 & 1860-66	102
New Zealand Police Long & Efficient Service Medal	233
New Zealand War Service Medal 1939-45	169
Newfoundland Volunteer War Service Medal 1939-45	172
North West Canada Medal 1855	113
Order of the British Empire for Gallantry, The Medal of the	12b
Order of the British Empire for Meritorious Service, The Medal	12c
Order of the British Empire, The Most Excellent	12
Order of the British Empire, The Medal of the	12a
Order of Merit, The	11
Pacific Star 1941-45	159
Permanent Forces of the Empire Beyond the Seas Long Service and Good Conduct Medal	217
Polar Medal	273
Police Long Service Medal	220
Punjab Medal 1848-49	93
Queen's Fire Service Medal	36a
Queen's Gallantry Medal	49
Queen's Medal for Champion Shots of the Air Force	270
Queen's South Africa Medal 1899-1902	129
Queen's Sudan Medal 1896-98	124
R.M.S. Carpathia and S.S. Titanic Medal	287
R.S.P.C.A. Life-Saving Medal	292
Rhodesia Medal 1980, The	179
Royal Air Force Levies Iraq Long Service & Good Conduct Medal	210
Royal Air Force Long Service & Good Conduct Medal	208
Royal Canadian Mounted Police Long Service Medal	229
Royal Fleet Reserve Long Service & Good Conduct Medal	188
Royal Household Faithful Service Medal	246
Royal Humane Society Medals	278
Royal National Lifeboat Institution Medals	275
Royal Naval Auxiliary Service Long Service Medal	191
Royal Naval Reserve Long Service & Good Conduct Medal	185
Royal Naval Volunteer Reserve Decoration	186
Royal Naval Reserve Decoration	184

Medal	Number
Royal Naval Volunteer Reserve Long Service & Good Conduct Medal	187
Royal Naval Auxiliary Sick Berth Reserve Long Service & Good Conduct Medal	189
Royal Naval Wireless Auxiliary Reserve Long Service & Good Conduct Medal	190
Royal Naval Dockyard Police (Hong Kong) Long Service Medal	193
Royal Navy Long Service & Good Conduct Medal	183
Royal Niger Company's Medal	114
Royal Observer Corps Long Service Medal	242
Royal Red Cross, The	23
Royal Ulster Constabulary Service Medal	221
Salford Humane Society Medal	289
Saxe-Gotha-Altenburg Medal for 1814-15, The	81
Scinde Medal 1843	90
Sea Gallantry Medal	53
Second China War Medal 1857-60	101
Seringapatam Medal 1799	60
Shanghai Municipal Police Long Service & Good Conduct Medal	234
Shipwrecked Fishermen & Mariners Royal Benevolent Society Medals	277
Sir Harry Smith's Medal for Gallantry 1851	95
Society for the Protection of Life From Fire Medals	279
South Africa Korea Medal 1950-53	175
South Africa Medal 1834-53	94
South Africa Medal 1877-79	106
South Africa Medal for War Service 1939-46	170
South Africa Permanent Force Long Service & Good Conduct Medal	219
South African Police Meritorious Service Medal	236
South African Police Good Service Medal	235
South African Prison Services Long Service Medal	237
South Atlantic Medal 1982, The	180
Southern Rhodesia War Service Medal 1939-45	171
South Vietnam Campaign Medal 1964	178
Special Constabulary Long Service Medal	222
Special Reserve Long Service & Good Conduct Medal	206
St. Jean d'Acre 1840, The	84
St. John of Jerusalem, The Order of	16
St. John of Jerusalem Life Saving Medal, Order of	282
St. John of Jerusalem, Service Medal of the Order of	244
St. John of Jerusalem, South African War Medal of the Order of	132
St. Michael & St. George, The Most Distinguished Order of	6
St. Patrick, The Most Illustrious Order of	3
Star 1914	145
Star 1914-15	146
Star 1939-45	155
Star of India, The Most Exalted Order of the	7
Sultan of Zanzibar's Medal 1896, The	128
Sultan's Medal for Egypt 1801	63
Sutlej Medal 1845-46	92
Tayleur Fund Medal	286
Territorial Decoration	199
Territorial Force Efficiency Medal	200
Territorial Force War Medal 1914-19	150
Thistle, The Most Ancient and Most Noble Order of the	2
Tibet Medal 1903-4	141
Transport Medal 1899-1902	138
Turkish Crimea Medal 1854-56	99
Ulster Defence Regiment Medal	203
United Nations Korea Medal 1950-53	174
United Nations Medals	182
Victoria Cross	17
Victorian Order, The Royal	10
Victorian Chain, The Royal	10a
Victorian Medal, The Royal	10b
Victory Medal 1914-18	148
Vietnam Medal 1964	177
Visit to Ireland Medal 1900	253
Visit to Ireland Medal 1903	257
Visit to Ireland Medal 1911	262
Visit to Scotland Medal 1903	258
Voluntary Medical Service Medal	245
Volunteer Decoration	197
Volunteer Force Long Service & Good Conduct Medal	198
War Medal 1939-45	164
Waterloo Medal 1815	77
Women's Voluntary Services Medal	243
Yorkshire Imperial Yeomanry Medal, The	135

TOAD HALL MEDALS

REGULAR MEDAL LISTS
EACH WITH SEVERAL HUNDRED FRESH ITEMS
Send 50p in stamps & large SAE for sample list
HIGH PRICES PAID FOR MEDALS & COLLECTIONS

TOAD HALL MEDALS
NEWTON FERRERS. Nr PLYMOUTH.
DEVON. PL8 1DH.
tel **01752 872672** fax **01752 872723**
e-mail th.medals@virgin.net
WE ALSO OFFER A PROFESSIONAL
MOUNTING SERVICE

Pen & Sword Books publish a wide range of Military History books to suit all interests; from the *Napoleonic Wars* to the *Falklands*; from *Collecting Militaria* to *Battlefield Guides*.

For our very latest catalogue
Telephone: 01226 734555
or write to:

Pen & Sword Books Ltd
47 Church Street, Barnsley,
South Yorkshire. S70 2AS

MILITARY BADGE Collecting

This book, updated many times, has now been in print for over twenty-five years. It is a collectors' unique guide to the subject

MILITARY BADGE COLLECTING
JOHN GAYLOR

New and revised sixth edition

ALMOST 800 BADGES ILLUSTRATED

✟

THIS UNIQUE REFERENCE BOOK HAS NOW ESTABLISHED ITSELF AS THE BADGE COLLECTORS BIBLE

£17.95

ISBN 0-85052-524-1

Available from
Pen & Sword Books Ltd
Church Street, Barnsley, South Yorkshire S70 2AS ~ Telephone: 01226 734222

The definitive guide for both the naval enthusiast and badge collector

A UNIQUE AND INDISPENSABLE REFERENCE WORK

✢

FULL COLOUR ILLUSTRATIONS

In compiling this book the author was assisted by most of the world's navies

SUBMARINE INSIGNIA & SUBMARINE SERVICES OF THE WORLD

Lieutenant Commander W M Thornton MBE RD* RNR (Rtd)

£16.95
ISBN 0-85052-536-5

Available from
─────── **Pen & Sword Books Ltd** ───────
Church Street, Barnsley, South Yorkshire S70 2AS ~ Telephone: 01226 734222

ANODISED CAP BADGES

COLLECTING ANODISED CAP BADGES
PETER TAYLOR

IDEAL FOR THOSE INTERESTED IN MILITARY INSIGNIA OF THE BRITISH ARMY

✢

COLLECTING ANODISED CAP BADGES IS A UNIQUE REFERENCE GUIDE

£7.95

ISBN 0-85052-637-X

Available from
Pen & Sword Books Ltd
Church Street, Barnsley, South Yorkshire S70 2AS ~ Telephone: 01226 734222

COLLECTING METAL SHOULDER TITLES

DATES OF FORMATION, AMALGAMATION, DISBANDMENT AND CHANGES IN DESTINATION ARE COVERED

✛

DETAILS OF AROUND TWO THOUSAND PATTERNS SHOWN IN TEXT

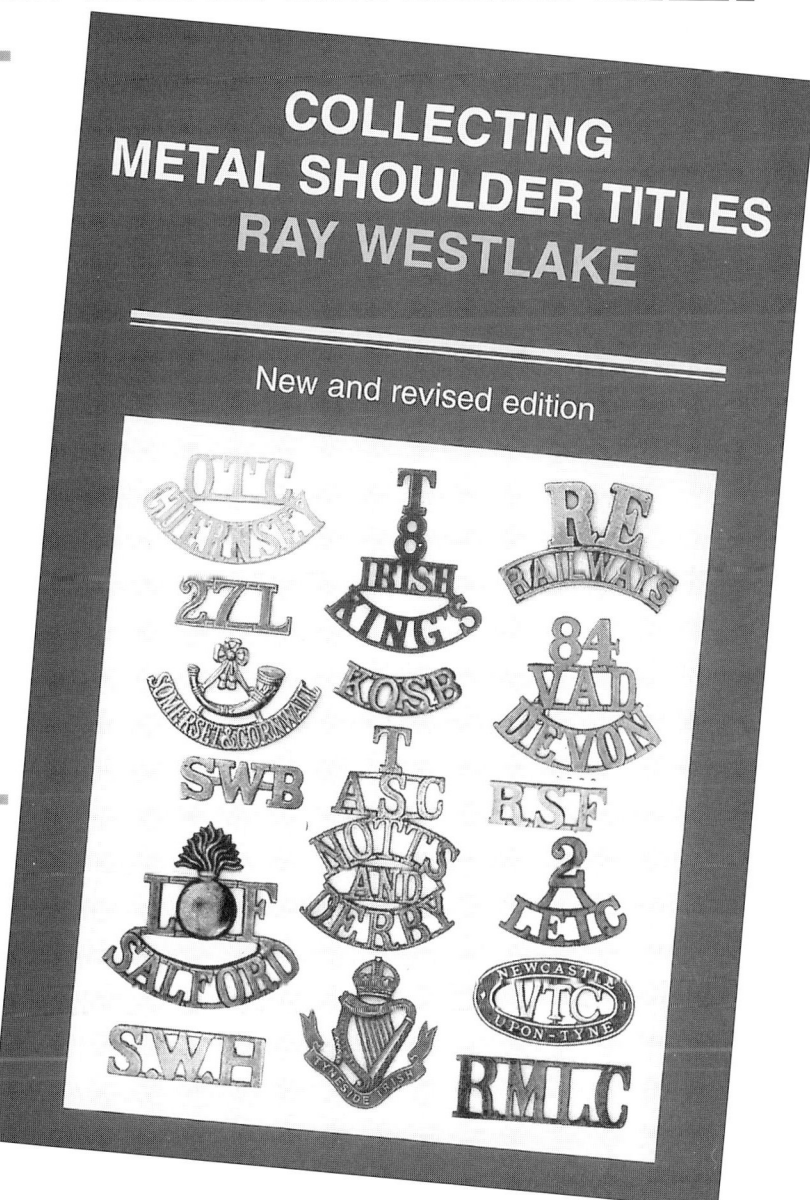

COLLECTING METAL SHOULDER TITLES
RAY WESTLAKE

New and revised edition

£19.95

ISBN 0-85052-505-5

Titles worn throughout the British Army Units of the Regular, Militia, Yeomany, Volunteer Territorial and Cadet forces are featured

Available from
Pen & Sword Books Ltd
Church Street, Barnsley, South Yorkshire S70 2AS ~ Telephone: 01226 734222